Selected Essays

Selected Essays

by

Protopresbyter Michael Pomazansky

Print shop of St. Job of Pochaev
Holy Trinity Monastery
Jordanville, N.Y.
1996

Printed with the Blessing of Archbishop
Laurus of Syracuse and Holy Trinity
Monastery

Published by Holy Trinity Monastery, Jordanville, N.Y.
13361-0036

ISBN 0-88465-062-2

Contents

Protopresbyter Michael Pomazansky

In Memory of
Protopresbyter Michael Pomazansky

*In everlasting remembrance
shall the righteous be...*

Father Michael Pomazansky, a quiet light of our Church, has departed. Modest, good, wise, and full of love, he has not been extinguished, but has merely departed. He has gone to a place "where there is neither sickness, nor sorrow, nor sighing, but life everlasting."

Every righteous man has one exceptional virtue. In Fr. Michael's case it was boundless humility. He was one of the outstanding theologians of our time, an excellent pedagogue, the author of many articles, books, a text on dogmatic theology, and the last living graduate of a pre-revolutionary Russian Theological Academy. Fr. Michael lived as if he were unaware of all this. Having fulfilled all that was commanded in the Gospel, he continued to think of himself as an "unprofitable servant."

Humility became for him second nature, although it was acquired by great labors. For many it is difficult to be humble, but for Fr. Michael it was painfully difficult for him to command others and tell them what to do. The acquisition of deep humility was the fruit of Fr. Michael's whole life, and its roots go back to the fertile soil in which he was born and raised.

Fr. Michael was born on the seventh of November, 1888, on the eve of the feast of the Archangel Michael during the 900th anniversary year of the baptism of Russia, in the village of Korist, Rovin Province, in Volhynia. His parents came from generations of priestly families. His father was Archpriest John, who likewise was the son of the priest John Amvrosievich, who was also the son of a priest. In the list of graduates of the Kiev Theological Academy, Fr. Michael found a number of people of the same last name at the time of the war of 1812. Fr. Michael's mother, Vera Grigorievna, was the daughter of a protodeacon in Zitomir, who later became a parish priest.

Fr. Michael's childhood was spent in simple village surroundings. A priest in those days served as judge, doctor, spiritual father and advisor for his parishioners. His grandfather, Fr. John, was strict, respected, and feared. Groups of rowdy boys would walk down the streets, and if he noticed one of them with a pipe, it would be necessary to either hide it or put it lit into a pocket. "Nevertheless, grandfather already felt a rift in the morality of the whole Orthodox Christian culture. Frequently from his lips were heard the words, 'something will happen, something will happen,' " in other words, "difficult times await us."

"Country life was simple," wrote Fr. Michael, "and one got along without any special forms of entertainment. In the summer a young boy rode horsey on a stick, galloping in the yard around the house, chasing himself with a homemade whip. When he grew up he would go out to the fields on a workhorse without a saddle or in a simple wagon.

"In a priest's family the church services were given the most attention. My father always used to take me with him to church. Outside it was still dark, and we walked along a narrow dam on our way to Matins. People gathered quietly in the church and one could hear only the whispering of prayers from many lips before the beginning of the service. There was frost and one's legs quickly numbed for the first half hour, but the church was gradually warmed by the breath of the congregation. Only a group of men sang. The people stood in an orderly fashion, the men on the right, the women on the left, with the young children in front, according to height. The little church was dedicated to the Great-martyr Demetrius of Thessalonica. It was well lit and painted in bright colors, which were appealing to the eyes of the children."

At the age of nine Fr. Michael entered the Theological School in Volhynia, where Bishop Anthony (Khrapovitsky) was especially attentive to him. The bishop left in his heart traces of his own wide social, intellectual, and moral influence. At every convenient moment, even during breaks, Fr. Michael hurried with like-minded friends to the Cathedral in Zitomir in order to hear the bishop's sermons. Once someone accused Bishop Anthony of heresy in front of Fr. Michael. Fr. Michael meekly but firmly responded, "We will not allow our Abba to be offended." Thus, till the end of his life he maintained a reverent attitude toward Vladyka Anthony as toward an Abba. Having left the diocese of Volhynia after finishing seminary, Fr. Michael continued to maintain contact with Bishop Anthony through letters. From 1908 until 1912 Fr. Michael studied at the Theological Academy in Kiev and also completed a one year pedagogical course offered by the Kiev Educational District. In 1913 he married Vera Feodorovna Shumsky, the daughter of a priest. She became his faithful and inseparable companion on the long path of life. After a brief experience in the anti-sectarian mission field in the town of Tiraspul near Odessa, Fr. Michael became zealously attached for the rest of his life to the study of the New Testament. In 1914, with the help of Vladyka Anthony, he was given a position in the Theological Seminary in Kaluga as instructor in Church Slavonic where he taught throughout the First World War (1914–17). The Revolution and the consequent closure of the theological schools forced him to return to his homeland — Volhynia. The bloody revolutionary whirlpool touched both his native land and his family. During the Revolution Fr. Michael's parents were away visiting their daughter and children, who had moved during the war to the area of the Dnieper. When they returned, instead of their home they found only a heap of ashes. But this was far from the last trial which was to visit Fr. Michael's relatives. In the fall of 1917 "my father was sitting at home alone at the table reading *Dogmatic Theology* by Metropolitan Macarius. Mama had not yet returned from her shopping trip to the town of Ostrog. Suddenly two men entered the house, one with a revolver and the other with a rifle and bayonet. One shot my father in the chest while the other speared him with the bayonet and said, 'It is finished.' Both of them turned and hid behind the door in the darkness. My father, covered with blood, was still able to flee outside shouting. Just as my mother arrived people were gathering, and right there, having covered and placed my father in the cart, they turned the horses around and rushed off into the night back to Ostrog, a two hour journey. There they placed him in the hospital. During the night all was done that was possible to save his life, and he survived. The coarse shirt (father never wore linen clothes) covered with blood was preserved by my father in remembrance of the incident."

Once I brought Fr. Michael the second volume of *The New Martyrs of Russia* by Fr. Michael Polsky. He read it through attentively, especially the part about the murder of the clergy in the Kiev diocese. He discovered many classmates, instructors, friends, and acquaintances among the new martyrs. At this point because of the humility that was a part of his nature he found a reason for self-disparagement, "They all suffered, became martyrs, and what have I done?" he asked. "I only live and burden others, and am of no use to anyone." Fr. Michael suffered no less than others, only his cross was different. In his youth a nerve in his face was injured. The meaning of pain from injured nerves can be understood only by those who have experienced it. The nerve pained him sometimes for days, letting up for only short periods. The pain frequently became intolerable and I sometimes found him in such a state. He was a living martyr. "This is for my sins," he would say, and not once did a word of complaint come from his lips.

From 1920 to 1924 Fr. Michael taught Russian Literature, Philosophy, and Latin at the Russian High School at Ravenna (Poland). During the same years he was closely involved in Church publications. This was difficult work in view of the persecution that had been begun by the Roman Catholics against the Orthodox. This was a period when Orthodox churches (in Poland) were either destroyed or converted into Catholic churches. During these events Fr. Michael published a bold article against Roman Catholicism but the issue in which his article was published was confiscated by the Polish police and the author was placed under special surveillance. Later, Fr. Michael edited the Church journals, *The Word* and *Sunday Reading*.

In 1936 Fr. Michael was ordained a priest and assigned among the clergy of the cathedral in Warsaw as the first assistant of Protopresbyter Terrenti Feodorovitch. He occupied that position until June of 1944.

"The conditions of my life fell into such an order," he wrote in his will, "that the first part of my social activity was in the secular academic field and the second part in the Church — the priesthood. In the world I experienced disappointments, but in the priesthood I saw only good will and in some circumstances great benefit."

After the evacuation of Warsaw, and the end of the war, Fr. Michael lived in Munich and was the editor of the Synodal journal, *Church Life*. He was also the secretary of the Missionary Committee. A disease of the lungs which he contracted during the German occupation of Warsaw periodically flamed up and interfered with his work. Fr. Michael tried to refuse the obedience placed on him because of his illness, but was answered by

Vladyka Anastassy with the words, "You must, therefore you can!" The Metropolitan served a Moleben before the miraculous Kursk icon of Our Lady of the Sign, Fr. Michael's illness took a turn for the better and he was strengthened.

From obedience grows humility. Fr. Michael always viewed himself as an obedient servant of the Church. Wherever the Church sent him, he went, never choosing his own way. Up to his very death he did not betray this principle. Already ninety years old, he continued to write articles, according to the wishes of Archbishop Laurus, dedicated to the glorious millennium of our Church. His eyes failed, he had to rest frequently, but the work was completed. After his death two new articles dedicated to the baptism of Russia were published.

Like Saint Tikhon of Zadonsk, Fr. Michael was able to find "a spiritual treasury" in everything, in the surrounding nature, in daily trivia, in meetings with people, in everything he saw the spiritual side and the opportunity to pass from contemplation of the earthly to the heavenly. From this it is obvious why Saint Gregory the Theologian was so close and dear to him, and why he never grew tired of reading him. More than once during our walks together he said, "One can learn to love the Creator from nature because He created it with love." Fr. Michael was a contemplative, a theologian, a practicer of silent and fervent prayer. He was also close in spirit to Theophan the Recluse. "I understand Theophan the Recluse, why even at Pascha he did not leave his seclusion; for me also it would be easier to celebrate Pascha alone in my cell, to quietly experience the joy of the Paschal night."

When Fr. Michael arrived in America in 1949 he was assigned by Archbishop Vitaly to teach at Holy Trinity Seminary. Fr. Michael arrived with his Matushka at Holy Trinity Monastery on the eve of the feast of Saint Job of Pochaev, the heavenly protector of Volhynia. The first years in the monastery were very lean, these were the years of building. It was not easy for Fr. Michael and Matushka. They moved into a house bought by the monastery in Jordanville. This house became the monastery guest house and Fr. Michael together with Matushka began to zealously fulfill their duty of receiving guests. Fr. Michael began his seminary work, teaching Greek, Church Slavonic and Dogmatic Theology. Fr. Michael dedicated sixty-six years of his life to teaching. It was not unusual that former students of Fr. Michael's would come to the monastery, having remembered him from the school in Ravenna and with tears would greet the ancient elder, and thank him for the unforgettable lessons in wisdom, patience, and goodness. As a teacher, Fr. Michael was indeed brilliant. As a rule, there were no discussions during his lessons. Not because he forbade them, but because no one was able to interrupt his lively, satisfying speech. Fr. Michael spoke simply, humbly, and knowledgeably about the dogmas of the Church in such a way that questions seemed to answer themselves. But if they appeared, then satisfying answers were found. Fr. Michael frequently repeated, "Much is hidden from us, and it is impossible to understand everything." His lessons passed as though they were orchestrated. He chose a theme, developed it, drew a conclusion, ended, and the bell rang.

After Matushka became ill, Fr. Michael moved into the monastery and lived like one of the brothers. He always tried to be unnoticed, and therefore chose a way of life that was semi-reclusive. He knew only the cell, church, seminary, trapeza, and for the last seven years only the church and his cell. He lived like an ascetic. Once during the first week of Great Lent, I asked him, "Batiushka, what can I bring you to eat?" He answered, "Nothing is necessary, I'll do as the brothers do." I answered, "The brothers at least eat a potato." He answered, "No thank you, God bless you." All the same I brought him two potatoes. On the following day I again asked him, "Batiushka, what shall I bring you?" "Nothing thank you, God bless you. One potato is still left from yesterday's lunch."

Prayer turned Fr. Michael into a theologian, though he himself was always afraid of such a title. "The Church knows only three theologians: Saint John, Saint Gregory and Saint Symeon the New. All the rest are superfluous." When Fr. Michael missed the daily services in the church, he read them in his room and besides this, he daily read the New and Old Testament, the New Testament frequently in Greek or Latin, and thus he continued until the last years of his life.

Concerning the meekness and compassion of Fr. Michael for his neighbor one could write much. I remember once having returned from digging a grave in the winter and went to see Fr. Michael. Again he found a cause for self-abasement saying, "I am worthless. I do nothing useful for the monastery. I am only a burden for the brotherhood, and on top of it, a grave will have to be dug for me. Oh, that only it would not be in winter! Look how difficult it is to dig in the winter." And for a long time he repeated this with great compunction.

I do not remember having ever heard Fr. Michael judge anyone, or have anything bad to say. I do not recall his ever becoming angry or irritated with my occasional carelessness in looking after him. If one forgot to bring him lunch or do the laundry and later did not remember, one could not expect him to remind one.

The last period, beginning around September of 1988, Protopresbyter Michael came to church less often. Previously, they drove him from the seminary building to the church on holy days. He attended the All-night Vigils and Divine Liturgies and as was his habit, received Communion. The last months he could not come to church and therefore received Communion in his cell. The last days of his earthly life Fr. Michael suffered terribly from his illness. Someone remained at his bedside throughout his last days: his daughter-in-law Natalia Sergievna, the monk Andrei, and others. Beginning with the twenty-sixth of October, Batiushka's condition worsened. Occasionally he lost consciousness. Even in such a state he repeated the familiar words, "My dear ones, my kind ones," and the kind sweet eyes of a child gazed at you. This was the soul of Batiushka — the soul of a joyful child who had entered into the sadness of life and was returning to the bosom of the Father, where there is neither sickness, nor sighing, but life everlasting.

On Friday, the fourth of November, at 6:30 in the morning, the feast of the Kazan Mother of God, I looked in on Fr. Michael and saw that he had reposed. Batiushka died alone. He was always an example for me of meekness, humility, attentive prayer, and continence, those very monastic traits which I could only strive for. He also reposed in a monastic way — alone. Soon Archimandrite Cyprian and Fr. Luke came in. They vested Fr. Michael and the brethren carried him in a wooden monastery coffin to the lower church of Saint Job of Pochaev. Fr. Michael remained for five days in the church where the Gospel and Psalter were read over him. The funeral was served by Archbishop Laurus on Wednesday, the ninth of November. Former students of Fr. Michael took part in the services. Memory eternal to our unforgettable pastor and teacher!

Is This Orthodoxy?

Or Modernism, Subverting True Orthodoxy,
and Unacceptable for the Orthodox Conscience?

A review of the book: *Orthodoxy in Life.*
A collection of articles edited by S. Verhovskoy.
Published by the Chekhov Society, New York, 1953, 405 pages.

As it may be seen from the opening lines by the editor of this collection, the book is intended for a wide circle of readers. Its aim is "to give brief information about Orthodoxy in teaching and life." However, a cursory examination is sufficient in order to see that little is said about the concrete features of Orthodoxy, and that the main part is full of abstract religious-philosophical matter; the other part is composed of articles of a theoretical character. The two articles by A. Kartashev giving church-historical material are an exception. The title *Orthodoxy in Life*, therefore, is in the latter case, completely unsuitable.

The participants in this collection [Prof. A. Kartashev, Fr. Alexander Schmemann, Fr. Serge Verhovskoy, V. Rev. V. Zenkovsky, Rev. E. Melia, Rev. A. Kniazev, B. Bobrinskoy, N. Arseniev, and N. Struve] are representatives, mainly as professors, of two theological schools: the Paris Institute and St. Vladimir's Seminary in New York. The book is arranged in a widely expanding plan: Orthodoxy and Today's World, Christianity, Christ, The Church, Faith and Knowledge, The Church and State, The Parish, Holy Scripture, Prayer and Services, Orthodoxy and Russia, Great Examples, Spiritual Traditions of the Russian Family. The Collection is internally united by a series of characteristic ideas which, evidently, must be their guide.

"Orthodoxy is Christianity in its purest form," we read in the first line of an introductory article by the editor. A further reading of the content of the articles of this collection permits us to accept these first words as the formula for the basis of the whole book. In this phrase, Orthodoxy is equated with the general, ideal image of Christianity. It follows that everything the authors say about Christianity, in its purest form, is Orthodoxy. The treatment of the subject of Orthodoxy in the basic essays of the book is guided in this direction.

Orthodoxy, however, has its own historical image, representing a way of life, and properly presenting itself as "Orthodoxy in Life." This image is touched on very lightly in the introductory chapter entitled, "Orthodoxy and Today's World." Here the picture is far from ideal... "Christians are weak, inactive, hypocrites; Church society is unchurchly in its spirit, in its life and conscience, often the only thing remaining of it is the form, with a predisposition towards compromise, even with bolshevism or racism. Beginning even with the Middle Ages, Church society ailed with all the illnesses of pharisaism, ritualism, scholasticism, insensibility to evil, an unwillingness to bring the light of Christianity into the essence of life..." (p. 23). "The condition of the Orthodox Church itself is very sad..." (p. 11). Thence follow the deductions: "it is necessary," "it is indispensible," "it is lacking," "it must be," "second necessity," "third necessity" — in a word, the correction of all sides of Church life is indispensible. Such is reality — to the author.

Let us return to the first phrase: "Orthodoxy is Christianity in its purest form." The phrase itself demands a series of rebuttals. A Protestant, of course, moved by an Orthodox service or captivated by the writings of the Holy Fathers, could express himself so: "Orthodoxy is the purest form of Christianity." His point of view is the relativeness of all Christian faiths. In other words, he holds the point of view of present-day ecumenism, and for him such a form of expression is completely natural. But when *Orthodox theologians* include Orthodoxy *in a long list* of Christian faiths, even though it is in the first place, the result is worse. First of all, this echoes of a clear subjectivity: to a Christian of any faith or sect, his understanding of Christianity *must* present itself as being the best, if he is faithful to it. Secondly, by such a listing the name "Orthodoxy" itself is implicitly crossed out. This name must imply to us that Orthodox doctrine is the true Christian doctrine, "the right faith," placed in opposition to "other religions". It is the *true* Church of Christ. In this collection there is no such direct and clear statement about Orthodoxy. For now, only a slightly noticeable move is made off the solid foundation. The switchman has only lightly separated the rails on the switch; but the brilliant express will now take another direction.

If Orthodoxy is the purest form in a line of other forms of Christianity, then where will the authors of this collection place the Church? Will not the *name* of the Church then be spread throughout all Christianity in the hundreds of its forms of confessions of faith? And if the Church is equated to Christianity in general, then in this diffused state, what does the Church add to Christianity? Is She in that case necessary? And where is She to be found in life, in a concrete incarnation?

Those are exactly the questions posed in the article by Fr. Alexander Schmemann, "Of the Church." "Why is so little said about the Church of the Gospel?" Is She not an "unnecessary, human obstacle" between Christ and those who love Him?* In order to begin to answer this question, the author deems it necessary first of all "to allude to that perspective, in which 'the problem of the Church' is placed and resolved by the Gospel itself." In presenting this perspective, the author speaks of the Kingdom of God, of "birth from water and the Spirit," of following Christ, of personal freedom, of faith, of renewal in Christ; of the Holy Spirit, Who is a) "the Life of the Father and the Son" and b) the Life "uniting me with the Son and adopting me to the Father"; of the Sacrament of the Eucharist, of love towards brothers in Christ, "of the service of one fulfilling the service of Christ, becoming the tie for all" [one could think that the theme here is the papacy, although, apparently, pastorship is the question at hand]. And, finally, the last chapter gives an answer about the Church. This answer is very unclear. We shall cite important thoughts from it. "New life, unity in Christ, the gathering of believers in the Spirit is the Church of God…" "The Gospel calls us to life; but the life announced by it is revealed as the Church. Christ came to the people and for the people. If He then did not remain alone, if even *two or three* heard and received Him, He is already in them and they in Him — and this oneness of Him with people the Gospel calls the Church: *I will build My Church and the gates of hell shall not prevail against it* (Matt. 16:18)…" "But many will pose the

---

* "Is it possible, that in order to be a Christian, it is not enough to believe in Christ and to strive to fulfill His commandments, but it is still necessary to fulfill incomprehensible ancient rituals, to understand difficult theological forms, to be drawn into church disputes and divisions, to accept all of the human incrustation, which during two thousand years has sullied the purity of the Gospel?" (p. 57).

last question: where then is She, the true Church? We see Her in divisions, in quarrels, in sin and temptations. How can one be sure what is of Christ in Her, and what is apostasy from Him? Here too we receive an answer from Christ Himself: 'Seek, and ye shall find. Knock, and it will opened for you — every one who seeks will find, to everyone who knocks it is opened...' One thing is certain: faith in Christ brings us into the Church and life in Him is life in the Church." The author then leaves the reader in this enigma, leaving him alone, with the Gospel in his hands, to search for the answer to the question of the Church.

On a parallel with the main theme, the Church, Fr. A. Schmemann in the same article conveys another thought, later more fully developed in the articles of S. Verhovskoy. This is the struggle with the seemingly false but ancient view of "the purest form of Christianity" — in Orthodoxy — that the substance of Christianity is "the salvation of the soul." Having reminded us that "the teaching about the Kingdom of God is opened to us in a somewhat double perspective," Fr. A. Schmemann writes, "We have already long ago reduced all Christianity to the teaching not of a new life, but of the salvation of the soul in a life beyond the grave" (p. 61). [We must note in passing, that such an expression, "the salvation of the soul in a life beyond the grave," is not generally encountered in an Orthodox church lexicon.] The author calls us to "examine our usual understanding of Christianity as the salvation of the soul" (p. 63). This thought of Fr. A. Schmemann puts us into a state of perplexity. All the writings of the Apostles, of the Holy Fathers, and finally all the Church services, beginning with the prayer "O Heavenly King" ["...save our souls, O Good One"], place the salvation of the soul in the center of our thoughts; whether this is right or wrong in the estimation of the authors of this work, such in truth is "Orthodoxy in Life," and without this, it is an illusory "Orthodoxy." Whoever reckons that the constant thought and prayer of the salvation of the soul is an unwanted element in Orthodoxy cancels out for himself Orthodoxy in general.

The author continues, "When we read the Gospel in the light of this question, we are convinced that the teaching of Christ is certainly not limited to the 'soul,' and that on the contrary, in His life He pays much attention to man's body. He 'heals all disease and sickness among the people,' returns sight to the blind, cures the lame, the paralytic, the hemorrhaging, and finally, raises the dead... He speaks of 'the luminous body.' He performs miracles and heals through the medium of His body: by touch, spittle, breath — and, finally, His very resurrection is the resurrection of His body. And even though age after age we search and await from Christ most of all especially healing, i.e., bodily help — still, *blinded by our own,* and not by the Gospel understanding of the salvation of the soul, we connect salvation to the soul alone, and limit it to the life of the soul beyond the grave" (pp. 63–64). Further the author writes, "And seeing that man lives in this union of the spiritual and bodily, and *outside of it discontinues being a man,* then…" (p. 64).

In answer to the reasoning of Fr. A. Schmemann one could turn to the Gospel, where it is said: *and fear not them which kill the body, but are not able to kill the soul* (Matt: 10:28); but it is not necessary to enter upon discussion of this sort here, since, as it is said elsewhere in this work, "you can prove anything through the Gospel" (p. 59). It is enough to turn one's attention to the fact that the truth of the soul's immortality, the truth of a knowledgeable life beyond the grave, after separation with the bodily "temple," is preserved in full force from Apostolic days to our time, namely by Orthodoxy, and this forms not only its distinctive characteristic from other faiths, but also its grandeur, strength, glory, its life. Hence, in Orthodoxy it is the exceptionally high regard for the dead and the heavenly Church, the Eucharist and general remembrance of the departed, an uninterrupted mindfulness of the saints and a prayerful communion with them, which astounds the heterodox. If a soul without the body is already not a personality, then how can we pray, "Give rest, O Lord, to the souls of Thy departed servants, where from eternity the light of Thy countenance shineth, and gladdeneth all Thy saints"? Fr. Schmemann calls his readers to that melancholy world-view into which Protestantism has already sunk, having almost lost its faith in life beyond the grave. Nobody denies the importance of the body and the bodily needs of man in earthly life, but the author evidently has a special purpose when he speaks of the meaning of the body. With such a world-view, two results are natural: 1) oblivion of the heavenly Church (and we see this in this work, where, in spite of its comprehensive character, the heavenly Church receives only several passing and pallid lines (p. 302), and 2) the idea of arranging "a happy life" on earth under the protection of religion. Fr. A. Schmemann does not elaborate on these points, but his second conclusion provides the inspiration for the two long articles of Serge Verhovskoy: 1) "Christianity," and 2) "Christ." These articles can be regarded as the heart of the whole Collection. We shall limit ourselves to a number of excerpts from them.

Serge Verhovskoy writes, "The substance of Christianity is the union of people with God, between themselves and with all beings," we read in the beginning of the first article (p. 277). What draws us to God? "In love, in understanding and creativity we can rise above life's problems. The understanding of nature and the contemplation of its beauty creates in us the ideal image of the world. Relationships with people...open to us the depth of man's spirit. In science and art we express all the riches of knowledge and beauty through which man is capable of living. If man could limit himself to spiritual riches which he finds in himself and in the world, he would not even begin to think of God. But in spiritual life man is never satisfied with his own accomplishments... Who of us will say, without falling into dull self-conceit: I love enough, I am holy enough; I know enough, everything beautiful is open to me, I am perfect!... In this consciousness of our limitedness, which appears to us on our endless road toward perfection, God is revealed to us; He is that All-Complete Being, to Whom we aspire; in Him is accomplished all that we seek..." (p. 278). [Here an observation must be made: is it really true that hunger for that which is greater than what is in our possession leads us to God? Is it not rather often the opposite; does it not lead us away from God?]

The author sees man's good in the attainment, during life, of Truth, Good, and Beauty. "In God we attain our Desire: Truth, Good, and Beauty," (p. 281); the triad of "Truth, Good, and Beauty," is used by the author on every page, but especial attention is allotted to Beauty. "There is only one Father, Son, and Holy Spirit, one good, one truth, one beauty in God" (p. 283). "The beauty of the outside world and the inner beauty of man leads us to the ideal beauty, in which we see primary shapes of beings, as they exist in God, for God placed within the universe not only wisdom, but also beauty" [page unknown, ed.]. "Whether we unite in the way of love or morality, knowledge of beauty, ideals, or creativeness, the summit of our way will be in God... Only a general living love for the one living God, only a general faith in absolute Good, Truth, and Beauty can completely unite people in the one and all-sided ideal of man's life" (p. 300). "Every individual Christian recognizes the truth from one angle, even though the Truth stands wholly before him in Christ. But Truth is fully open for the unity of all. The same can be repeated also concerning beauty. One should not forget that in multi-unity, i.e. in a complete unity of singleness and multitude, of originality and sameness, lies the foundation of good and truth and beauty, and of Being itself, and that is why God is the complete Tri-Unity" (p. 304). "Why are we so persistently speaking of good, of truth, and of beauty? Isn't there here a poor abstraction? No, the whole irreplaceable and necessary value of good, truth, and beauty consists in the fact that in them we are united with reality itself, i.e. with God, people, and the world... The perfection of life is revealed to us in beauty, more than in anything else. The perfect is always beautiful. It follows then that in beauty we also enter into communion with Reality itself — with God and everything existing... For this reason the Kingdom of God can be but a Kingdom of good, truth, and beauty" (pp. 306–307).

The author of the article cited does not see any difficulties in the fact that the idea of serving truth, good, and beauty is also used by irreligious humanism, pantheism, and atheistic philosophy. The article suggests to us that no matter what unites searchers of the fullness of life, whether in creativity, in love, or in beauty, the summit of their road will be in God, they will be united by faith in "the Absolute Good." "Everything positive already in fact belongs to Christianity, *even though it may not recognize this*. Sooner or later everything will be gathered into the Church, and at the end of world history the Universe will become the Kingdom of God" (p. 308). The arts of the world, even though non-Christian, are rated by the author as an integral part of the Kingdom of God, when he says: "The arts of the world of the past (not only Christian) were the treasure houses of the beautiful" (p. 321). So, if we follow the thought of the author, the ideals of godless humanism flow together with the Christian building of the Kingdom of God, and the Christian concept of the Church diffuses into total vagueness.

The fullness of life in Christ, as represented by the author, seems to be easily attainable. "Who loves Christ," we read here, "will want to belong to Him and live a common life with Him. Continually remembering Christ, we will turn to Him with our thoughts and feelings and search for personal communion with Him, at first possible in answerless prayer to him, and afterwards in prayerful conversation with Him and internal contemplation of His actual presence in us. When we do feel the presence of Christ, we will see Him in all the positive content of the spiritual life, as well as in

all that is good in the world" (p. 294). "The first sign of grace is the presence in us of a force surpassing our strength; we perceive that our actions
and experiences contain in themselves more than our own capability.
Grace inspires and warms our soul: it is light; it is joy; it is love; it is the
fire which burns us and gives life to us, and this fire we can transmit to
others…" (p. 295). [Do these words not suggest an empty self-delusion? Is
this not self-flattery? Is it fitting to use the word "we" in representing the
heights of spiritual experience? And, is this in fact what the saints, who
have reached these heights, experienced?]

The essence of the Church, according to the author, is multi-unity.
"No human differences of sex, conditions of life, profession, education,
class, nation, or race can divide the Church. All Christians, parishes, dioceses, and churches must be one, notwithstanding any differences which
are possible among people. We should not forget that the essence of every
being from the Most-holy Trinity to the atom, and also the essence of
good, truth, and beauty is multi-unity…" (pp. 312–313). [The author
does not make mention of the dogmatic distinctions; it may be that they
are to be understood in the expression: "notwithstanding any differences
which are possible among people." He places a mark of equality between
the "Church" and "all Christians"; on the other hand, he speaks of the
(seven) Ecumenical Councils of the Orthodox Church, as the highest
authority of the Church (p. 312). We cannot know whether by the words
"all Christians" he means only the Orthodox Church or, on the contrary,
whether "Church" is to be understood as Christians of all possible confessions, sects, and doctrines.]

The author understands Christian activity as "creativity" — "according to that ideal which we find in Christ": "to transform your own or other
souls, to cleanse and transfigure them, to elevate them to the fullness of
the life of the Kingdom of God — cannot be the work of mechanical effort
or book learning; only an extreme effort of the will, mind, artistic sensi-
tivity, a continual inspiration and illumination from God, can give us success… Christ, the prophets and apostles, left everything for the sake of this
creativity, and God and the World glorified them more than all other
genus of mankind" (p. 314).

Such a lofty spiritual state, an uninterrupted existence in Christ, etc.,
according to the author, are fully compatible with ordinary forms of life
and activity. He writes: "From what has been said, it does not follow of

course (to come to the conclusion) that Christians should not give their efforts to those types of creativeness which are usually spoken of in the world, i.e., social activity, science, art, etc. They are justified in so far as they serve good, truth, and beauty" (p. 315).

"The spiritual life" is understood by the author as "love for God, people, and the world, the recognition of truth and beauty" (p. 312). "The understanding of spiritual life is constantly being reduced among Christians to a plain concentration on a religious or prayerful-ascetic life. The apostolic understanding of spirituality was not such," he writes (p. 315).

Only from the point of view of the breadth of Christianity does the author tolerate the right of monasticism's existence. "The Church counts it permissible to renounce these forms of life (political, family, cultural, and household) for those who want to concentrate on an inner life, in solitary prayerful labors: such is the ideal of monasticism." "It is understood," the author finds it necessary to warn, "that love for one's neighbor and the duty to help him remains in force even for a monk" (p. 37).

The pinnacle of Christian attainment is the feeling of "happiness on earth." "If three unite in the name of Christ, they will be strong and happy. If thousands gather in the Kingdom of God, here on earth, the Christian world will begin to be transfigured... The happiness of man is in unity with God and people, in a nearness to all beings, in love, truth, and beauty, in beneficent creativity. On earth all of this is accomplished in the Church; in it resides the Kingdom of God..." (p. 329).

Church services are offered by the author as one of the kinds of Christian art (pp. 287–311).*

A dangerous philosophy is observed in his expression of the relationship of God to the world: "It is also evident, that *God is inseparable from the world.* He Himself united Himself with us, desiring to be our Creator, Guide, and Saviour. He, too, Who is the Perfect Spirit, is also the Creator of the Universe. *We must not divide God. Therefore, it is erroneous to separate,* in our religious life, our relationship to God from our relationship to created beings (p. 305).

---

*The author writes: "It is a fact that Orthodox church services, in their text as well as their structure, are real artistic productions... In general, Orthodoxy summons one not only to inner beauty; it aspires that the whole life of the Church and believers have a beautiful form; of course, this outer beauty has an inner sense and impels us to the spiritually beautiful" (p. 311).

"God is actively present in the material world, in the body of Christ, in Church, in icons, in the Cross, in sacred articles, in priestly actions, in the relics of the saints" (p. 311).

What does "actively present" mean? Does He dwell "in the body of Christ" and "in the material world" on an equal footing? Does the omnipresent God "dwell especially" in sacred articles and in the relics of saints? Can He dwell in priestly actions?

A special article, as the author writes, is "dedicated to our Lord Jesus Christ" (p. 293). Former themes are partly repeated here.

Beauty: "For Christ it was most important to create an internal spiritual world, in which the souls of mankind would be united one with another in one truth, verity, holiness, love, beauty" (p. 345).

"Christ says nothing about arts, but in the image of God and man, which is revealed by Him, are shown the foundations of all beauty. It does not follow that Christ regarded with animosity all forms of our earthly life, repudiating them in the name of pure spirituality" (p. 345).

The body: "Christ's body had an enormous meaning in His theanthropic life...His miracles, transfiguration, resurrection, ascension, were connected with His body... and in general, Christ disclosed His Divinity through His body... Thanks to His body, Christ was in direct communication with the material world" (p. 350).

Asceticism: "Poverty and persecutions forced Christ to experience bodily sufferings and deprivations, but premeditated asceticism occupies a secondary place in the life of Christ; we know only of His forty-day fast after Baptism" (p. 352). [We ask: Where does asceticism not occupy a secondary place? Did the circumstances of life really "force," i.e., compel the Saviour against His will to suffer deprivations and poverty? Do not the words of the Saviour call one to an ascetic regard of life: *whoever wishes to follow Me, let him deny Himself and take up his Cross*? The author, it is evident, forgot the ascetical example of Saint John the Baptist.]

The author thinks it is necessary to suggest to readers that Christ loved life in all its entirety. "Being Himself the Wisdom of God, Christ sees wisdom and beauty in nature, in the Scriptures, in the ordinary life of people... He is ready to accept accusation even from an evil slave; Christ does not scorn any man: neither the loyalty of the fishermen, chosen by Him, nor the children, nor the plain family of Lazarus, nor the entertainment of publicans and pharisees, nor the anointing and tears of a sinning woman"

(p. 358). "Not justifying sin, He loved sinners with a special love and occupied Himself more with them than with the righteous" (p. 361). He "rejoiced with parents whose children were cured of sickness or sin, [rejoiced over] the birth of a baby, a wedding, a shepherd finding a sheep, and even the woman who found a coin" (p. 361). "Christ regarded pagans with condescension: they know truth poorly, but can follow the simplest morality" (p. 367).

Concerning the fact that the Saviour *came to bring to earth not peace, but a sword*, not a word. Christ loved sinners not with a "special love," but of publicans and sinning women He said: *Verily I say unto you, that the publicans and the harlots will go into the Kingdom of God before you; for John came unto you in the way of righteousness, and ye believed him not, but the publicans and the harlots believed him.* It is strange even to read such an expression: "did not scorn the loyalty of the fishermen, chosen by Him"; to read of the Saviour, praying for them before the sufferings on the cross: "I sanctify Myself for them."

The author's understanding of Christian humility is certainly original. He writes, "Humility is usually understood very one-sidedly — not in substance, but in its ascetic expression — as self-abasement, the regarding of oneself as nothing, the emphasizing of one's sinfulness." The essence of humility, according to the author, is not in the above, [rather]: "My good is in all good, my life is in unity with all, my truth and good and beauty is the same truth, good and beauty for all, my worth is measured by a common measure — this is the essence of humility" (p. 357).

It is evident that with such "humility" it will not be difficult to be "reconciled" even with evil. And this we do read further. "Every manifestation of Christ's humility is explained by His condescension to everything alive — to the worst sinner, to the slightest good" (p. 358).

"Why do the humble avoid external strife with evildoers? Because, in them they are ready to see some good, and fear to destroy the good together with the evil… In every being there is at least a drop of good and for this reason God tolerates even those who knowingly become evil" (p. 359).

Not justifying, then, strife with evil, the author does justify egoism. "Love naturally arises from humility, because it is natural to love that which you recognize as good for yourself (!). Love is a yearning to live one life with the loved one, to give yourself to him, to possess him (!). Only he really loves God, people, truth, good, beauty, who not only takes from them and makes use of them, but who also gives himself to them. However, it is true that love is also possession, for if I do not have possession of something, then how can I be in unity with it? It is justifiable also to love one's self, for it is natural to want to possess and live for yourself" (p. 359). [In the final analysis, then, humility leads to the desire to "possess," to love for oneself, and to "live for yourself."]

There are many separate phrases in the article which catch the eye with their inappropriateness to Christian truth; others are so unclear that it is difficult to appraise them.

"Riches and power seemed to Christ and the apostles to be dangerous for spiritual life" (p. 341). [Is it possible to apply to Christ the expression "seemed?"]

"Those who fulfill the word of God are more blessed than His Mother" (p. 343). [Where did the author get this? The Gospel does not say this.]

"Christ was the Righteous One, and His righteousness was first of all internal holiness" (p. 346). [What does "first of all" mean? What other kind of holiness can there be?]

"To follow Christ is the first step of Christianity; a higher step is to live by Him" (p. 347). [Does this mean that to live by Him is already not being a follower of Christ?]

Thoughts which are plainly contradictory to dogmas of faith are expressed in the following deliberations.

"In His love for the Father and the world, Christ gave them His life and His soul [?]. The death of Christ in itself was not related to His body alone, but also His soul" (p. 366). (This is something entirely new in theology, for we know that every person's soul, not only Christ's, is immortal. "In the grave bodily, but in hades with Thy soul as God…," we hear in the Paschal service.)

Just as far from Orthodox theology are the following words: "Christians have but one God — Father, Son and Holy Spirit; one Lord — Christ is our Lord not only in that He is a divine, perfect Personality, but also because in Him is opened to us a new world of being and a perfect ideal of life; the true meaning of life is opened to us… In Christ we have reached the comprehension of what man is; we have learned to appreciate the wealth of the spirit and its indivisibility from the body" (p. 369). So says S. Verhovskoy. But we have been taught by the Church not to separate God the Son and Christ the Lord, for in Him mankind is united to God "inseparably" and "indivisibly." There is no God the Son separately from Christ the Lord. And concerning the assertion by the author about the indivisibility of the spirit from the body — *the dust will return to earth, as it was, and the spirit will return to God, Who gave it* (Eccles. 12:7), and according to the Apostle: *There is a natural body* (of the present age), *and there is a spiritual body* (of the future age); *Now this I say,* continues the Apostle, *that flesh and blood cannot inherit the Kingdom of God, neither doth corruption inherit incorruption* (I Cor. 15:44, 50).

Both articles of Professor S. Verhovskoy, to whose pen belongs more than a quarter of the whole Collection, contain a number of subjective elements, which can be found only in modernistic "theological" literature or in publications of extreme Protestant doctrines. The internally contradictory understanding of the essence of Christianity, the artificial, touched-up picture of Christianity strikes the eyes. It may be that this picture, as well as the style of exposition, was intended to meet the taste of a definite circle of readers by its novelty and originality; it may be that some who are little acquainted with Christianity will indeed find such a picture satisfying. In any case, this is far from authentic Orthodoxy, and we can say with confidence, that Orthodoxy is not in need of such an embellished view.

We will now proceed to a short survey of other articles in this collection following in order from general to particular themes.

"Faith and Knowledge," by V. Rev. V. Zenkovsky — The author presents this question: How are miracles possible in our world of strict causal dependence of phenomena? He proposes to resolve this question by applying the teaching of Cournot about the confines of causality, explaining the appearance of "chance" in the world of causality. Chance is the result of the collision of two "independent causative series," as the collision of two moving machines at the point of intersection of two paths (i.e., to the collision of a train and an auto). But the will of the engineer can forestall the collision. Does not the will of God in the same way invade the course of causative series, creating a favorable junction of events, without violating the laws of causality, and this appears in our eyes to be a miracle? However, in the opinion of Fr. V. Zenkovsky, there is one exceptional miracle which does not conform to such an explanation: this is the miracle of the resurrection of Christ. "In the matter of the resurrection of the Saviour, on the contrary, the question of its very *possibility* is difficult, but the question of its authenticity and reality…is decided simply and categorically... The reality of the resurrection of the bodily dead Saviour is certified, not only by its complete possession of the mind and heart of His followers, but especially by its entrance into the souls of the Lord's disciples in its victorious radiance, that their preaching kindled endless masses of people with a fire unquenchable until the present day. This force lives in mankind till now..." (p. 50). The reader of the article draws the inference that the very reference to the *one fact of* the resurrection, as the deciding argument in the question of the miracle, namely the fact of Christ's Resurrection, pushes aside as superfluous all discussions of the relationship of miracles to the law of causality.

Continuing in the appointed order, we will speak briefly about the two articles of Anton Kartashev, "Church and State" and "Orthodoxy and Russia." Both articles, expressing thoughts already known from previous articles of A. Kartashev, are distinguished by the author's knowledge of the history of the Eastern Church and love of Russia's past.* He speaks about the symphony of the Church and state in Byzantium and in Russia with sympathy, notwithstanding all historical sins, and speaks sorrowfully of the present "divorce" of Church and state. In conclusion, he contrasts the laudable old symphony to the present "most absurd compromise" between a godless state and the Church, "on the terms of reciprocal service, to which, in the darkness of a Bolshevik hell, a terroristically-harassed and freedom-bereft part of the episcopate lowered itself. This nightmarish absurdity is accepted with unfeeling stupidity as something normal and tolerable by foreign general church opinion, ecumenical circles, some Eastern Orthodox hierarchs, and — what is most unforgivable — even by a small handful of Orthodox Russians, living here, in the blessed lands of human and Christian freedom" (p. 171).

The second article of A. Kartashev concerns the ideas of "Holy Russia" and "Third Rome." In it the belief is expressed that, in spite of all the terrifying reality, these two ideas even today have not lost their meaning. "Let us pre-assume that we have already been pushed into eschatological times... We are called with all the more anxiety to a stronger stand with the banner of Christ even in rear-guard battles" (p. 202).

---

*We would like to think that the application by the author to the relationship of the Church and State of the "Chalcedon dogma — without confusion and without change," is only verbal decoration.

Referring to the past of the Eastern and Russian Churches with understanding and love, the author acknowledges that you cannot return what is lost. At the end of the first article, he writes: "In the belief that the archaic Eastern system of the symphony is ideal, we do not weaken ourselves with inactive, romantic longing for the irrevocable past" (p. 177). At the end of the second article: "Raising the banner of Orthodox Russia and rendering her becoming honor for her attainments in the past, we count it neither obligatory nor wise to take upon ourselves the thankless and utopian role of restorers" (p. 204). In the light of these reservations, more strange but characteristic is the reaction by the editor of this work to the ideas of the author about the monarchic order of Orthodox kingdoms in the past. In the most intimate sections of the article the editor of this collection retorts with the following remarks in the footnotes: "The intervention of Christian monarchs in the administration of the church is a negative fact" (p. 204); "We do not think that at the present time all Orthodox people must be monarchists" (p. 207); "...that the constant and principle intervention of Christian monarchs into church affairs was evil" (p. 161). On the question of the USSR the editor remarks, "One can imagine that far from all the Russian hierarchy in fact serves the interest of the Soviet authority..." (p. 202).

The article, "The Small Church: The Parish as a Christian Community," by Rev. E. Melia, gives a series of theoretical, but in practice, useful ideas about the organization of the internal life of a parish. Built on the plan: unity, holiness, conciliarity, and apostolicity of the Church, by its very plan it traces the idea that every Christian community is a small Church, retaining all four signs of the Church.

A series of thoughts in the article appears as a fresh and good stream in comparison to the prevailing spirit of this work. Such are: a) the idea about the "*unsuitability* of Christianity with the *natural* reality of the world, about the foreignness of Christianity in respect to the world" (p. 112); b) about monasteries: "the monastery is a likeness of a parish or even of a diocese, it has such an accumulation of spiritual power that it does not yield to the latter in its allotted importance in the Church" (p. 115); c) the priesthood: "like a prophet, the priest is subjected to reproach, mockery, and even to a hidden anger because — just like every Christian, but in the first rank, where he offers himself voluntarily — he appears as a *monk* on earth, i.e., with all his being, witness of life, and service, as also in his outer appearance. In the name of the Church he reminds all of the corruption of this world, and of the coming age" (p. 105).

"What is Holy Scripture?," by Rev. A. Kniazev contains the chapters: Books of Holy Scripture. Their origin. The place of Holy Scripture as the source of the knowledge of God. The nature of Holy Scripture. The mutual relationships of the Bible and science. The composition of the Bible. Holy Scripture and the prayerful life of the Church. The article represents an introduction to the usual course on Holy Scripture.

"Prayer and Services in the Life of the Orthodox Church," by B. Bobrinskoy: The first part of the article deals with prayer, its forms, the meaning of the rule of prayer. The second part speaks of public services: of the Christian icon, of reading and singing in church, of the daily, weekly, and yearly cycle of services. The central place is here occupied by an explanation of the Eucharist. The author explains the Eucharist symbolically. The Eucharist is a *symbol* of our redemption by the Saviour and is presented here as a reproduction of the Hebrew Paschal feast, celebrated as a remembrance of the kindness of God during the leading out of Egypt of the Hebrew people. The lamb on the table of the Old Testament Passover, the bitter herbs, the chalice, were to the Hebrews symbols of historic remembrances. Having expounded in detail and in succession the Old Testament rituals of the Passover foods, the author writes: "*Christ placed into the rituals...a new meaning*" (p. 261). "And so this bread and this wine, of which all partake according to rank, is none other than the Body and Blood of Christ. As this bread — His Body will be broken. As this wine — they will spill His Blood. This chalice is the symbol of the sufferings of Christ; the lamb is Christ Himself. The bitter herbs are the bitterness of His Passion and desertion. There are no more doubts. At the Supper the disciples are experiencing the very death of Christ" (p. 261). In such a fashion, the significance of the lamb on the Paschal table and of the bitter herbs is placed here on the same level with the bread and wine of the Eucharist, and all of this together is interpreted as a symbolic image of the sufferings. *Of the change in essence in the Sacrament of the Eucharist the article says nothing.* Although on the earlier pages one finds the expression "the communion of the Body and Blood of Christ," a phrase following this, "in the Liturgy we break the bread and drink from the common chalice with Christ and His disciples" (p. 255), does not give the basis for understanding the explanation of the Eucharist in the Orthodox sense.

This is extreme Protestantism. We Orthodox Christians do not drink from a common chalice with Christ when we accept Communion of His Body and Blood.*

"The Spiritual Traditions of the Russian Family," by N. Arseniev — This chapter is from the book: *Of Russian Spiritual and Creative Traditions*. Here is presented the life of the Russian family, properly of a family of the upper class, satiated with cultural tradition, a tradition where the contemporary was blended with the old religious ways and with the living world of the past, where the main person, even though often unnoticed, and the guardian of the firm principles was the mother. This literary illustration only obliquely approaches the general theme about Orthodoxy; it touches on general Russian life, an integral part of which was the Orthodox way, and is confined only to the social stratum of old Russia.

The last article in this collection is an outline by Nikita Struve entitled "Great Examples." The aim of this essay is "to prove from examples of the most diverse epochs," that Christianity is "a great vital and creative force." Contained in it are short biographies of the Apostle Paul, Ignatius the God-bearer, St. Justin the Philosopher, St. Athanasius the Great, St. Anthony the Great, Vladimir Monomachus, Metropolitan Philip, and St. Seraphim of Sarov (all of whom, except Vladimir Monomachus, are glo-

---

*The *New Testament* is established by the Eucharist of the Mystical Supper ("this is My blood of the New Testament"). If we acknowledge that before the institution of the Sacrament of the Eucharist, the eating of the Old Testament lamb took place (this is denied by many contemporary exegetists: see Clarendon Bible, Oxford, the explanations of the text of the Gospels of Matthew, Mark and Luke), then it is necessary to acknowledge that giving the disciples of the Body and Blood of Christ in the form of bread and wine at the Mystical Supper was accomplished after the Old Testament rite of Passover and independently of it.

If the Mystical Supper had been in fact the Hebrew "Passover," fulfilled once a year, then the words of the Saviour *this* (i.e. this same kind of Supper) *do in remembrance of Me* would have been received as meaning that the Eucharist be accomplished once a year, whereas the disciples of Christ gathered for the "breaking of bread" each week (on the first day of the week) from the very beginning of the institution of the Eucharist. The Passover rites were fulfilled strictly by a ritual established by custom, but here they were not applied: the blessing of the bread and wine took place at the end of the Supper, while the Hebrew Passover ritual demands the blessing at the beginning of the supper; the one presiding at the Hebrew Passover table blesses not one chalice (as we see at the Mystical Supper), but four cups. The name of the supper as "Passover" possibly has a conditional meaning for the synoptic evangelists, transferring us to an understanding of the "New Testament Passover." The "lamb" of the New Testament Passover, the Lord Jesus Christ, was slain on the next day after the completion of the Mystical Supper.

rified by the Church as saints, though in the text the title of "Saint" is given only to some of them). The features of these great personalities are presented concisely, but expressively. But here something is characteristic. They are composed in the form of ordinary biographies of "historic personalities." This fully harmonizes with the general one-sided direction of this collection. Where else, if not here, could we have expected the idea of the heavenly Church, of the everlasting blessed life of these pillars of the Church, of their ties with those living on earth? But the biographies of the saints here end with a dull "laid down his soul" for the Truth; "died in bed"; "went the way of his fathers"; "fell in an unequal battle and by martyrdom won the victory."*

Such is the collection as a whole. Its themes are varied, but one-sided in content, and almost completely avoid many essential elements of Orthodoxy. There is no mention of life beyond the grave, of temperance and asceticism, of penitence, of the writings of the Holy Fathers, etc. In fact very little is presented of "Orthodoxy in Life" and instead, too much is given concerning Orthodoxy "outside of life," in the form of a questionable subjective philosophy of Christianity. But what is most important is that many points here do not represent authentic Orthodoxy, both from the point of view of dogmatics and of history, as it came into being in life, with its constant striving for the heavenly. The "Orthodoxy" of the collection longs intensely for the earth.

In vain does it sorrowfully proclaim that "we have long ago reduced Christianity to life beyond the grave" and to the Kingdom of the age to come. No, we have not "reduced" it. Christians know that when they believe in the Kingdom of Heaven and search for it, then the Kingdom of Heaven is already entering "inside them" and into the world through the Church. But if they intend to build a happy life of the Kingdom of God now on earth for themselves or even for future generations, not only will they fail to build it on earth, but they may lose it in Heaven as well.

---

*The author speaks — as of one of the revealed truths — of "the identity of Christ with those believing in Him," on the basis of the words: "Saul, Saul, why persecutest thou Me?" (p. 375). How we are to understand this is unknown. If Christ is the believers, then where is Christ Himself?

Children in Church

Every Christian mother considers it one of her primary obligations to teach her child prayer as soon as his consciousness awakens — prayer that is simple and easy for him to understand. His soul must be accustomed to the warm and fervent experience of prayer at home, by his cradle, for his neighbors, his family. The child's evening prayer calms and softens his soul, he experiences the sweetness of prayer with his little heart and catches the first scent of sacred feelings.

It is harder for a child to assimilate in the atmosphere which prevails in church. At first he just observes. He sees people concentrating and rites he does not as yet understand and hears incomprehensible words. However, the very solemnity and festivity of the church have an uplifting effect on him. When a two year-old child wants to take part in church, to sing, speak or make prostrations — we can see in this his uplifted state of soul, wherein he is involuntarily influenced. We say this from simple observation.

But there is also something higher than our sense perceptions. Christ is invisibly present in church and He sees the child, blesses him, and receives him into the atmosphere of the Grace of the Holy Spirit. Grace envelopes him as a warm wind wafts over a blade of grass in a field, helping it to grow up slowly, gradually, to put down roots and develop. And so the mother hastens to bring her child to Christ, to His Grace, regardless even of whether he has any understanding at all of this contact with the gift of Grace. This is especially true concerning the Eucharist, the very closest union with Christ. The mother brings her infant to this Mystery while he is still a baby lying in her arms. Is the mother right?

Suffer the little children to come unto Me, for of such is the kingdom of God. Can you really say with certainty that there and then in the fields of Palestine these children had already understood Christ's teaching, that they had been sitting at the Teacher's feet and listening to His preaching? Do not say this, for the Evangelist himself remarks that *they brought unto Him also infants, that He would touch them: but when His disciples saw it, they rebuked them.* In bringing their little ones, the mothers' purpose was simply that His hands should touch the children, and not that He should teach them divine knowledge.

Allowing children to have contact with spiritual Grace is one of the first, basic concerns of a Christian who thinks about his children, and the task of Christian society, which is concerned about its youth. Here is the door to a correct Orthodox Christian upbringing. Enlightenment, compunction, and joy, as they awaken in the infant's growing consciousness, are an external indicator of the fact that the little Christian is feeling warmth from the divine source in himself. And even if he does not feel it, the invisible action of God's Grace does not stop; only we do not see it, just as we do not instantly see the effect of the sun on our own health. In Russian literature we have edifying examples of the disposition of children's souls during preparation for Confession and Communion, after Confession and after Communion of the Holy Mysteries.

Nevertheless, how often it is forgotten that herein lies the key to organizing religious education. How often, on seeing the inadequacy of religious education, we pick up the programs and rework them, lay the blame on the textbooks and the teachers — and forget about the importance of the church and the influence of the services; certainly we do not always ask ourselves the question: "But did the children go to church?"

As the child grows up, he should enter more deeply into the life of the Church. The child's mind, the youth's mind must be enlightened by the church services, learn from them, become immersed in them; the church should give him knowledge of God.

The matter is more complex. The task of religious education will be fulfilled only when we teach our children to *love church.*

When we, the adults, organize church services, make arrangements for them, shorten or lengthen the order of service and so on, we are accommodating ourselves to our own concepts and needs, or simply convenience, understood in adult terms. But in so far as the concepts, needs, and spiritual strivings of children are not taken into account, the surroundings are often not conducive towards making children love church. This is, nevertheless, one of the most important means of religious education: let the children come to love the church, so that they may always attend church with a pleasant feeling and receive spiritual nourishment from it. And since parents often cannot help here, if only because not infrequently they are irreligious themselves, we are often compelled, when we think about our Orthodox children, to place this work into the hands of the community, the hands of the school, the hands of the Church.

Just as we are not afraid of destroying a devotion to learning and books, or love for our national literature and history by making our children come running to class at the sound of a bell and sit at desks, and by immersing them in an atmosphere of strict discipline and compulsion, so also, one might think, we would have no reason to be afraid of using a certain amount of compulsion in the matter of attending church, whether it be part of a school regime or an expression of self-discipline on the part of youth organizations — both those that are connected with school and those that are not. If, however, this remains just compulsion, and to such an extent that it creates a psychological repulsion in the young people — this will certainly show that the aim has not been attained, that the method has proved to be inadequate and the compulsion fruitless. Let the child brought by our will express a desire to remain there through his own will. Then you will have justified your action.

Again we say: not only natural, psychological effects take place in children's souls in church, but the action of Grace. Our whole concern should be that the soul of the baby, child, or youth should not be closed to holy impressions, but should be opened freely. Then it will no longer need effort, force, or any other form of self-compulsion, but it will be nourished freely, easily and joyfully.

There is one thing that must not be forgotten: human nature requires at least a minimal degree of active participation. In church this can take the form either of reading, or of singing, serving in the altar, or of decorating and cleaning the church, or of some other activity, even if it is only indirectly connected with the services.

The indisputable importance of the church and of communal church services in the religious upbringing of children constitutes one of the arguments in favor of the Orthodox understanding of the Mystery of Baptism: that is to say, an argument in favor of baptizing children at a very young age, as we do in the Orthodox Church. Baptism is the door through which one enters the Church of Christ. One who is not baptized — which means he is not a member of Christ's family — has no right to participate in the life of this family, in its spiritual gatherings and in its table — the Lord's Table. Thus our children would be deprived of the right to be with us in church, to receive the blessing in the name of the Holy Trinity, to partake of the Body and Blood of Christ. And however we may influence them in our family at home, however much we might teach them the Gospel, we would be depriving them of the direct action of heavenly Grace, and at best we would arouse a thirst for faith in them — but we would still be keeping them far from the heavenly light and warmth, which comes down, regardless of our human efforts, in the Mysteries, in all the services, in holy prayers. How grossly mistaken are those religions which recognize only adult baptism!

The holy maidens Faith, Hope and Charity, and the holy young bride Perpetua, who became martyrs, are witnesses to the fact that adolescence is an age prepared even for the highest active participation in Christ's Church. The baby in his mother's arms in church who cried out, "Ambrose for Bishop!", and by his exclamation determined the choice of the renowned Ambrose of Milan for the episcopal cathedra — this baby is a defender of children's rights to an active participation in Christ's Church.

And so let us take some trouble over our children: first let us give them the chance to participate more in church — in a wider and more elevated form than just giving the censer to the priest; and secondly, let us adapt ourselves somewhat to our children when praying together with them.

Let the children be conscious that they are members of Christ's family. Let the children come to love church!

On the Rite of Churching an Infant

and the Prayer for a Woman Who Has Given Birth

The question is often raised as to why the Church does not permit the mother of a newborn child to enter a church or approach the Mysteries of Communion before the fortieth day following the delivery of her baby — the day on which the "churching" of the newborn child is performed. We consider it best to respond to this question by way of an explanation of the rite itself.

The fundamental purpose of the Rite of Churching is the reception of a new person into membership in the Church of Christ, just as an adult passes a set period of time in preparation before entering the Church of Christ, standing in the ranks of the catechumens, which of old occupied, and today still occupies, a period of about forty days. Usually this was the period of the Great Fast before Pascha, or another fast, likewise forty days, prior to the feast of Theophany — the Baptism of the Lord, which was later moved after the feast of the Nativity of Christ. The Church has recognized that such a length of time is also necessary for the infant, though in a somewhat different sense, namely, that having been accounted worthy within the first few days after his physical birth of a new, spiritual birth in the Mystery of Baptism, he might be prepared, throughout the succeeding days until the fortieth, for his entrance into the ranks of the members of the Church; and this means that the parents themselves are assured that the child will be able, in the arms of his own mother, to receive the Communion of the Holy Mysteries of Christ at the Divine Liturgy. Although as a newborn infant he as yet does not have a Christian consciousness, he nevertheless stands on the path which leads to the appearance and strengthening of this consciousness, under the Grace-bearing influence of the Church and Her divine services with the good influence, of course, of the family lifestyle. The infant is still in need of physical strengthening. He must enter upon conditions of earthly life unknown to him, become familiar with the method of partaking of nourishment and respond normally to the sensations he receives — in a word, he must show himself capable of a new form of life. The child is already baptized, already cleansed, spiritually washed; sponsors have made the Orthodox confession of faith for him and have promised to guide him spiritually in that confession. In Chrismation, the second Mystery, which immediately follows that of Baptism, he received the "seal of the gift of the Holy Spirit," and is thus open to the influence of the Holy Spirit's gift of Grace upon his soul.

The Church has done all that is within Her power in this sphere to open the path of salvation to him. He has been clothed in spiritually radiant garments. Adult catechumens who have received Baptism remain for eight days thereafter in their white robes as an expression of their radiant spiritual state. Here, also, concerning the infant, we ought to be especially attentive to the purity and noble aspect of his external appearance and environment. What else should follow?

Those first steps toward the fulfillment of the confession of faith and the promises given in the infant's name should be made. He has been received by the Church: let him enter therein. Churching is that first step: the child enters, is carried into the temple. Under the conditions of our way of life it is far from possible always to keep exactly the forty-day period of time for bringing the child into the church, since parish churches are often open only on Sundays and feast days. This matter, of course, is purely a formality: the Sabbath is for man, not man for the Sabbath.

This rite of Churching is not lengthy, and the fulfillment of the duty of bringing the child to church is not complicated. But for the one who does so, it is a profound obligation in the Christian upbringing of a new member of the Church.

Who shall bear him for the first time, as is fitting, into this divine chamber where the Mystical Supper is performed? "I behold Thy bridal chamber, O my Saviour, but have no garments that I might enter therein." Who, if not the mother? To whom, if not to her, does this right, this spiritual obligation, belong? In actuality she will yet further nourish him physically and spiritually. Forty days is sufficient for her to become strong in body and spirit, just like her child, and she is able to fulfill that duty, which is a joy to her: to bear her child into church and hand him to the priest, that with prayer he might lay him spiritually before God, might bear him before the altar and the holy things of the temple; that in the shortest possible time she may commune of the Mystical Supper of the Lord, not only herself, but with her child.

Once the All-holy Virgin, accompanied by her betrothed, the righteous elder Joseph, bore her divine Infant into the temple in Jerusalem precisely on the fortieth day — the temple was then open for prayer. She bore Him there to offer Him to the heavenly Father, in accordance with the prescription of the law of Moses that firstborn sons be specially consecrated to the Lord. And we honor this day among the great feasts of the Church, calling it The Meeting of the Lord.

For the woman who has given birth, these forty days as they pass are not simply days of waiting: they are a period for the restoration of her physical strength, and her spiritual equilibrium as well. For many hours and perhaps for many days she was completely in the hands of other people, most likely unknown to her. There were times when she could not pray. Was the medical and other aid accorded her always pure in the moral sense? Does her own conscience not accuse her of sin committed then in spiritual confusion? After the recovery of her strength there were new concerns; the former style of her domestic life has had to undergo certain modifications. If she has experienced a long lapse in the fulfillment of the duty of Confession and Communion of the Holy Mysteries of Christ, then it is beneficial for her to accept this on her soul as a period of penance similar to those imposed at Confession in accordance with the Church's canons.

The period of time comes to an end and the mother, child in arms, enters the church. At this point we should note that in the Church's rules there is no strict prohibition forbidding a woman who has given birth from entering the church before the end of the forty-day period. Circumstances may arise when such must take place before the fortieth day; in these cases, what is important is spiritual benefit, spiritual nourishment.

The mother enters the church with the thought of having her child receive a blessing for the rest of his life. She is conscious of the fact that the child is pure of soul, but she can no more say the same of herself than can we. It is significant that all home rules of prayer, as well as the divine services, begin with the words of repentance: "Have mercy on us, O Lord...cleanse us of our sins...forgive our transgressions...visit our infirmities...." For this reason the Church, blessing the infant, does not leave the mother bereft of attention, but goes beforehand to meet her feeling of lowliness.

In the following beautiful prayer it is suggested to us all in general that we each make our morning entry into church: "Glory to Thee, O King, Almighty God, Who through Thy divine and man-loving providence hast vouchsafed me, a sinner and an unworthy one, to rise from sleep and obtain entry into Thy holy house" — with such words it begins; and further on: "Deign that, through my defiled lips, but from a pure heart and humble spirit, praise may be offered to Thee so that I also,...may become a companion of the wise virgins..."

For the believer, attending church is a precious privilege, a joy, and he yearns when deprived of it. Having every possibility of attending church, it may happen that we underrate it, so it is at times profitable to arouse this feeling by delaying this possibility for a short period of time.

But in the given case we have in mind there is another reason: the strengthening or even the rousing of feelings of humility and repentance. Although *marriage is honorable in all, and the bed undefiled* (Heb. 13:4), yet life remains life: married life has its weaknesses and stumbling blocks. Thus, the Apostle Paul saw grounds for placing celibacy above marriage. *Come together again, that Satan tempt you not for your incontinency* (I Cor. 7:5). Psalm 50, with its words: *For behold, I was conceived in iniquities, and in sins did my mother bear me*, is part of nearly every rite of the Church performed in the home.

It is clear that the short restriction on the entry into the church of a woman who has given birth and on her receiving the Holy Mysteries casts no shadow on her, and thus should not elicit any bitterness on her part. A Christian woman should not here introduce the now popular demand for the "equality of women" to the rights of men. In Christianity these rights are always equal and always lofty; only their spheres of activity are different because of the difference in several of the attributes of their respective natures. There are no grounds for personal distress. Whoever might harbor such a feeling of discontent should realize that it is only an indication of self-importance, of too great a confidence in oneself, of the languishing in the soul of pride which is the root of our moral discontent. In this decision of the Church it is precisely the particular concern of the Church for the mother, its care for her, that is evident. In and of itself, the desire to partake of the Mysteries is always blessed, but only insofar as the reception of the Mysteries does not bring condemnation upon the communicant.

Thus, according to the Church Slavonic text of the Rite of Churching, we read:

> *On the fortieth day the babe is brought to the church by its mother, the babe having already been cleansed and washed... And when she hath inclined her head and the infant, the priest maketh the sign of the Cross over them, and, touching the child's head, he saith the prayer:* "Let us pray to the Lord. O Lord God, Ruler of all,...by Thy will Thou hast saved Thy handmaid, *N.*, who cometh to Thy holy temple, cleansing her of every sin and of every impurity, that without condemnation she may be vouchsafed to partake of Thy Holy Mysteries. The babe born of her do Thou bless, sanctify, enlighten, render chaste, and make of right mind,...that he (she) may be vouchsafed the noetic light at the time which Thou hast ordained, and may be numbered among Thy holy flock by Thine Only-begotten Son. With Him art Thou blessed, with Thine all-holy, good and life-creating Spirit..." *There follow then several brief prayers of similar content, and then the priest, taking the infant in his arms, bears it into the depths of the church, saying:* "The servant (handmaid) of God, *N.*, is churched...; he (she) entereth into Thy house...; In the midst of the church he (she) will hymn Thee.. " *Such is the essence of this short rite.*

It may be that the infant was baptized before the fortieth day. In general, however, if it is in no danger and is healthy, the mother comes to church for the prayers of remission without the baby; and the infant is brought to church for its churching immediately after the Mystery of Baptism has been performed. Hence, the chronological significance of several of the prayers is altered.

Let all things be done decently, and in order (I Cor. 14:40).

The Glorification of Saints

What, in essence, is the Church's formal glorification of saints? In the Holy, Catholic, Orthodox Church the prayerful memory of each of her members that has departed in faith, hope, and repentance is cherished. This commemoration of the majority of the departed is limited, comparatively, to the narrow circle of the "Church of the home," or, in general, to persons of close blood relation or acquainted with the departed. It is expressed by prayer for the departed, prayer for the remission of his sins, that "his soul be numbered among the righteous," that "his repose be with the saints." This is a spiritual, prayerful thread which binds those on earth to the departed; it is an expression of love which is beneficial both for the departed and, likewise, for those that pray for him. If, after death, he is not deprived of the vision of the glory of God because of his personal sins, he responds with his own prayer for those close to him on earth.

Persons who are great in their Christian spirit, glorious in their service to the Church, beacons illumining the world, leave behind themselves a memory which is not confined to a narrow circle of people, but which is known throughout the whole Church, local or universal. Confidence in their having attained the glory of the Lord and in the power of their prayers, even after death, is so strong and unquestioned that the thought of their earthly brethren is not channeled into prayer for the forgiveness of their sins (since they are holy before the Lord without such), but towards the praising of their struggles, towards accepting their lives as models for ourselves, towards requesting their prayers for us.

In witness to the profound certainty of the Church that a reposed righteous man is with the Lord, in the choir of the saints in the heavenly Church, she composes an act of "numbering among the saints," or of "glorification." By this the Church gives her blessing for the change from prayers for the reposed to prayer requesting for us his prayerful assistance before the throne of God. The unanimous voice of the Church, expressed through the lips of her hierarchs, the conciliar voice, confirms the conviction of her ordinary members concerning the sanctity of the righteous man. Such is the essence of the act of glorification itself. Nothing in the Church should be arbitrary, but "proper and orderly." The concern of the Church in regard to this is expressed in offering a uniform prayerful supplication to the righteous one.

At times the commemoration of a departed righteous one does not extend beyond the bounds of a particular province. Other saints of God become famous and renowned throughout the Church even during their earthly activity; they are her glory and show themselves to be pillars of the Church. An ecclesiastical resolution on their glorification confirms this commemoration forever in its proper domain, i.e., in the local Church which has made the resolution, or throughout the universal Church.

The assembly of saints in the heavenly Church of all times is great and beyond enumeration. The names of certain saints are known on earth; others remain unknown. The saints are like stars — those closest to us are more clearly seen; yet, countless other points of light stretch through space, beyond the eye's reach. Thus, in the Church's commemoration, saints are glorified in large groups and whole assemblies, as well as individually. Such are the commemorations of martyrs that were slain by the hundreds and thousands, the Fathers of the Ecumenical Councils, and, finally, the general celebrations of "all saints," both annual (the first Sunday after Pentecost; the second Sunday after Pentecost for all the saints of Russia), and weekly (every Saturday).

How has and does the Church's glorification of her great and glorious hierarchs, ascetics, and others recognized as saints, occur? On the basis of what principles, by what criteria, by what rite — in general, and in individual cases? Research by Prof. E. Golubinsky, *The History of the Canonization of Saints in the Russian Church* (2nd ed., Moscow: University Press, 1903), is dedicated to these questions. In the following exposition we will, for the most part, make use of Professor Golubinsky's treatise.

While using the term *canonization of the saints*, Prof. Golubinsky admits in the first lines of his book that, although this term is etymologically derived from the Greek word *canon*, it forms a part of the terminology of the Latin Church and is not employed by the Orthodox Greeks. This is an indication that we need not use it; and indeed, in his own time Prof.

Golubinsky was reproached for using it too assiduously, especially since the spirit and character of Orthodox glorification is somewhat different from the canonization of the Roman confession. The Roman Church's canonization, in its contemporary form, consists of a solemn proclamation by the pope: "We resolve and determine that Blessed N. is a saint, and we enter him in the catalogue of the saints, commanding the whole Church to honor his memory with reverence..." The Orthodox "numbering among the choir of the saints" has no special, fixed formula, but its sense might be expressed thus: "We confess that N. is in (numbered with) the choir of the saints of God."

In the first centuries of the Christian Church, three basic types of saints were recognized. These were: a) the Old Testament patriarchs, prophets (among whom St. John the Forerunner is pre-eminent) and the New Testament apostles; b) the martyrs, who gained crowns of glory through the shedding of their blood; and c) outstanding hierarchs who served the Church, as well as people acclaimed for their personal struggle (the righteous and the ascetics). As concerns the patriarchs, prophets, apostles, and martyrs, membership in any one of these categories carried with it recognition as a saint.

It is known from history that prayer meetings were held in honor of the martyrs as early as the first quarter of the second century (cf. St. Ignatius of Antioch). In all probability, they were begun in the period immediately following the first persecution of the Christians — that of Nero. It is apparent that no special ecclesiastical decree was required to authorize the prayerful veneration of this or that martyr. A martyr's death itself testified to the reception of a heavenly crown. But the numbering of departed hierarchs and ascetics among the choir of the saints was done individually, and was naturally carried out on the basis of each one's personal worthiness.

It is impossible to give a general answer as to which criteria the Church employed for recognition of saints belonging to this third classification. As regards the ascetics in particular, without a doubt the fundamental, general basis of their glorification was and still is the working of miracles as supernatural evidence, which is free from human whim or bias. Prof. Golubinsky considers this indication the sole basis for the glorification of ascetics in the history of ecclesiastical canonization. Despite his opinion, however, one may conclude that the commemoration of the great Christian desert dwellers of old, the leaders and guides of monasticism, was kept by the Church for their didactic gifts and their lofty spiritual attainments, apart from a strict dependence on whether they were glorified with the gift of working miracles. They were numbered among the choirs of the saints strictly for their ascetic life, without any particular reference to such a criterion [miracle working].

The ancient Church's glorification of holy hierarchs should be viewed somewhat differently. Their lofty service itself was the basis of their glorification, just as the martyrs' holy ends were for them. In the Carthaginian Calendar, which dates from the seventh century, there is the superscription: "Here are recorded the birthdays (i.e., the dates of martyrdom) of the martyrs and the days of the repose of bishops whose annual commemoration the Church of Carthage celebrates." Thus, judging from ancient Greek liturgical calendars, one may surmise that in the Greek Church all Orthodox bishops who did not sully themselves in any way were numbered amongst the choir of the local saints of their diocese, on the basis of the belief that as intercessors before God in this life by their vocation, they remain such even in the life beyond the grave. In the ecclesiastical calendars of the Patriarchate of Constantinople, all the patriarchs of Constantinople who occupied that see between AD 315 (St. Metrophanes) and 1025 (St. Eustathius), with the exception of those that were heretics or for one canonical reason or another were deposed, are recorded in the list of the saints. This compilation, however, was scarcely done in the sequence in which the patriarchs occupied their see. In all probability, the most renowned bishops were recognized as saints immediately following their repose; in the other cases, this inclusion was carried out at some other time.

The names of all departed bishops were entered in the local *diptychs* — the lists of the departed which were read aloud at the divine services, and every year, on the date of the repose of each of them, their commemoration was kept with special solemnity. Sozomen, the church historian, states that in individual churches or dioceses, the celebrations of their local martyrs and the commemoration of their former priests (i.e., their hierarchs) were observed. Herein he uses the term "celebration" in reference to the memory of the martyrs, but "commemoration" in reference to the hierarchs, leaving it to be understood that in the ancient Church the latter events (if one may speak of an overall plan and not of individual cases) were of lesser stature than the former. Prof. Golubinsky conjectures that, as regards hierarchs, after a certain number of years of fervent prayer *for* them, the annual celebration of their memory was transformed into a day of prayer *to* them. According to the testimony of Symeon of Thessalonica, from the earliest times in Constantinople the hierarchs were interred within the sanctuary of the largest church, that of the Apostles, like the relics of the saints, because of the Grace of the divine priesthood.

In the Greek Church, until the eleventh century, only a very few of the choir of hierarchs were saints universally venerated throughout the entire Church. The greater portion of the hierarchs remained local saints of the individual Churches (i.e., dioceses), and each individual diocese/Church celebrated only its own local hierarchs, with a very small number of hierarchs venerated universally throughout the Church. With the eleventh century the transformation of the choirs of hierarchs from local to universal came about, as a result of which there are a great number of names. This was probably the reason why, from that century on, the numbering of hierarchs among the choirs of the saints was carried out more strictly, and as the criterion for the numbering of any of the patriarchs of Constantinople among the saints it was declared necessary to have irrefutable evidence of their miracles, as was also required for the glorification of ascetics.

In local Churches (dioceses) the right to recognize individuals as saints belonged to their bishops and their clergy or officials subject to their authority. It is also quite possible that the bishops did not perform such an act without the knowledge and consent of the metropolitan and the synod of bishops of the metropolitan province. At times the laity determined beforehand the future glorification of ascetics, even while the latter were still alive, and in witness of their determination erected churches dedicated to such ascetics, apparently in the certainty that the blessing of the hierarchy would be forthcoming.

When Symeon the Pious, St. Symeon the New Theologian's elder and guide, reposed in the Lord after forty-five years of ascetic labor, St. Symeon, knowing the intensity of his struggles, his purity of heart, his closeness to God and the Grace of the Holy Spirit which overshadowed him, composed in his honor a eulogy, as well as hymns and canons, and celebrated his memory yearly with great solemnity, having painted an icon of him as a saint. Others, perhaps, both within and outside the monastery, followed his example, for he had many disciples and admirers among monastics and laity alike. St. Sergius II, then Patriarch of Constantinople (reigned 999–1019), heard of this, summoned St. Symeon to appear before him, and questioned him concerning the feast and the Saint who was being so honored. But perceiving that Symeon the Pious had led such an exalted life, he did not prohibit the reverencing of his memory, and even sent lamps and incense himself in Symeon's memory. Sixteen years passed without incident. But later, a certain influential retired metropolitan who resided in Constantinople objected to any veneration conducted on private initiative. Such a thing seemed to him blasphemous and contrary to church order. A few parish priests and some layfolk agreed with him, and disturbances began over this point, lasting for about two years. To attain their goal, St. Symeon's opponents did not stop at slander, directed at both the Saint and his elder. St. Symeon was ordered to appear before the patriarch and his synod to give an explanation. His reply was that, following the precepts of the apostles and the holy fathers, he could not refrain from honoring his elder, that he did not compel others to do so, that he was acting according to his own conscience, and that others could do as seemed best to them. Satisfied by this *apologia*, they nevertheless ordered St. Symeon henceforth to celebrate the memory of his elder as modestly as possible, without any solemnity. The controversy continued for about six years, however, and a full-scale vendetta was launched against the icon of Symeon the Pious, in which he was depicted in the company of other saints, with an inscription referring to him as a "saint," and overshadowed by Christ the Lord in an attitude of blessing. The result of this was that, for peace of mind and the establishment of peace, St. Symeon decided to leave Constantinople and settled in a remote spot near the ancient church of St. Marina, where he later built a monastery. Concerning the question of the veneration itself, the previous decree remained in force, viz. the celebration was permitted so long as it was not conducted with solemnity (cf. "Life of St. Symeon the New Theologian" in his *Discourses*, ed. Bishop Theophan, 2 vols. [Moscow: Ephimov Press, 1892], Vol. I, pp. 3–20).

The incident cited above demonstrates, from one point of view, that knowledge of an ascetic's righteous life in and of itself leads to a firm conviction regarding his sojourn in the company of the saints after his death and to his veneration; on the other hand, it witnesses to the fact that, at that time (the 11th century), the custom and procedures of the Church required definite confirmation by higher church authorities and a special synodal decree sanctioning public veneration.

In the future the Greek Church was to know two classifications of newly glorified saints: martyrs and ascetics. Under Turkish rule, the Greek Church had no small number of martyrs who were put to death for their exceptional zeal for the Christian faith and for publicly denouncing Islam. The later Greek Church, and the universal Church with her, has regarded and continues to accept her martyrs just as the ancient Church regarded the martyrs of the early Christian era, acknowledging martyrdom as sufficient foundation for glorification, irrespective of the gift of working miracles, although miracles did have a place in many cases. A great many Greek martyrs were not proclaimed as saints in any official manner and were often honored as "zealots," without any deliberate inquest or proclamation on the part of the Great Church of Constantinople, for such would have been difficult to carry out under the conditions of the Turkish Yoke. St. Nicephorus of Chios, who composed a "General Service to Any New Martyr," explaining the need for such a service, states: "Inasmuch as the majority of the new martyrs do not have a service to celebrate, and whereas many people are desirous of such a service — one, to honor his fellow countryman; another, to honor someone known to him personally; yet another, to honor someone who has helped him in some need, I have therefore composed a general service for any new martyr. May he that so desires sing such a service to that martyr for whom he has a veneration." The author of *A History of the Canonization of the Saints in the Russian Church* believes that generally martyrs honored without official glorification were also intended in the above case. Whether or not his supposition is accurate is difficult to determine.

As before, in the Eastern Church the criterion that had to be met for the glorification of ascetics, be they hierarchs or monastics, was the gift of working miracles. Patriarch Nectarius of Jerusalem (reigned 1661–1669), gives lucid testimony concerning this. He writes: "Three things witness to true sanctity in people: 1) irreproachable Orthodoxy, 2) perfection in all the virtues, which are crowned by standing up for the faith, even unto the shedding of one's blood, and finally, 3) the manifestation by God of supernatural signs and wonders." In addition to this, Patriarch Nectarius indicates that at that time, when abuses in reporting miracles and virtues were common occurrences, yet other signs were required, i.e., the incorruption of bodies or a fragrance emanating from the bones.

In the East, the right to glorify a saint for local veneration belongs to the metropolitans of the metropolitan sees; for general veneration throughout the Church of Constantinople, the patriarch of Constantinople with his synod of bishops gives the blessing. Athos, apparently, constitutes an exception in this regard, glorifying its own ascetics for local veneration on the Holy Mountain through the personal authority of the brotherhoods, or of individual monasteries, or by the synodia of the Protaton for the entire Athonite community. Also, the gift of working miracles can hardly be considered obligatory as a basis for glorification, yet one may deem an ascetic life, confirmed afterwards by the sign of fragrance emanating from the bones, as such a basis.

From the compilation of documents of the Patriarchate of Constantinople relating to the glorification of the saints, which is appended to the second edition of *A History of the Canonization of the Saints in the Russian Church*, one may form for oneself an idea as to by what sort of decree glorification has been carried out.

From the fourteenth century a decree has come down to us from Patriarch John XIV (reigned 1333–47) addressed to Theognostus, Metropolitan of Kiev and All Russia (reigned 1328–53, resident in Moscow), dated July of 1339, concerning the numbering of his predecessor, St. Peter, Metropolitan of Moscow (reigned 1308–26), among the saints: "...We have received the letter of Thy Holiness, together with the notification and attestation concerning the hierarch of the holy Church who was before thee, that after death he hath been glorified by God and shown to be one of His true favorites, and that great miracles are worked by him and every disease is healed. And we rejoiced concerning this and were exceedingly glad of spirit, and rendered unto God fitting glorification. And inasmuch as Thy Holiness hath sought guidance from us as to how to act with such holy relics, we reply: Thy Holiness doth thyself know, nor art thou ignorant of the manner of ritual and custom the Church of God holdeth to in such cases. Having received a firm and incontestable attestation concerning this Saint, let Thy Holiness in the present event act in accordance with the Church's rite. Honor and bless God's favored one with hymnody and sacred doxologies, and bequeath these to the future ages, to the praise and glory of God, Who glorifieth them that glorify Him..."

In the eulogy of Patriarch Philotheus of Constantinople (reigned 1354–55, 1364–76) for St. Gregory of Palamas, Archbishop of Thessalonica, concerning the numbering of the Archbishop among the choir of the saints, after an account of ten miracles performed at the saint's tomb, we read: "Hence [i.e., owing to the fact that many miracles had taken place at the Archbishop's tomb], the most God-loving and pre-eminent of them here present [the citizens of Thessalonica], and especially of them that are priests, having taken counsel together, have set up a sacred icon of Gregory and are celebrating a radiant festival for all the people on the day of his repose, and are hastening to erect a church for him, for he is a glorious disciple of Christ. They are not waiting for the assemblies of great men or any general councils to proclaim him [a saint], for such things sometimes are a hindrance, a burden, an obstacle and a care, and are all too human, but they are content, as is laudable, with a proclamation from on high, with the luminous and irrefutable contemplation of his works, and with faith." From the discourse of Patriarch Philotheus it is clear that: 1) St. Gregory Palamas was numbered among the saints because of the miracles performed at his tomb, and 2) his glorification was performed by the Metropolitan of Thessalonica.

Decrees of much later origin clearly speak of special inquiries of synods relative to glorification. Thus, in a decree of Patriarch Cyril I (reigned 1621–23, 1624–32, 1632–33, 1633–34, 1637–38) concerning the glorification of St. Gerasimus of Cephalonia, following a dogmatic explanation of the Orthodox teaching concerning the Saint, we find: "And we, on the one hand, ready before God to render unto divine men the honor that befitteth them in recompense, and on the other hand, caring for the common good of the faithful, in accordance with the divine fathers that were before us, and following the universal practice of the Church, we do synodally resolve, appoint and command in the Holy Spirit, with the approval also of the blessed Patriarchs of Antioch and Jerusalem who live in Constantinople, of the most sacred metropolitan, and our beloved brethren, the archbishops and bishops, most honored in the Holy Spirit, of the most worthy and learned clergy, that the above-named St. Gerasimus be venerated yearly with sacred services and psalmody, and be reckoned in the number of the venerable and holy men, henceforth and forevermore, not only on the island of Cephalonia, but throughout the Church of the pious, from one end of the world to the other. But he that doth not accept this synodal decision, or that hath in general dared to gainsay it, after the first and second admonition let him be cut off from the community of the pious, and let him be unto all as a heathen and a publican, in accordance with the word of the Gospel." There then follow the signatures of the three patriarchs and seven other hierarchs. In the copy which bears the seal, the request addressed to the Patriarch by the inhabitants of the island of Cephalonia is placed before the decree. Therein, they request, through the mediation of a certain bishop, that a decree be issued by the Patriarch, authorizing the veneration of Gerasimus, and that he be included in the list of venerable and holy men.

Another decree of the same Patriarch, dated 1633, concerning the numbering of St. John of Crete and his ninety-eight fellow ascetics among the choir of the saints, contains a dogmatic explanation followed by this statement: "Inasmuch that long before our time, in the divinely built city of Crete, the venerable John the desert-dweller and his fellow ascetics, ninety-eight in number shone forth... whose life the Lord hath glorified with miracles... having assembled in the Holy Spirit all the hierarchs to be found in Constantinople, and having called upon the Promised One to be with us all our days, we do ordain that these holy ones be glorified with yearly festivals and sacred hymnody, and be numbered among the rest of the saints, both on the island of Crete, and in all the churches throughout the whole world. Strange and surpassingly foolish it would be if God were wondrously to glorify them as saints and we were not to delight in honoring them, or were even to deprive ourselves of the benefit derived therefrom, especially since we are needful of such intercessors..." This decree ends with the signatures of twenty-one hierarchs.

Finally, the decree of Patriarch Gabriel III of Constantinople (reigned 1702–70), issued in 1703, concerning the numbering among the saints of Dionysius, ascetic Archbishop of Zakynthos, contains a decree on the local celebration of a local saint. The inhabitants of the two islands which comprised the diocese of Cephalonia and Zakynthos requested permission from the Patriarch to institute an annual feast for the Saint and to make of this a solemn celebration. The synod of bishops, presided over by the Patriarch, decreed: "We command and decree in the Holy Spirit that Kyr Timotheus of Cephalonia and Zakynthos, beloved of God, and the sacred assembly of the clergy — priests and hieromonks — and all the people of the Lord with him, rulers and subjects, have express permission to institute henceforth an annual feast, and to celebrate the solemn memory of our venerable and God-bearing father Dionysius, hierarch and wonder-worker, with canonical services on the day appointed for him, i.e., on the seventeenth day of the month of December, in the sacred Monastery of the Transfiguration situated on one of the Strophades islands where his relics are located... and on these two islands in particular, that the annual feast and the solemn service of the saint be confined to these islands alone, where the divine Grace descended, and that this sacred service established for the saint be kept until the end of the ages, unbroken in its continuity and hindered by none..."

The act of numbering among the choirs of the saints is, for the most part, combined with the uncovering of relics of the righteous one who is being glorified. In these cases one must then distinguish three specific acts. The examination of the relics may be reckoned as one of the actions that precede the act of glorification, on par with the verification of the accounts of his miracles. Then follows the synodal decision concerning the glorification. In our days, the solemn removal of the relics is usually one of the first sacred actions in the realization of the act of the glorification which will take place. With the removal of the relics and the enshrining of them in a specially prepared place in a church, the prayerful commemoration in honor of the newly-glorified favorite of God begins. However, the presence of relics and their actual uncovering are not absolutely essential to a glorification. The relics of many saints have not been preserved, and the bodies of others have been subject to corruption, as are the bodies of ordinary people. As regards the relics of a considerable number of ancient saints, certain of these constitute entire bodies — bones with flesh; others, bones devoid of flesh.

The removal of bodies from the ground began in the early Church. As is known from documents from the second century, Christians gathered yearly at the tombs of the martyrs on the days of their repose to celebrate these days with solemnity. St. Basil the Great and St. Gregory the Theologian mention the exhumation of the relics of the saints. In his *Life of St. Anthony*, St. Athanasius reports the extraordinary reverence the Christians of Egypt had for martyrs' remains. It is well known that Emperor Constantius (reigned 337–61), son of St. Constantine the Great, enshrined the relics of the Apostles Andrew, Luke and Timothy in the Church of the Holy Apostles, in the years 356 and 357.

In the matter of the glorification of saints, the Russian Church has followed the belief and practice of the Churches of the East. The general rules

regarding this have been and remain the following: the basis for the numbering of one of God's departed favorites among the choir of the saints was
the gift of working miracles, either during his lifetime, examples of which
are known, or, as in the majority of cases, after death. In the ancient
Church, as has been stated, exalted service to the Church or a martyr's end
were in and of themselves such bases. In the Russian Church similar occasions of ecclesiastical glorification, aside from the working of miracles were
but rare exceptions.

The following differ according to the degree of the territorial extent of
veneration: 1) local saints in a more narrow sense, whose celebration began
only on the very site of their burial, be that in a monastery or a parish
church (of which there are several examples); 2) local saints in a wider
sense, i.e., those whose veneration was limited virtually by the boundaries
of the diocese; and finally 3) universal or general saints of the Church,
whose celebration was begun throughout the Russian Church. The right of
glorifying local saints of the first and second categories belongs to the
diocesan bishop, apparently with the assent of the metropolitan or patriarch; the right to general glorification belongs to the head of the Russian
Church. The execution of the glorification of the saints consisted of receiving accounts of miracles and of a corresponding verification of these testimonies. The essence of glorification of the saints lies in initiating an annual celebration of a saint's memory on the day of his repose or on the day of
the uncovering of his relics, or both. For the celebration of a saint's memory a service to him is required, as well as a written "life." The ecclesiastical
authorities saw to it that the services and the readings from the Prologue
(Synaxarion) concerning the saint were composed "according to pattern,"
i.e., that they conformed to a set form and were satisfactory from the literary stylistic point of view.

The veneration of a newly-glorified saint began with a special, solemn
divine service in the church at which or within which the bodily remains of
God's saint were located.

From ancient times until the present, the glorification of the saints has
been conducted in the same manner in the Russian Church; for this reason
there have been no periods in its history which might have depended on a
change of condition or of the method by which the glorification was carried out. Regardless of an official glorification, and in other cases before the
glorification, there existed yet a "veneration" of the departed virtuous

ascetics. In many instances a chapel was erected over the grave of the departed, and in it there was set a grave slab or reliquary (if the departed one was interred within a church, the reliquary was positioned over the place of burial; usually this "cenotaph" was an empty sarcophagus which held no body, since the body was underground). Pannykhidas were chanted at the tomb and, at times even molebens to the departed. Such a capricious declaration of such a person as a "saint" by the chanting of molebens has been forbidden by the ecclesiastical authorities as illicit. There have been cases in the life of the Russian Church when services have been composed to saints not yet glorified by a special synodal decision; these have passed into private use. Thus, in the sixteenth century, Photius, a monk of the monastery of Volokolamsk, composed a service to the departed Joseph of Volotsk and submitted it to Metropolitan Macarius of Moscow (reigned 1543–64). "The great beacon and teacher of the whole world, His Eminence Metropolitan Macarius," the superscription of the service states, "having reviewed this service, blessed the Elder Photius to use it in his cell prayers until the celebration of a synodal exposition." Similar occasions of the blessing by the higher ecclesiastical authorities of personal initiative in the composing of services to ascetics as yet not glorified by a synodal decree were hardly frequent. In one of the *sborniki* (anthologies) of St. Cyril's White Lake Monastery is found an article "On the Vainglory of Young Monks that Compose New Canons and Lives of the Saints." The anonymous author of the article opposed monks who, "striving for earthly glory and desirous of attracting the attention of those in authority, compose canons to, and lives of, the departed whom God hath not glorified." In his conclusion, the author admonishes compilers of canons and lives, saying: "O ye childish ones, do not compose new canons and lives to be sung by individuals at home or in monastic cells, without the blessing of the Church."

In essence there is no distinction between saints celebrated by the whole Church and local saints. Saints of both classes are glorified by a resolution of hierarchal authority. The faithful turn to both with their prayerful entreaties for assistance. The Church calls both "saints." In the Russian Church, as among the Orthodox Churches of the East, local saints in many instances pass on to the category of saints of the universal Church. One of the marks distinguishing universally venerated saints from local ones is that the names of saints generally revered are included in the divine service books. It is true that until the mid-sixteenth century, there were in general no names of Russian saints in the official listings, but after the sixteenth century they began to appear. In the *Book of Epistles (Apostol)* printed in Moscow at the end of the sixteenth century, there are seven Russian saints to be found: St. Sergius of Radonezh, St. Peter, Metropolitan of Moscow, St. Alexis, Metropolitan of Moscow, St. Leontius, Bishop of Rostov, St. Cyril of Byelozersk, the Holy Great Prince Vladimir, and the Holy Passion-bearers Boris and Gleb. But beginning with the first printed *Liturgikon (Sluzhebnik)* of 1602, a required listing of generally celebrated saints was introduced into the monthly listings in the *Typicon* and in the lists of saints in other liturgical books. During the Synodal period, in the Holy Synod's resolutions concerning general ecclesiastical glorification, the following indication is found on several occasions: "...and in the printed church books permission is required to insert names into the lists with the rest."

In the Russian Church, the first to be numbered among the choir of the saints were the holy princes Boris and Gleb (named Roman and David at their baptism); there then followed St. Theodosius of the Kiev Caves Lavra; then, perhaps, St. Nicetas, Bishop of Novgorod, and the holy Great Princess Olga. In all, until the sixteenth century, there were about seventy names of glorified Russian saints, of whom twenty-two were celebrated by the whole Russian Church. The Councils of 1547 and 1549, convoked under the presidency of Metropolitan Macarius, instituted the celebrations of several new saints, and raised the rank of others by adding thirty-nine names to the twenty-two that were already receiving general veneration, bringing the number of the latter to sixty-one. Between these councils and the establishment of the Holy Synod, as many as one hundred and fifty new glorifications took place in Muscovite Russia, of which the exact dates of about a third of them are known; of the remainder indirect references, such as the construction of churches and side altars dedicated to them, and some passing mention in literature of the period, provide us with evidence of some official sanctioning of their veneration.

The names of the saints of south-west Russia should be placed in a category of their own, headed by the saints of the Kiev Caves Lavra. Historical circumstances, particularly the subjugation by foreign powers (Lithuania and Poland), resulted in far fewer glorifications of saints in that region. A general service to saints of the Kiev Caves was commissioned by Metropolitan Peter Moghila (ruled 1633–46), to whom it was presented in 1643.

Prior to this, but also under Peter Moghila, the *Patericon of the Caves* was compiled, as well as an account of the miracles performed at the Lavra and in its caves during the forty-four years preceding the compilation of the book.

From the life of St. Job of Pochaev, written by his disciple and assistant in governing the Monastery of Pochaev, we know how the glorification of the venerable one came about, whose memory is especially revered in the Russian diaspora. The uncovering of his relics was performed seven years after the saint's repose, by Metropolitan Dionysius (Balaban) of Kiev (reigned 1657–63). The immediate cause of this was a thrice-repeated apparition of the venerable Job to the Metropolitan while he was asleep, informing him that it was pleasing to God that his relics be uncovered. After the third apparition, the Metropolitan (who apparently knew St. Job and the Monastery of Pochaev from his tenure as Bishop of Lutsk) "thus understood that this matter was in accordance with the Providence of God and, not delaying, he hastened to the Monastery of Pochaev, taking with him Kyr Theophanes (Krekhovetsky), Archimandrite of the Obruchsky Monastery, who happened to be with him at the time. Arriving at the monastery with all his clergy, he inquired earnestly concerning the honorable and pure life of St. Job in detail. Ascertaining that this was a good work and pleasing unto God, he straightway commanded, with the consent of the brethren, that the saint's tomb be opened. Therein, in a state of incorruption, as though at the hour of burial, they uncovered the relics of the venerable one, which were full of an inconceivably sweet fragrance. In the company of a multitude of people, they bore the relics with fitting honor to the great Church of the Life-creating Trinity, and there, in the narthex, positioned the reliquary, in the year of our Lord 1659, on the twenty-ninth day of August. Then did a vast multitude of people afflicted with divers ailments receive healing, for St. Job was in this life adorned with every virtue; and thus, after death, ceased not to do good unto them that approached him with faith" (cf. *The Service of the Venerable Job and His Life,* Jordanville, NY).

After the unification of Muscovite and Kievan Russia, Russia's saints should then have been referred to as "saints of all Russia" — both those of Northern and Western Russia. This was in fact the practice, though it was not until 1762 that a decree was published by the Holy Synod permitting the insertion of the names of Kievan saints into the general monthly listings at Moscow, and allowing their services to be printed in the Menaion. This decree was repeated twice thereafter.

In the Synodal period, the following saints were glorified for the veneration of the whole Church (they are presented in chronological order, according to the dates of their glorifications): St. Demetrius, Metropolitan of Rostov; St. Innocent, first Bishop of Irkutsk; St. Metrophanes, first Bishop of Voronezh; St. Tikhon of Zadonsk, Bishop of Voronezh; St. Theodosius, Archbishop of Chernigov; St. Seraphim of Sarov; St. Joasaph, Bishop of Belgorod; St. Hermogenes, Patriarch of Moscow; St. Pitirim, Bishop of Tambov; St. John, Metropolitan of Tobolsk; St. Joseph, Bishop of Astrakhan.

There were also local glorifications of saints during the Synodal period. But even for this era there are no accurate lists or reliable facts concerning the circumstances and dates of their glorification, as the decisions for local canonization were made without formal proclamation in the general record of the Holy Synod's decrees, for until the appearance of the official publications of the Synod — *The Church Register* and the *Diocesan Registers* — these were not published at all.

In the Russian Church, as in the Orthodox East, the wider the area of the proposed veneration, the higher the ecclesiastical authority needed to confirm it.

When, in 1715, the priest and parishioners of the Church of the Resurrection in Totma (Vologda Province) turned to the archbishop of Veliky Ustiug with the request that, in view of the many miracles which had occurred at the grave of Maximus, a priest and "fool for Christ" of that town, who had reposed in 1650, the archbishop blessed the construction of a church dedicated to St. Paraskeva over his grave, "as is customary for the saints of God, and also to construct over his relics a sarcophagus and a holy icon to cover it." In reply to this request, the archbishop decreed "that a monument be constructed in that church and that molebens be chanted to St. Maximus in a holy manner, as for the other favorites of God." Thus, one may conclude that the archbishop blessed the local veneration on his own personal authority.

The brethren of the Monastery of Solovki turned in 1690 to Archbishop Athanasius of Kholmogora with the request for permission to celebrate the memory of St. Herman in their monastery, who had been a founder of their monastery together with Sts. Zosima and Sabbatius and who had reposed in 1484 (Sts. Zosimas and Sabbatius had already been glorified for general celebration at the Council of 1547 under Metropolitan Macarius). The Archbishop, expressing his personal willingness, but keeping in view the important general ecclesiastical implications of this act, replied to them indicating the order that exists and that should be employed on such occasions: "Not denying his sanctity i.e. that of St. Herman, but preserving the fullness of the dogmas of the Holy Church, from of old they have been accustomed in our Holy Orthodox Faith to require first reliable testimonies concerning the lives and miracles of the saints of God. On this testimony, and with the general blessing of the Archpastor and the Orthodox monks, services and canons are composed for them, and in this manner a veneration is established; but without evidence and without the blessing of the sovereign and His Holiness, the patriarch, this can in no wise be firmly initiated." Permission for the local glorification of St. Herman occurred in that year or the following.

As examples of how a synodal execution of matters pertaining to the righteous departed came about, we shall cite several extracts from acts related to the glorification of saints "of all Russia."

Regarding the institution of the general ecclesiastical celebration of the memory of St. Joseph of Volotsk, the following statement is found in one of the anthologies of Volokolamsk: "By order of the right-believing and Christ-loving Sovereign Autocrat, Tsar, and Great Prince Feodor Ivanovich of All Russia, and with the blessing of his father, His Holiness Job, first Patriarch of Moscow and All Russia, the troparion, kontakion, stichera and canon, and the whole service for the Liturgy to our venerable father and Abbot Joseph of Volotsk were corrected under Abbot Joasaph on June 1, 7099 (i.e., 1591). And the Sovereign Autocrat, Tsar, and Great Prince Feodor Ivanovich of All Russia, and His Holiness Job, Patriarch of Moscow and All Russia, and the whole council, in general assembly witnessed the singing of the troparion, the kontakion, the stichera, the canon, and the service at Liturgy to the venerable Joseph. On the advice of the whole council, the Tsar and the Patriarch commanded the service to be chanted and celebrated in all places on September 9, the day of the repose of our venerable father Joseph the Wonderworker, which is the day of the commemoration of the holy and righteous ancestors of God, Joachim and Anna. The Sovereign, Tsar and Great Prince Feodor Ivanovich commanded that in the printed menaion and in all menaia on the same day the kon-

takion, stichera, canon, and all the service to the venerable Joseph be printed, together with that of the feast of the Nativity of the Most Holy
Theotokos and that of the Ancestors of God, thus instituting and confirming that this feast be celebrated in this manner, unchanging, in all places,
forever. Amen." The veneration of St. Joseph was thrice instituted — twice
locally, once generally. His relics were not uncovered and have remained
until the present day beneath a slab.

From a decree of Patriarch Job (reigned 1586–1605) dated 1600 and
located in the Korniliev Monastery in Vologda Province, we know how the
establishment of the general veneration of St. Cornelius of Komel came
about. Abbot Joseph of the Korniliev Monastery reported to the patriarch
that a side chapel had been constructed in the monastery in honor of St.
Cornelius, that it had not been consecrated yet, and that "for many years
they that requested healing from St. Cornelius had received it, and the
blind, the lame and they that were afflicted with divers ailments were
cured." With this, Abbot Joseph submitted to the patriarch in council the
stichera, canon, and life of St. Cornelius. The patriarch, bishops, and all
others attending the council questioned Archbishop Jonah of Vologda
concerning the miracles of St. Cornelius and received a reply from him to
the effect that "at the reliquary of St. Cornelius the Wonderworker many
ineffable miracles take place, and it is well known that the miracles worked
by him are not false." Later, they all listened to the stichera, canon, and life
of St. Cornelius and found the life to be written "according to the image
and likeness." After this, the patriarch and the council referred the matter
to Tsar Boris Feodorovich Godunov (reigned 1598–1605), and the sovereign, having conferred with the patriarch and the council, commanded that
"Vespers be celebrated and the All-night Vigil, and the Liturgy of God be
served in the catholic and apostolic church of the Most Pure Theotokos,
dedicated to Her Dormition, in the capital city of Moscow, on the day of
the commemoration of the Holy Martyr Patricius, Bishop of Prusa, May
19, and in the cathedrals of the metropolitan provinces, the archepiscopal
and episcopal sees throughout all of Great Russia, as is done for the rest of
the saints; and in the monastery of St. Cornelius, and at the cathedral
church of Sophia the Wisdom of God in Vologda, and in the suburbs, and
in the holy churches of God in outlying districts and throughout the surrounding cities and all the territory subject to the archbishop of Vologda,

it is commanded to celebrate the memory of Cornelius the Wonderworker on May 19."

We see from these extracts that the institution of the glorification of God's saints was treated with great attention and zeal. More than once the ecclesiastical authority denied requests for the glorification of the revered departed if it did not see incontestable and firm proof on which to base such a glorification.

The words of synodal decrees concerning glorification of the saints clearly show us the Orthodox understanding of this action as a universal, conciliar confession on the part of the Church of a firm belief or certainty that God has glorified His favorite in the heavens, and that therefore we on earth must glorify him also, joyously. This thought is expressed in the acts of the Synodal period, as has been fully and exactly noted.

In the official account of the glorification of the Holy Hierarch St. Metrophanes of Voronezh, we read: "When by the investigation which had been conducted a true act of God, Who is wondrous in His saints, became sufficiently apparent to the Holy Synod in the incorruption of the body of the Holy Hierarch Metrophanes and the healings that took place through his relics, the Holy Synod no longer delayed in solemnly revealing to the Church this gift of God, i.e., with a hierarchal blessing it permitted what until that time had been an act of personal zeal, the calling upon the intercession of our father among the saints Metrophanes in his prayers to God, and the placing of the wonder-working and healing relics of his body as a candle, not under a bushel, but on a candlestick, that all may be illumined. The annual ecclesiastical celebration of this Holy Hierarch has been fixed on the date of his repose — November 23."

The decree on the glorification of St. Tikhon of Zadonsk says: "The memory of His Grace Tikhon, Bishop of Voronezh…has been honored with reverence among the Russian Orthodox people who have streamed to the Monastery of Zadonsk and the grave of the Hierarch from far-distant places in a great multitude, praying for the repose of the soul of this hierarch and hoping for his prayerful intercession before God. Memory of the lofty Christian virtues with which he shone throughout his earthly life, news of the evangelical wisdom remaining in his divinely illuminated writings, and the miraculous healings of divers ailments performed at his grave have drawn many believers to the veneration of the Holy Hierarch. On all of this a pious hope was founded that this Hierarch who has been glorified by God be numbered among the choir of the saints. Even at the end of the last [18th] century such a hope was expressed in petitions submitted to His Imperial Highness and to the Most Holy Synod…" Archbishop Anthony of Voronezh, on the very day of his [St. Tikhon's] repose, wrote a letter to Emperor Nicholas concerning the universal fervent desire of innumerable pilgrims "that this great beacon of faith and good works which now lies beneath a bushel, be set before the eyes of all…" The Synod, in its report to the sovereign, announced its decision, beginning it with the following words: "Recognizing the late Bishop Tikhon of Voronezh as among the choir of the saints that have been glorified by the Grace of God through the fragrance of sanctity, and his incorrupt body as holy relics…"

The resolution concerning the glorification of St. Seraphim of Sarov is expressed in like manner: "Recognizing the pious elder Seraphim, who reposed at the Hermitage of Sarov, as being in the choir of saints glorified by the Grace of God…"

As is well known, and still remembered by certain people, in the last decades before Russia's downfall, the glorification of saints of the Russian Church, such as St. Theodosius of Chernigov, St. Seraphim of Sarov and later cases, were great national religious festivities, at the center of which was the uncovering of the relics of these saints of God. Generally, the glorification of Russian saints from the eighteenth to the twentieth centuries was marked by the uncovering of their holy relics. This shows that these two acts were closely bound internally, although, as has been said, the uncovering of the relics was not an absolutely essential condition and did not always follow immediately after the act of glorification.

From all that has been said, we may draw several conclusions. Essentially, according to the understanding of the Church and according to the principles of the glorification of saints, the glorification of saints has always been the same in the Orthodox Church. In these questions, the Eastern Orthodox Churches of the second millennium have followed the tradition of the Church of the first millennium and its ancient period. The Russian Church of the pre-Petrine era followed the path of the Greek Church; the Russian Church of the post-Petrine era remained faithful to the customs of the pre-Petrine era. The glorification of the saints consisted and consists of a general statement of faith by the Church that God Himself has united the departed one to the assembly of His saints. This faith is founded on the facts of a death by martyrdom, or upon a righteous life which is apparent to the whole Church, or upon the glorification of the saint of God by instances of wonderworking during his lifetime or at his tomb. Glorification is usually an expression of the voice of the people of the Church, to whom the higher ecclesiastical authority, after due verification, gives synodally the final word, establishment, recognition, confirmation and sanction of the Church.

The glorification of the saints is among the most important activities of the Church. In its basic, elementary aspect, glorification consists of turning from prayers "for the dead" to requests for a saint's intercession before God, and in his prayerful glorification by services from the general menaion or with specially composed services. The glorification of a saint and the uncovering of his relics do not constitute a single, inseparable act, although they often are performed together. The Orthodox Church does not maintain that it is essential that a fixed period of time pass between the repose of a righteous man and his numbering among the choir of the saints, as is accepted in the Roman confession, which has instituted a period of several decades (usually fifty years from the date of death for "beatification," a process which corresponds roughly to local veneration, and eighty years for canonization).

In the miracles worked through the prayers or at the tombs of the righteous of God, the Orthodox Church sees the will of God in the glorification of these strugglers. When no such signs exist, the Church does not see the will of God in their solemn glorification, as one of the resolutions of Patriarch Adrian of Moscow (reigned 1690–1700) expresses in regard to a certain request for glorification: "If our Lord God, the Creator of all, glorifieth anyone in this life, and after his death declareth this to His people through many miracles, then the miracles of this person become clearly known, for many holy wonderworkers were found in the Holy Church, whose memories the Church always hymns and their relics it contains. They that are not known, whom God Almighty Himself hath not been well pleased to glorify with signs and wonders, even if such lived righteously and in a holy manner, are not such as the Church glorifieth. The names of many are not remembered, and the whole world cannot contain the books of their names that could be written."

Catholicity and Cooperation
in the Church

Catholicity — this is not merely a sonorous word, but a theological concept of the loftiest significance. It is, of course, used in the Nicene Creed as one of the non-biblical terms to define the Church as one, holy, *catholic*, and apostolic. What does the original Greek word mean of itself? The main root of this word, ὅλος, means, according to Lampe (G. W. H. Lampe, *A Patristic Greek Lexicon*, Clarendon Press, Oxford, 1965), "whole, entire, complete." The prefix καὺ has as one of its three meanings the intensification of the word to which it is joined. Thus, in sum, the meaning is that of an unlimited fullness, all-inclusiveness, a "pleroma." "Catholicity" expresses what the Scriptures state of the Church, that in her *there is neither Greek nor Jew, nor circumcision, nor un-circumcision, nor Barbarian, Scythian, bond nor free, but Christ is all in all* (Col. 3:11). And again, *the Father... gave Him to be the head over all things to the Church, Which is His body, the fullness of Him that filleth all in all* (Eph. 1:22–3). And again, *That at the name of Jesus, every knee should bow, of things in the heavens, things in earth, and things under the earth* (Phil. 2:10). Catholicity refers to the fact that the Church is not limited to space, by earthly boundaries, nor is it limited in time, that is, by the passing of generations into the life beyond the grave. In its catholic fullness, in its catholicity, the Church embraces both the Church of the called and the Church of the chosen, the Church on earth and the Church in Heaven. Such is the Orthodox understanding of the essence and elements of the Church in its perfect form, as our Orthodox services make especially clear.

A problem has arisen in some Russian theological circles due to the misinterpretation of the Russian word for catholicity, *sobornost*. This word, whose adjectival form has been used in the Slavonic translation of the Symbol of the Faith for a thousand years, is related to the Slavonic word for a council, *sobor*. In its present form as a noun, *sobornost* is indebted to the Russian Slavophiles, who employed it to define the uniquely lofty connotations of the Slavonic *sobornuyu* as used in the ninth article of the Creed: "I believe in One, Holy, Catholic, and Apostolic Church." "I will not presume to say," writes the Russian Orthodox thinker and devoted son of the Church, A. S. Khomiakov, "whether this profound realization of the essence of the Church (to translate the word 'Catholic' with the word 'Sobornaya') was taken by the first teachers of the Slavs from the very sources of truth in the schools of the East or whether it was yet a more lofty inspiration granted by Him Who alone is Truth and Life, but I boldly affirm that this one word contains in itself a complete confession of the faith" (A. S. Khomiakov, *Theological Works*, p. 313). One must bear in mind that in Greek there is no philological or linguistic connection between the concepts "catholic" and "council" (ecumenical). A council of the Church is called in Greek Σύνοδος, and an ecumenical council, οἰκου-μενικὴ Σύνοδος. In the secular usage, the dictionary meaning of Σύνοδος is "a gathering, meeting, congress."

Concerning the Russian and Slavonic word *sobor*, one can readily see its relationship to the concept of catholicity in its usage as a term for a large church or cathedral. A *sobor* is a church with two or three altars, which thus more fully expresses the union with the heavenly church, whose lofty iconostasis portrays the choirs of the saints, where the daily services are constantly being celebrated in memory and glorification of the heavenly Church, and where the vessel of Grace and the bond with the hierarchy of heaven and earth, the bishop, serves and has his seat.

What is the Catholicity of the Church on Earth and How Is It Expressed?

Catholicity is the unceasing prayerful communion with the celestial Church. The radiant bonds of prayer go in all directions: we on earth pray for one another; we ask the saints to pray for us; the saints, we believe, hear us and lift our prayers unto God; we pray for our reposed fathers and brothers in Christ; we ask the saints to assist us also in these appeals to the Lord.

Catholicity is expressed in the fact that the ancient Fathers and Teachers of the Church continue to be as relevant in our times, and are just as instructive, memorable and valuable as they were in their own time. The

Church is nurtured by One Spirit, and therefore temporal divisions between generations of Christians are irrelevant. The Christian who studies the Apostolic Scriptures, the writings of the Holy Fathers and Ascetics, or the texts of the divine services, we believe, enters into a spiritual communion outside of time, with the very authors of these writings, fulfilling the behest of the holy Apostle John the Theologian: *That which we have seen and heard declare we unto you you, that ye also may have fellowship* (communion) *with us; and truly our fellowship* (communion) *is with the Father, and with His Son Jesus Christ* (I John 1:3).

Catholicity is expressed in the fact that members of the Orthodox Church living at various ends of the earth have one common faith. This is why in the ancient Church the faith itself was called the "catholic faith" and "catholic truth." All have one and the same Mysteries; all commune of the one Body of Christ in the Mystery of the Eucharist, no matter where or when they live; all have one priesthood, which takes its one succession from the Apostles; all Church life is built on the common foundation of the canons of the Church.

Catholicity, finally, is expressed in the fact that all true members of the Church treasure her. We grieve for the Church in her times of difficulty. For the members of the small community of a parish, she is just as close whether in part or as a whole. "For the welfare of the holy churches of God and the union of all," we pray at every liturgy. A Christian who makes the salvation of his soul the goal of his personal life in the Church demonstrates concern for the peace and welfare of his own local church, working towards this according to the measure of his own capabilities and strength. Of course, such an ecclesiastical cooperativeness is also an expression, although more remote, of the concept of the catholicity of the Church.

It is, generally speaking, with these characteristics that the Russian Slavophiles received into their hearts the concept of the catholicity of the Church; such was the understanding which they had of the term "the *sobornost* of the Church." Expressing by this formula the fullness of the spiritual unity of the Orthodox Church, regardless of her geographical and national separations, they underscored the *ethical* aspect of Orthodox catholicity which is free from compulsion and legalistic concepts. It is this ethical aspect of Orthodoxy which contrasted with the legal principle of "rights and privileges" in the structure of the Roman Church, and likewise, to the cold rationalism, sometimes replaced by mysticism, in Protestantism. The Slavophiles did not associate with the concept of *sobornost* any kind of elective lay organs of Church government.

Catholicity in the Usual Vernacular Sense

With the passage of time the meaning of the term *sobornost* began to narrow. At the beginning of this century when talk arose of the need for calling a council of the Russian Church, due to the similarity of the Russian words for council (*sobor*) and catholic (*sobornaya*), this term began to be used in everyday polemics as virtually identical with the concept of a council of bishops, local or ecumenical. Subsequently it came to be identified with conciliar government in the Church in general, which, incidentally, was conceived of by different people in different ways: for some a patriarchate in conjunction with periodical, frequent convocations of the bishops; for others on the contrary, a continuation of conciliar government by the Synod; still others saw in a patriarchate an immensely unifying moral force which eliminated the need for collegial forms of ecclesiastical government.

During the sessions of the Russian Church Council of 1917–18 this term took on a new significance. At that time one could already foresee and sense the approach of the brutal blows against the Russian Church from the enemies of the Orthodox Church, of Christianity, and of religion in general. It was imperative to seek out means of uniting all the vital forces of the Church, an authentic alignment of firmness and the faithful forces of the believers in accordance with the principle of the catholicity of the Church. The Church must be defended; a moral confirmation of the episcopate and the parish pastors was required, so that they would not be left isolated. This goal could be realized only by attracting the faithful to an active participation in the protection of the Church through representatives of the laity who were self-sacrificing and well-tested. The vast majority of these turned out to be people who were also prepared to be confessors when this choice sooner or later presented itself. The consciousness of this necessity and the corresponding summoning of the people was reflected in the resolutions of the Council of 1917–18. This mobilization of Church forces at that moment was truly an expression of the idea of the catholicity of the Church in a profoundly ethical sense.

In the period of the Russian emigration after the First World War, the term *sobornost* began to be used in an extremely simplistic way and acquired a special connotation. The idea was spread abroad that the lay members of the Church were being deprived of their rights; that the time had come to put elected persons into diocesan government, both from the laity and from the clergy. As long as this was lacking in the ecclesiastical framework, it was said, the doctrine of the Creed was not being implemented. From time to time these voices grew more shrill and they were even given a hearing in the press. Before the Second World War a pamphlet published throughout the emigration entitled *For Sobornost* (in Russian), expressed this kind of understanding of the word.

The Church in the Sea of Life

The historical path of the Church has not been an easy one. The Holy Fathers represented it by the image of a ship sailing on the sea of life. Its lot is such that even when the sea is calm, the vessel must move *against the current*. What then must be said about the moments of storm? The Church is forced always to maintain a resistance against the sinful world. The world possesses power, authority, the instruments of compulsion and punishment, as well as the seductive pleasures of life. The Church in and of herself possesses nothing except moral influence. Whence could she draw on the strength that she requires, were it not that the Lord protects and has mercy on her?

The Orthodox Church is *the inheritance of Christ.*

The Lord protects as well the little vessel which is called the Russian Church Outside of Russia, the offspring of the once outwardly magnificent Russian Orthodox Church. Should the Church in the homeland be re-born, then this free part of her will return to her bosom.

Within the diaspora, our little Church watches over, to the fullest extent, the canonical structure that she inherited from of old, and sets for herself as one aspect of her duties to maintain the entire inheritance of Orthodoxy inviolate, undiminished, and undistorted. To keep watch over oneself in this way in foreign lands is more difficult than at home, however, she has not only succeeded in this, but even shows certain encouraging signs in comparison with the past in Russia.

In old Russia the ruling bishop had under his jurisdiction a thousand or more parishes; this meant a population of millions in a diocesan flock. Could he have visited each and directed it personally? Could he have been as close to it as are our archpastors here? Our bishops here know the parishes committed to them, with their own eyes they see their members and, one can say, bear them all within their hearts, rejoicing and weeping together with them. All the more painfully, of course, do they experience disturbances in the parishes, and it may be that only God sees their suffering of soul for their flocks. One must also say the same concerning the parish pastors. How often both bishop and priest quietly reconcile themselves to the most adverse conditions of life, concerning which many of the flock, being themselves well provided for in life, perhaps do not even take the trouble to consider...? And frequently those who serve the Church face, instead of cooperation, only cold analysis and criticism — a very discouraging phenomenon.

Nonetheless, the negative aspects do not overwhelm the spiritual consolation which accompanies service to God and the Church. Those living amid the vanity of the world do not even imagine the existence of such consolation, and for this reason so few are prepared to embark on the pastor's way of life. Because of this, there is in our day an acute lack of clergy, and the number of parishes not tended by their own pastors continues to grow.

The apostolic epistles provide us with a sketch of the image of pastoral sorrows. The Apostle Paul writes to the community of Christians which he founded: "You are already filled; you have grown rich; you have begun to reign with us... We are fools for Christ's sake, but you are wise in Christ; we are weak, but you are strong; you are in glory but we are in dishonor... O, if only in fact you had begun to reign, so that we might reign together with you!" (cf. I Cor. 4:10, 8) What then? Is this grief of the apostle a cause of despair and indecision? Not in the least! Note the outstanding spiritual state of the Apostle: "Who can separate us from the love of God: grief or deprivation? or persecution or hunger or nakedness? or danger or the sword?... All this we overcome by the power of Him Who loved us" (cf. Rom. 8:35, 37).

Catholic Unity and Cooperation in the Church

The biblical image of the Church in the world is that of a human body. In the body there is an innumerable number of parts that work together, both visibly and invisibly. They all have their value and their purpose. *The foot does not say: I do not belong to the body, because I am not a hand... the ear does not say: I do not belong to the body because I am not an eye...* (I Cor.

12:15–16). So also in the Church; for each of her members there is a place for union with the other persons who serve her. But just as the body is in need of outer coverings, clothing, and other necessary items which are not a part of the body, so in the serving of the Church there are also two spheres: the internal sphere, truly ecclesiastical, catholic; and another — the outward, on the surface, temporary, passing. We must distinguish between the "essential" and the "non-essential," at least in practice and in indispensable matters. Since we live in a material world, a world of relativity, the external often becomes indispensable. In the Church this constitutes the organizational aspect — besides the Grace-bearing hierarchal structure; there is also the need to maintain the church building and clergy, parish meetings, finances, organizations associated with the Church: schools, publishing, and so on. Life summons us to participate in both spheres. However, it is of no benefit to a person's salvation to take part in the outward without participating in the internal.

Which of our activities, then, represents the full and authentic expression of the catholicity of the Church?

It is manifested, namely, in congregational prayer in the church building. The church is the Christian center of our lives. Setting out for the services, we say, "Let's go to church," or "Let's go to the cathedral"; thus we express half-consciously by these words the fact that catholicity and the Church are fully manifested in the church building.

Is the priest, standing before the gates of the sanctuary or within it, praying for himself alone? No, these prayers of thanksgiving for the past day and the approaching night, these petitions for the mercy of God are completely catholic. "Incline Thine ear, and hearken unto us, and remember by name, O Lord, all that are with us and pray with us, and save them by Thy might... Give peace to Thy world, to Thy churches, to the priests and to all Thy people." "Teach us, O God, Thy righteousness... grant us to behold the dawn and day in rejoicing,... Remember, O Lord, in the multitude of Thy compassions, all Thy people that are with us and pray with us, and all our brethren, on land, on the sea, in every place of Thy dominion, needing Thy help and love for mankind... that always remaining saved in soul and body, with boldness we may glorify Thy wondrous and blessed name..." One after another, these prayers reach ever higher unto the "Treasury of good things, the Ever-flowing Fountain, the Benefactor of our lives, Who is Holy and Unattainable." The majority of these prayers could be read aloud. But experience has proven that people in church are not able to maintain sufficient concentration and attention to become absorbed in the meaning of these prayers — the fruit of the lofty, Grace-filled inspiration of the great Fathers of the Church. In particular, this must be said of the principal section of the Divine Liturgy, that of the Faithful. Therefore, the Church has found it better to place in our thoughts and mouths as often as possible, the brief prayer of contrition and request, "Lord, have mercy." This prayer expresses the Church-inspired catholic consciousness of the primary importance for a Christian: sincere repentance.

Is not the whole Church meant to pray through the mouth of the choir? We must add that the readers and chanters, as well as those who listen, should bear in mind the communal character of the praises, petitions, and thanksgiving of the services, and mutually strive to realize common prayer. In at least certain parts of the divine services it is possible for the whole congregation to participate actively in the chanting. Undoubtedly, in the future Russian Church, reborn through sufferings, this aspect of ecclesiastical catholicity will attain a more complete expression.

At the conclusion of each service we leave the church. At the end of the vigil service we hear the concluding prayer of the First Hour: "O Christ the True Light, Who enlightenest and sanctifiest every man that cometh into the world..." And, indeed, our departure from the services is, in fact, a passing over "from the Church into the world." We depart to our worldly cares and interests. The Church and catholicity recede for a time into the background, into the past. Completely? That depends on us. Not completely, if we preserve them within ourselves, in our soul, in our consciousness, in our actions; in a word, if we maintain ourselves in piety. Thus, even in the world it is possible to work together with the Church, as a reflection of that same catholicity. It cannot be said here that the Church's path is narrow.

What activities of the members of the Church, then, can and do express the spirit of catholicity?

One of the first modes of activity is directly associated with the church building itself. This includes the construction of the church, the providing of it with all that is necessary, acquisition of icons and frescoes. In terms of moral value, acts of love and philanthropy in the name of Christ have an even greater significance. The manifestations of Christian faith and love can be extremely diverse. For example, personal Christian missionary activity springs from devotion to Christ and the Church, upholding the right, compassionate defense of the persecuted and abused. Christian service through lectures, reports, the printed word, work in church schools, scholarly activity in a Christian spirit — all this constitutes a broad, open and, here outside the Communist world, a free field for Church cooperation, both as individuals and in groups.

These forms of activity and those like them are loftier and more worthy than plans for participating in the administrative side of the Church. The peaceful and prosperous management of the house of God rests not on legal foundations but on the rock of right faith and ethical, voluntary obedience to the rules of the Church by all her members, both clerical and lay. One cannot imagine how such an approach to the question of catholicity could be considered conventional or boring.

Vladimir S. Soloviev and the Catholic Aspect of the Church

So that the skeptical reader might not think that the concept of catholicity found in the ninth article of the Creed and set forth here is one-sided, and to make it clear that such an understanding is not limited to a single group of persons or to that movement whose spokesman was A. S. Khomiakov (the Slavophiles), let us avail ourselves of the opinions of Vladimir S. Soloviev on this question. We consider him here not as a theological authority, but as a free-thinker who did not confine himself to the traditional theological frame of reference. In many of his opinions he went far beyond the bounds of the Gospel's truths. However, he was a sincere Christian, and he had a well-intentioned, if vain, hope that by an originality of conclusions he might interest the Russian intelligentsia in the questions of faith, towards which it had grown so indifferent. But his devoted followers, when they began to introduce certain philosophical speculations into theology and develop them, made him the source of one more heresy. In his work *The Justification of the Good*, Soloviev, commenting on the characteristics of the Church given in the Creed, writes in agreement with the conception generally accepted by the Orthodox Church:

> Catholicity ($\kappa\alpha\theta\acute{o}\lambda o\nu$ — as a whole, or in agreement with the whole) consists in this, that all the forms and activities of the Church join separate persons and separate nations with the

entire God-Manhood, both in its individual concentration — Christ, and likewise in its collective circles — in the world of the bodiless hosts, the saints who have departed and live in God, and the faithful struggling upon the earth. In so far as all within the Church is brought into harmony with an absolute whole, all is catholic. Within her all the exclusions of national and personal characteristics and social status fall away, all the separations and divisions cease, and all differences are left behind, for godliness requires that one perceive unity in God not as an empty indifference nor bleak uniformity, but as the unconditional fullness of every life. There is no separation, but rather there is preserved the distinction between the invisible and the visible Churches, for the first is the hidden active power of the second, and the second is the first becoming manifest; they are one with each other in essence, but different in condition. There is no separation, but rather there distinction is preserved in the visible Church between the many races and nations, in whose unanimity the one Spirit by various tongues witnesses to the one Truth and by various gifts and callings imparts one Good. There is not, finally, any division, but rather there is preserved the distinction in the Church between those who teach and those who are taught, between the clergy and the laity, between the mind and the body of the Church, just as in the distinction between husband and wife there is not a barrier but a basis for their perfect unification.

(*The Justification of the Good*, Pt. III, Sec. VIII, pp. 473–4)

Everything Has Its Time, Its Place

Like everything in the world, human nature is wisely constructed. We are capable of acquiring and preserving knowledge, and we are capable of forgetting. Often even forgetfulness is useful and laudable.

Have you met with failure? Do not be too long in lamenting. Forget it! Consider it to be a lesson for the future. You have lost something and cannot find it? In this transitory world there is nothing eternal. Forget it!

Someone offended you without cause, they hurt your feelings? Do not let your memory dwell on it. Humble yourself; it will be good for you.

You have a bad habit? In our souls a constant process of renewal is in effect. Determine to turn away from your bad habit and God Himself will help you to forget it.

Are you troubled or attracted by seductive memories or desires? Join your heart to the words of the prayer: "Guard me, O Lord, from vain thoughts and evil desires"... It will be fulfilled, and you will forget them.

Forget what is useless, acquire positive knowledge and preserve it. Do not think: I will never find that useful. "Give here that bit of rope; even a bit of rope can come in handy" (from Gogol's *Inspector General*). In the course of your life each item in the storehouse of your memory will prove useful, even it it is only once.

Look ahead. Choose what is best. Think of that moral countenance which you would like to see on yourself in the last decade of your life. You have heard which is good, and you have read a fair amount. If you are acquainted with Church history, imagine to yourself the images of those people whom you find most attractive and close to your soul by nature. Do not strive to race ahead prematurely.

Forgetting those things which are behind, and reaching forth unto those things which are before (Phil. 3:13).

How Each of Us Can and Ought
to Serve the Church

If we love the Church, if She is dear to us, then how can each of us serve Her? And if someone were to ask you: "How have you served Her?" what activities can you boast of?

When this question was put to the holy Apostle Paul and he had to defend his authority before the Corinthian Christians, he answered in this way: *I will glory of the things which concern mine infirmities* (II Cor. 11:30). Glory in our infirmities? Without question, the humble realization of our infirmities is beneficial for each of us, but how can we serve the Church in this way? At the same time, the holy Apostle insists on his answer and explains: *For when I am weak, then am I strong* (II Cor. 12:10).

Then, this is no paradox, no play on words, no contradiction. The Apostle shows no trace of being "imaginative" or "witty." He writes from the fullness of his heart, from deep conviction. His meaning is direct. He speaks of the Christian principle of life.

Christianity upset the usual concepts dominant in the world, and in particular the concept of power. According to Christianity, power is what "seems" to the world to be impotence, what appears to its short-sighted view to be a contemptible weakness. Christian power is meekness. Meekness is the law of the new life and action, under whose banner the Gospel declared war on the world: *Blessed are the poor in spirit. Blessed are they that mourn. Blessed are the meek, for they shall inherit the earth.* The poor in spirit, the mourning, the meek — is this not infirmity (weakness) in the usual human understanding?

Yes, "in the world," without Christ, without faith, outside the Church and apart from Christianity one cannot pit meekness and spiritual poverty (humility) against the mighty, against all that has power and authority in the world; nor can they oppose the proud power of the will, so often brutal, hardened, and harsh. They cannot stand against sheer physical power, the power of naked force; nor can they withstand the power of a refined and clever mind or the power of the simple majority. How is it possible to take up arms against the entire arsenal of this world armed only with the weapons of "meekness and temperance, purity and chastity, love of brother and the poor, of patience and vigilance," as we hear, for example, in the prayer to St. Job of Pochaev, one of the strugglers for the life, rights, and dignity of the Orthodox Church in Western Russia against Roman Catholicism.

But He of Whom the prophet said *A bruised reed shall He not break, and the smoking flax shall He not quench* (Is. 42:3), Who bore His obedience, *being obedient even unto death, even to the death on the Cross*: He, our Lord, stated even before His sufferings on the Cross, *Be of good cheer, I have overcome the world.*

The meek Christian virtues are a mighty power in God's world — they are an artery by which the power of God comes down into the world. In order to understand this, we must pull back the veil from our own personal world-view. A veil usually hangs before our mental eye that limits our thoughts and our actions in earthly life. But when we pull back the veil, before us open perspectives of eternity, with faith in the immortality of our soul, with faith in God, with faith in the radiant kingdom of eternal life. In the face of eternal life, concepts are completely changed: much that is great becomes of no consequence, and the insignificant becomes great. He who believes and beholds the Kingdom of God with spiritual eyes is like a giant whose head reaches the heavens. Who has strength enough to throw him down? They can slay his body, they cannot kill his soul and spirit. The words of St. Paul can be applied to such spiritual giants: For *I am persuaded, that neither death, nor life, nor angels, nor principalities, nor powers, not things present, nor things to come, Nor height, nor depth, nor any other creature, shall be able to separate us from the love of God, which is in Christ Jesus our Lord* (Rom. 8:38–39). Here there is an authentic feeling of his power, which the Apostle expresses in the words: *We then that are strong ought to bear the infirmities of the weak, and not to please ourselves* (Rom. 15:1).

And so two contradictory laws of life stand against one another, two kingdoms: the kingdom of the meek and the kingdom of the powerful. The kingdom of the meek is forced to wage war against the kingdom of power while located in the midst of it and surrounded on all sides by the kingdom of power and force.

The struggle continues. It is difficult for the Church. It is not surprising that the human powers of the Church weaken towards the end of the struggle. But the end has been written beforehand in heaven: victory is on the side of the kingdom of the meek. And should it not turn out this way by the laws of logic? For the Church has been standing against the kingdom of the world for two millennia now. If meekness were not power, then how could she have survived for even the shortest time in the struggle? Still, there come moments in the history of the Church when Her powers, exposed to popular view, weaken in the struggle. Why? Is this because the meek Christian weapons turn out to be useless or insufficient? No! This happens when, under the influence of discouragement and weakness of faith, those who serve the Church forget their true armament and adopt a foreign kind. The evil world urges its own weapons on them: worldly power, force, deceit. If those who serve the Church yield to the enticement, they weaken and bring Her internal sufferings as well. History gives us sufficient examples of this sort.

The world creeps into the Church by an even simpler method: by human passions, self-love, and ambition, love for the first place, insistence on one's own will. The world of the proud creeps in with the wish to submit the Church to one's own plans, to make her an instrument that is political, national, even partisan. It creeps in through indulging our weaknesses of the flesh, through replacing authentic virtues with seeming ones; in a word, through the help of those powerful, poisonous means which are called the spirit of flattery (or deceit).

By nature the Church is meek and it is easy to insult Her. If we attentively read the history of the Church, we can see how many have insulted Her from within, entering into Her very heart and thus all the more painfully wounding Her. But it is insufficient to say that there have been offenders: it is more grievous that so-called scientific history attributes the actions of those offenders to the Church and blames and blasphemes Her for these actions.

We should all remember this when our thoughts are directed to the Russian Orthodox Church Abroad. Someone may think: this is a peculiar little handful of Orthodox scattered over the far ends of the earth. What kind of social force do we represent? If the numerically, materially, and morally powerful branches of historical Christianity are withstanding the powers of this world with difficulty, then what are we to think of our Church? In answer to such a thought, we must remember that the power of the Church is not in numbers. Rather that in order to preserve inner, spiritual strength one should stand apart, and such is the situation of the Russian Church Abroad. Thus, if we are children of the Russian Church Abroad, if we are devoted to Her, if we love Her and wish to see Her internally mighty and glorious, then how can each of us serve Her?

Of course, the fullest form of serving the Church is for a person to give himself to Her completely for his entire life as a pastor or in another life of service, close to the pastorate. But we must not feel that only the ordained servants of the Church are called to be Her soldiers while the others are only observers — some sympathetic, others critical. Each of us has a place in the ranks of the soldiers of the Church, and the forms of participation in service to the Church are varied. The Apostle writes: *Let every man abide in the same calling wherein he was called* (I Cor. 7:20). Translating this quotation into contemporary concepts, we can say that there does not exist a constructive, honest profession and a social position where a good person could not at one time or another contribute his good mite to the work of the Church. Look at how the fruits of pagan higher education were used to great advantage by the great hierarchs Basil the Great, Gregory the Theologian, and John Chrysostom. What a precious heritage they gave to the Church!

The Church is meek. For this reason She is in need of protection and defense. Only they must be good means for her defense. In the past, both the Byzantine and Russian Churches had external defenders: a governmental system, the emperors, the tsars; although one must admit that there were times when this defense was worse than none. Times have changed. Now the care of the Church is entrusted by the Lord to the people of the Church Herself, and so to each Orthodox Christian. In this regard we are returning to the times of the first Christians. Our times call us all to a conscious, constant sacrificial "stand for the Church," each with his talents and means. However, the principal power of service does not lie in our knowledge, abilities, and callings. The principal power is in the "infirmity" through which the power of Christ comes to abide. It is in our morality, in our living according to the law of the Gospel, according to the law of the Church.

How we are to bring this about in a practical way is taught by the most perfect example of the holy martyrs and ascetics; it is demonstrated also by the Orthodox monasteries, the builders of Russia, such as the Trinity-Sergius Lavra, the Optina Hermitage, the Lavra of Pochaev and others that existed before the Revolution. But since all this remains in the past, in order to find an example in the present, let us look at least to the handful of modest monastic communities of our Church in the corners of the Russian diaspora — to these small groups of people, both men and women, who have given themselves over to the law of meekness and obedience. Concerning them we can say rightfully with the Apostle: *For ye see your calling, brethren, how that not many wise men after the flesh, not many mighty, not many noble, are called; but God hath chosen the foolish things of the world to confound the wise; and God hath chosen the weak of the world to confound the things which are mighty; and base things of the world, and things which are despised, hath God chosen, yea, and things which are not, to bring to nought things that are* (I Cor. 1:26–28). The quiet, meek, laborious life of the monastery sheds such a beneficial and varied influence far beyond its own physical limits! And what a good result is granted just by contact with this world, as many different persons can testify! Of course the same can also be said about the Orthodox monasteries that are not of Russian background.

Those who think that prayer, fasting, temperance, ascetic labor, and the struggle with vices have only the goal of personal salvation and thus those who practice these good works, as it were, conceal in themselves a subtle spirit of egotism, are gravely mistaken. Rather, internal work on oneself is an investment in the Church. This is a gathering in of the powers of the Church, a collecting of the Church's wealth, which does not consist in the number of persons, not in large and opulent church buildings, not in sonorous choirs, not even in impressive statistics about philanthropy — but rather in the moral life of Her members.

One must serve the Church as the one body of Christ, a single organism, a single substance. Each one's personality is the plot of land entrusted to him for him to labor over, clean up, and produce fruit on. In working on ourselves, we work for the whole, for the entire Church, for Its Head, the selfless Saviour. In letting one's plot grow over, neglecting it, condemning it, we bring harm not only to ourselves but also to the

Church. By not gathering for our own soul, we scatter what belongs to the Church.

Our service to the Church consists in this: that through our personal Christian life the spirit of the Gospel values flows into the life of the world, thus putting the enemies of the Church to shame. In our personal qualities lies the pledge of the internal unity of the Church as a whole and of the parish in particular; from this source come mutual understanding, obedience, unanimity in goals, friendly labor for the glory of God and the glory of the Church. Thus a completely unique Church atmosphere is established. In such an atmosphere a person feels that he is in a special world, which gives rest and joy to the soul, refreshing and renewing it. One strives to come to it as if to a new earth, the earth of the meek. In it one feels the beneficial power of the Church within oneself. It is easier in such circumstances for the soul to open up to the reception of the breath of the Grace of God that abides in the Church. But if this spirit is absent; if within the groups of the Church there are divisions, discord, the struggle of ambition and self-love, then can one, in such circumstances, speak of the power of the Church.?

Therefore, to the question of how we can serve the Church, the answer is simple: by active obedience to Her. Active obedience to Her is a life according to the rules of the Church, observance of moral laws, zealous attendance at church services, prayer at home, a Christian foundation and direction in home life. We can say then, in general, that for us it consists of the joy of belonging to the Russian Church Abroad as a true confessor of the Orthodox Catholic faith and a herald of righteousness, and a corresponding attitude in our personal life which worthily reflects that membership.

An Outline of
the Orthodox World-View of
Father John of Kronstadt

Based on His Own Words

There is an unusually attractive power, particularly for the pastor, in the personality of Father John of Kronstadt, even in his portrait, the attraction of his writings, in his diary *My Life in Christ*. There is a peaceful and consoling quality in the notes of his diary, not to mention the very subjects of his talks, which spiritually exalt, uplift, and strengthen. Once you have opened the book, the eye is drawn aside only with great difficulty, and the hand seems by itself to turn one page after another. Whence comes this attraction of hearts to Father John? Undoubtedly of great significance is the fact that Father John is our contemporary. He made his notes for himself and at the same time for us. He brought into his diaries his personal thoughts, answered the questions of his own soul, but to a certain degree these were also our questions, answers to our perplexing problems, here often is the confirmation of our own conclusions. What he himself writes down in his diary is justified: "We often hear from others, or frequently read in their writings, that which God has placed in our own mind and heart, what we ourselves have wished, that is, often we find our most beloved thoughts in others." He then offers an explanation: "Is not there one Lord God of minds; is not there one Spirit of His in all those who seek Truth? Is not there one Enlightener, enlightening every person who comes into the world?" (*My Life in Christ*). Here you have the basic reason for the attraction toward Father John, as he himself indicates. He answers the questions of our own personal spirit. As a person of strong faith, of deep Orthodox religious thought, and of complete unity in word and deed, he answers in a most perfect manner, becoming our friend, our counsellor, comforter, reviver, and spiritual teacher.

The theology of Father John, his world-view, is deeply Orthodox. Can it therefore be the object of any special study? Is it not already given in the Orthodox catechism? What new thing can be revealed in it?

Of course, Father John's thinking concerning God, in its essence, is that which is transmitted from the Fathers of the Church, catholic, apostolic, and based on the Gospel. In him we do not find any sensational novelty, no modernism in faith. Nevertheless, it is precisely this tradition that attracts special attention, it attracts because it is the basis on which Father John expresses his broad world outlook, that which may be called a personal Christian philosophy.

Believers react differently to the truths of faith which they accept. Some accept them without any doubts as indisputable authority. Others strive to unite them with their own general world outlook; faith together with reason. But in either case each must unite his faith with his life, with his deeds. If the content of our faith does not affect the content of our deeds, their essential nature, if our conduct is unaffected by what we believe, then faith ceases to be alive. A synthesis of faith and life is needed, and better yet — of faith, reason, and life — faith, reason, heart, and life. The more completely one lives the life of the Church, the more complete should this synthesis be. It is quite evident how much this is needed by the pastor. In the person of Father John we are given an example of harmony between theological knowledge and practical understanding of life, together with personal spiritual experience. Before us is the purposeful, deep, harmonious world outlook on which foundation the Christian personality of an ideal Christian pastor was formed.

What influence shaped the world-view of Father John? He himself speaks concerning this.

The basic structure of his world-view was Sacred Scripture. "From the first days of my high service to the Church," writes Father John, "I began reading the Sacred Scripture of the Old and New Testaments, drawing from it all that is edifying for myself as a human being in general, and as a priest in particular " (Brief autobiography in the journal *North* for 1888). In his talk with pastors he relates : "When free from personal service and duties, I read the Sacred Scripture of the Old and New Testaments and especially the New Testament — this most invaluable good tidings of our salvation. While reading I try to ponder over every paragraph, every phrase, even separate words and expressions, and then through this careful attentive relation to the Sacred Book, there arises such a wealth of thoughts, such a wealth of themes for sermons, that no preacher can exhaust this vast depth of God" (A talk with clergymen at Sarapule in 1904). When reading the diary of Father John, we notice that all the books of Sacred Scripture are presented in the diary by extracts, but in such a manner that nowhere can one feel intentional grouping of texts, there is no overstatement with texts; unusually natural is the union of the personal and divine elements. The usual method of Father John is to conclude his own personal talks with an extract from the Word of God, and close his writings in the same way that the word *amen* confirms the words of prayers taken from the service book.

The other part of the structure of Father John's world-view was the reading of the Lives of Saints. "Having read the Bible, the Gospel, and many of the writings of St. John Chrysostom and other Ancient Fathers, and also the Russian Chrysostom, Philaret of Moscow, and other Church writings, I felt a special attraction towards the calling of a priest, and began to ask God that He might make me worthy of the Grace of the priesthood, and worthy of being a pastor to His sheep..." (A talk on the 25th anniversary of his priesthood). Father John rarely mentions the Fathers of the Church in his diary and one must at least be somewhat well acquainted with their writings in order to feel the power of their influence on the formation of Father John's thought, and on the very style of expression in the diary, in particular the influence of Sts. John Chrysostom, Basil the Great, Gregory the Theologian, and the writings of the great Ascetics. In his often-used conversational form of writing, one feels the spirit of St. John Chrysostom; in his discourse on the Holy Trinity — St. Gregory the Theologian; in the completeness of thought, as expressed by rich synonyms and epithets — St. Basil.

We know how highly Father John valued all the Church service books. He himself said: "I always read the canons at Matins myself. What riches are found here; what deep content, what wonderful examples of fervent faith in God, patience in sorrow, self-denying fidelity to conscience under conditions of merciless torture the Church daily presents to us! By reading the canons the soul gradually becomes filled with the inspired feelings and mental attitudes of those Saints whom the Church praises; it lives within a perpetual church environment, and thereby it becomes accustomed to church life. I was trained, it may be said, in the church life by this reading, and for this reason I advise all who sincerely desire to acquire spiritual riches to pay serious attention to the reading of the canons according to the church service books — the Octoechos, Menaion, and Triodion."

All these influences so affected the person of Father John that God, Faith, and Church became the foundation of his entire life, and these contents united with his pure, healthy, harmonious development, and the full lively energy of his physical and spiritual being. Exalted contents filled a worthy vessel. One of the consequences of this was that for Father John the truths of Faith were presented not as abstract propositions, but as life forces, expressed in practical living. Father John thinks in terms of images, and he teaches us this manner of thought. He writes: "They say that we soon get tired of praying. Why? It is because you do not picture before yourself the Living God as being nearby, on your right side. Look upon Him always with the eyes of your heart, and then you will be able to stand all night in prayer, and you will not become tired. What am I saying — night! You will stand three days and three nights and not become tired. Recall those who stood in prayer on pillars for long periods of time." He writes elsewhere: "In praying, it is necessary to imagine all creation as nothing before God, and the One God as All, upholding all, Omniscient, active, giving life to all." For this reason his thoughts are so rich in comparisons, likenesses, and symbols dealing with the most exalted objects of faith.

As a lens can burn wood when it has concentrated the rays of the sun at its focus, in like manner during prayer the heart is set afire when "the Sun of the Mind — God, images of the Blessed Virgin Mary, the Saints, the Angels with fullness and power, are concentrated at the center of our soul, at the heart."

The spontaneous incarnation of faith in corresponding Christian activity, the moral application of each point of faith to life: these comprise the characteristic feature of Father John's understanding of the world and of life. In him one meets theology in thought and in practice.

How then does Father John present his theology to us?

God is One, of One Essence, Self Existent. "For the true believer God is Omnipresent and is All, and creatures are as though non-existent; every earthly substance and that of all visible worlds are as though non-existent, and for him there is not even a single line of thought without God." God is unchanging and everlasting, angelic spirits and souls of men also. "Everything else is like a soap bubble. By these words I do not underestimate that which has been created, but I speak of it in comparison to the Creator and the blessed spirits." From this there proceeds a clear moral deduction for us: not to cling to material, temporal life.

"God is closer to us than any person, at all times; closer than my clothing, closer than air, closer than my wife, father, mother, daughter, son, or friend. I live by Him in soul and in body. I breathe by Him, I think by Him, I feel, imagine, plan, speak, undertake, and act by Him, *For in Him we live, and move, and have our being* (Acts 17:28). As in the ocean, lake, or river, every drop of water is connected with other drops of water and surrounded by them, or as in the air, every part is surrounded by others and united by them, so likewise we earthly inhabitants are surrounded by God from all sides, and the pure in heart among us or those who are being cleansed are united with Him, and are everywhere with Him." "The Omnipresence of God is spatial and mental, i.e., God is everywhere, in spatial and mental relationship. Wherever I go in body or thought, everywhere I meet God, and everywhere God meets me."

Throughout his entire diary, Father John constantly reminds us of God — that God is Self-Existent, of One Essence — as do the Church Fathers (for example St. Gregory of Nyssa). Namely as a Pure Being, God is Omnipresent, Omniscient, all-permeating, and all-filling. For this reason God is so near to the world and to people. "God is simply love." "The Lord in His infinite nature is by simplicity such a Being that He is all in the name *Trinity* or in the name, *Lord*, or in the name *Jesus Christ*."

If that is so, then in order for man to be in union with God it is necessary by His Grace to attain that perfect simplicity of goodness or holiness of love. And one "should believe simply, saying to oneself: I believe all this which is asked in simplicity of heart, and I ask all simply." "Love without reasoning: love is simple. Likewise believe and hope without reasoning. For faith and hope are also simple." "Truth is simple." Consequently from the thought about God there proceeds a general commandment of life, which is to be simple in everything and in particular in relation to people. "May simplicity go before you everywhere; especially be simple in your faith, hope, and love, for God is an Essence of Simplicity, a

Unity that is worshiped everlastingly, and our soul is simple. The simplicity of our soul is hindered by our flesh, when we please it." "Endeavor to attain the simplicity of a child in your relation to people and in prayer to God. Simplicity is the greatest good and dignity of a person. God is completely simple, because He is perfectly spiritual and completely good. And let not your soul be divided into good and evil."

God is a Trinity in Unity. "God the Father is Life, God the Son is Life, and God the Holy Spirit is Life: the Holy Trinity is Life." "What a fullness of Infinite Life!" exclaims Father John, when speaking about the relationship of the three Persons in God, and then again in the same notes he repeats: "What a fullness of life," and about their unity, for the third time: "What a fullness of life!"

The fullness of divine life is reflected in the richness, the variety of life and of the created world, in the kindness of God, spread throughout the whole world. The world as the product of a Live, Wise God is full of life: everywhere and in all there is life: as in the whole, so in all parts. This is a real book from which one can study God, although not as clearly as from revelation. Before the world was created, only the infinite God of Life existed; when the world was created out of nothing, God, of course, did not become limited; this complete fullness of life, and His infinity remained with Him. The fullness of life and infinity were expressed in creatures that are alive, limited, and possess life, of which there are innumerably many.

However, the world is limited, and in its limitation serves as a support for living creatures, that they may not disappear into limitless space.

"Just as the soul supports the body, so does God uphold the whole universe, all the worlds, and yet is not bound by them; the soul is in all the body, and the Spirit of God is transcendent and fills all nature; only the soul is limited by the body, although not completely, because it is able to be everywhere; likewise the Spirit of God is not limited by the world, and is not contained by the world, as in a body."

In observing the world we are astounded by how generously, how bountifully the Creator has endowed His creations with capabilities, with art, delicate and beautiful forms, gave them creative capacity. "*Wondrous are Thy works, O Lord! At every step, at every moment in life.*" "Involuntarily one becomes aroused to praise God when one sees the infinite variety of everything created on earth in the animal kingdom, and in the plant and inorganic kingdoms. What a wise arrangement in all, in that which is great and small. Involuntarily one praises God and says: *Wondrous are Thy works, O Lord; in wisdom hast Thou made them all; glory to Thee, O Lord, Who hast made them all.*"

"Who is it that forms the flowers so wisely, so delicately, arranges so splendidly, gives form to the disordered, i.e., the shapeless, formless substances of the earth? Who gives it such wonderful form? O Creator, grant us the opportunity through flowers to embrace Thy wisdom, benevolence, and Thine almighty power."

"The Lord is the cause and everlasting support (strength) of my organic, physical life through the activity of the lungs, stomach, heart, veins, muscles, and spiritual-organic life through the mind, and thought, through the enlightenment of the heart by His Light."

And here again in the midst of ideas dealing with the fullness of life, the bountifulness, and wisdom of God, Father John gives a corresponding moral lesson.

"The Lord has complete consideration for nature created by Him, and for its laws, which are the product of His infinite, most perfect wisdom; and therefore He usually realizes His will through the means of nature and her laws, as, for example, when He punishes people, or blesses them." This is one deduction. The other: If the Lord is so generous a Creator, if there is no end to His goodness, if the earth by His will furnishes food and clothing in abundance for man, then "each Christian, especially a priest, should follow in example the goodness of the Lord, that everyone should be invited to dine at your table, the food is the Lord's. The miser is an enemy of the Lord."

From here comes the call towards the fullness of pastoral activity; from here comes the fullness of his personal pastoral work. As a pastor, he warns himself and his co-pastors of being one-sided in Christian effort. "It is not necessary to ask whether one should spread God's glory by writing, speaking, or by good deeds. It is obvious. This we are obliged to do according to our strength and our ability. Talents must be used in action. If you should stop to think of this simple matter, then the devil will try to suggest an absurdity…that you need only inner work." "A priest must also remain in the spiritual world, in the sphere of his flock, as the Sun in nature; he must be a light for all, the living, kind hearted soul of all." "My sweetest Saviour! Thou didst come to serve mankind; not in the temple only didst Thou preach the Word of Heavenly Truth, but wandering through cities, towns, Thou didst not shun anyone; Thou didst go into the homes of all, especially those in whom Thou didst foresee full repentance with Thy divine glance. Thou didst not sit at home, but had love for all. Grant us that we may show that love toward Thy people, that we pastors may not exclude ourselves from Thy sheep, in our homes, as in castles, or prisons, coming out only for service in the church, or for urgent call in their homes because of duty, mechanically repeating the same prayers. May our lips be opened in the spirit of faith and love in free conversation with our parishioners. May our Christian love spread and be strengthened towards spiritual children through attentive, free, fatherly discourse with them."

In the spirit of the ancient Fathers, Father John has recourse in examining for dissimilarity the Three Persons of the Holy Trinity. He represents God the Father as Mind or Thought, God the Son as the Word of the Father, and God the Holy Spirit as the Divine Deed. "God is a Spirit... And in what way does a Spirit manifest Himself? By thought, word, and deed. For this reason, God as a Simple Being does not consist of a series or multiplicity of thoughts or multiplicity of words or creations, but He is all completely in one simple thought — God the Trinity, or in one simple word — Trinity..., but He is all, and all-existent, all-permeating, and all encompassing..."

In the unity of the Holy Trinity, an image is also given to us. As the Trinity, our God is One in Being — "so should we be One. As God is simple, so should we be simple, so simple as though we all were one person, one mind, one will, one heart, one goodness, without the slightest admixture of malice, in a word, one pure love, as God is Love."

Let us concentrate our attention on how Father John expresses his Christian teaching about God the Father. How often God the Father is presented as distant from the world! In philosophical religious teachings about God the Word, or Logos, it is explained in another sense, that God the Father, as the Absolute, is incommensurate with the relative world, and therefore cannot have direct contact with it, and consequently, is in need of an intercessor between Himself and the world, and that such an intercessor is God the Word, God the Son (Son of God). Such an outlook, incidentally, was expressed in the philosophical system of Vladimir Soloviev. This view penetrates often also into our common religious ideas:

God the Father, living in unapproachable Light, has reserved the right for this same reason to be remote from this earthly world and from us people. In a similar manner, the thought of the remoteness of God the Father from people is felt in the Roman Catholic teaching about atonement (redemption) where the redemption of mankind with the Blood of the Son of God, is explained by the necessity of appeasing, satisfying God the Father for His being insulted through the sin of man.

Father John teaches an entirely different idea:

God, Father of the Word, is also our benevolent and loving Father. When saying 'The Lord's Prayer,' we must believe and remember that the Father in heaven never forgets and will not forget us, for what earthly father forgets or does not care for his children? Remember that our Heavenly Father constantly surrounds us with love and care, and not in vain is He called our Father — this is not a name without meaning and force, but a name with great significance and power." "Should we not recognize Him as all the more benevolent, because He gave...the greatest gift of His benevolence, wisdom, and omnipotence — by this is meant freedom..., not being shaken by the ingratitude of those who received the gift, in order that His goodness could shine brighter than the sun before everyone? And has He not shown by His deed His boundless love and unlimited wisdom by bestowing upon us freedom, when, after our fall into sinfulness, and our withdrawal from Him, and spiritual ruin, He sent into the world His Son, the Only-begotten One, in the likeness of perishable man, and gave Him to suffer and die for us?"

"Christian! Remember and constantly bear in mind and in your heart the great words of the 'Lord's Prayer': 'Our Father, Who art in the Heavens.' Remember Who our Father is. God is our Father, our Love: who are we? We are His children, and among ourselves, brothers; in what manner of love ought children to live among themselves, having such a Father? If you were children of Abraham you would have done the deeds of Abraham; what kinds of deeds must we do?" "Our life is that of love — yes, love. And where there is love, there is God, and where there is God, there is all good... And so with joy feed and delight everyone, please all and depend in all things upon the heavenly Father, the Father of mercies, and God of all consolation. Bring to your neighbor in sacrifice that which is dear to you..." And so, we see, Father John converts the fundamental dogmas into immediate moral admonitions; he shows that every truth of Faith contains in itself a moral purpose.

Father John, in his theology about the Father teaches, first of all, about divine thought. "From God's mind, from God's thought, proceeds every thought in the world. In general everywhere in the world we see the kingdom of thought, as in all the structure of the visible world, so also, in particular, on earth, in the rotation and life of the earthly planet, in the distribution of the elements of the world: air, water, fire, whereas other phenomena are distributed in all animals, in birds, fish, snakes, beasts, and in man, in their wise and purposeful formation, and in their capabilities, morals, habits; in plants, in their adaptation, in nutrition, and so on, everywhere we see the kingdom of thought, even in the inanimate stone and sand."

God's thought has its reflection in man's thought. "We are able to think on account of this, because there exists the Infinite Thought. We are able to breathe because there is boundless space with air. That is why pure thoughts dealing with any subject are called *inspired*. Our thought constantly flows under the condition of an Infinite Spirit's existence. That is why the Saviour says: — *Take no thought how or what ye shall speak: for it shall be given you...what ye shall speak.* You see, thought and even word (inspiration) comes to us from an outside source; this takes place in a Grace-filled state and in case of need."

What kind of edification does Father John draw from his thinking on God's Thought? The reminder that we must avoid all kind of thought that is not true, fear lies, not to sin in thought, because false thoughts themselves draw us away from God, and incline us to surrender to the devil's power. Sins of thought in a Christian are not to be considered a small matter, because, according to St. Macarius of Egypt, all our pleasing of God consists of thoughts; for thoughts are the beginning: from them arise words and actions, words, because they give Grace to listeners, or are corrupted words and serve as a temptation to others; they corrupt the thoughts and hearts of others.

The second person of the Holy Trinity, God the Son, is the Hypostatic Word of the Father. This dogma gives Father John the inspiration to often express in his writings the power and action of every word, not only God's word but also man's.

"The Word is the Creator and our God; every word of His is Truth and action. Such should our word also be, (for we are created in the image of God)." "The Word is the expression of truth, the very truth, the life, and the deed. The Word precedes every creature, everything, as the cause of existence, in the past, present, and future." "How much then must one cherish especially all that which comes forth from the Very Hypostatic Word, the Gospel words, the writings of the Church Fathers, the prayers." "Christian! cherish every word, be attentive to every word; be firm in word; be trusting toward every word of God, and the words of saintly persons, the words of life. Remember that the word is the beginning of life." "The word must be revered strongly because in one word there is the Omnipresent One, and One that fulfills all, one and undivided Lord,... in one name is He Himself, the Lord..." "Remember that in the very word is contained the possibility of action; only one must have strong faith in the power of the word, in its creative capacity. With the Lord the word and deed are inseparable. So ought it to be with us also, for we are images of the Word, in its creative capacity. With the Lord the word and deed are inseparable. So ought it to be with us also, for we are images of the Word..." "The word is power... And of people it is said: he has an extraordinary power of words. So you see, the word is power, spirit, life." "Every word, every kernel will bring you spiritual benefit. Who from among those who pray has not experienced this? Not in vain did the Saviour compare the seed with the word, and the heart of man with the earth." "One must believe that as the shadow follows the body, so action follows the word; as with the Lord, word and action are inseparable; for He speaks and it is; He orders and it is done... The trouble is that we are of little faith, and separate words from deeds, as body from soul, as form from content, as shadow from body."

It is evident that in the majority of thoughts expressed, Father John speaks about prayer, about the power of prayerful words spoken with faith.

In action not every word retains its power. Father John observes: "The word on the lips of some is spirit and life, and on the lips of others, dead alphabet (for example during prayer or sermon)." Finally, the word can be a negative force. "With the devil, who fell away from God, there remained only the shadow of a thought and word without truth, without the essence of a deed, a lie, a shadow; and as the true word being the image of God the

Word, and proceeding from Him, is Life, so a false word from the devil, being his image, is death; a lie is inevitable death, for, naturally, that brings death to the soul which itself had fallen from life into death."

The Second Person of the Holy Trinity is also called Hypostatic, i.e., Personal Wisdom of God. Why do we believe that the Wisdom of God has a Personal attribute? Father John answers: "How could God be without Wisdom, and not be Personal, how could God not be the Creature, how could He be without His own living self-existent Wisdom? Glance upon all in this world, how wonderful it all is!... Imagine how God, having created innumerable reasonable, personal, wise, living creatures, could not Himself generate from within Himself Personal Wisdom? Is this wise? Is this possible? Is this in conformity with the perfection of God? In God there must be the Hypostatic Wisdom, or the Hypostatic Word of the Father, equal as the life-creating Spirit, Who proceeds from the Father and rests in the Son."

The Holy Spirit is the third person of the Holy Trinity, indivisible, "Within you, there is breath, material, impersonal in nature, but in God as Life Itself, breath is a Personal Spirit, indivisible, simple, that gives Life to everything." "You will ask further: Why is the third Person called Spirit, and why is He a separate Person, when God, even without Him, is Spirit? I answer: The Holy Spirit is called Spirit in relation to creatures: the Lord breathed with His Hypostatic Spirit, and there appeared, by the power of His Life-creating Spirit, an innumerable host of spirits: In the power of His Spirit lies their strength; He breathed with His Spirit into man's body: and now man became a living soul, and from this Breath, until now, people are born, and will be born until the end according to the commandment: increase and multiply. If the Lord created by His Spirit so many personal separate beings, then why is it impossible for the Holy Spirit Himself to be a Person, or a personal creative Being? If there are countless numbers of created personal spirits, then is God Himself to remain without Spirit, without His Independent, Hypostatic Personality?"

"The Holy Spirit, like air, is everywhere and penetrates all." "The Lord Jesus Christ Himself likens the Holy Spirit in His action to the substance of water (John 7:38–39), air, or wind (John 3:8)." "As the air in the room is identical with the outer air, comes from it, and necessarily presupposes the air spread out everywhere, so in like manner, our soul, the breath of the Spirit of God, presupposes the existence of the omnipresent, transcendent Spirit of God." It is the Spirit that quickeneth (John 6:63). "The life in creatures belongs to God, from the time of their creation, and to God the Son, their creator, bringing them from non-existence to existence... The Holy Spirit creates us in the womb of our mother; our spiritual wealth belongs to the Holy Spirit."

Our soul lives by the Holy Spirit, through Him we pray, through Him we become purified, through Him we save ourselves. "As breath is necessary for the body, and without breathing man cannot live, so without the Breath of the Holy Spirit the soul cannot live the true life. What the air is for the body, that the Holy Spirit is for the soul. Air is likened to the Spirit of God. The Spirit breathes wherever It wishes." "He who prays prays by the Holy Spirit." "Prayer is the breath of the soul, as air is the breath of the natural body. We breathe by the Holy Spirit. You cannot say a single word of prayer from your heart without the Holy Spirit."

"As in a conversation with people the sound-conveying medium between our words and the words of another is air, which is everywhere and fills all space, and through air the words reach the ear of another, and without air it would be impossible to speak and hear: so in a spiritual manner, in communication with spiritual beings the mediator is the Holy Spirit, omnipresent and transcendent."

"We are filled with One Spirit: Do you see how the Holy Spirit surrounds us like water and air on all sides?"

"For a long time I did not know with full clarity how necessary was the strengthening of our soul by the Holy Spirit. And now the Most Merciful One gave me the opportunity to find out how indispensable it is. Yes, it is necessary every minute, as is breathing, necessary at prayer, and throughout life. It is necessary that our heart rest on a rock. And that rock is the Holy Spirit."

"All upright people are filled by the One Divine Spirit, similarly as a sponge is saturated with water. The comforting Holy Spirit, filling the universe, penetrates through all the believing, humble, good, and simple souls of men, and living in them, revives and strengthens them; He becomes all for them: light, power, peace, joy, success in deeds, especially in an upright life — He is all goodness."

Thus we see that the dogma of the Holy Spirit in the thought of Father John is closely connected with life. The teaching about the Holy Spirit is at the same time teaching about the life of the world, about the source and nourishment of all uprightness and holiness.

Such is the teaching of Father John about the Holy Trinity. In God, the Triune Unity, is found all the fullness of life and the life of the world. The reflection of the attributes of God is represented by the universe, the material world, and in particular, man. From here, we will make a general deduction from the words of Father John: "In order to become pure images of the Holy Trinity, we must try to attain holiness in our thoughts, words, and deeds. Thought corresponds to God the Father, the word to the Son, and deeds to the Holy Spirit, the all active Creator."

"Your Lord is Love: love Him and in Him all people, as His children in Christ. Your Lord is Fire: do not be cold at heart, but burn with fire and love. Your Lord is Light: do not walk in the darkness of your mind without reason and understanding or without faith. Your Lord is a God of mercy and kindness: you also be a source of mercy and kindness to your neighbors. If you will be so, you will attain salvation with eternal glory."

Such should our life be, for we carry within ourselves the image of God.

But actually most of the time we live in doubts, lack of faith, in unbelief, *having eyes and seeing not, having ears and hearing not, and having a hardened heart.* "We notice within ourselves the struggle of faith and disbelief, of good and evil, the spirit of the Church against the spirit of the world. Do you know from whence this comes?" asks Father John, and he answers:"From the struggle of two opposing forces: the power of God, and the power of the devil. And I also feel within myself this struggle of two opposing forces. When I begin to pray, at times an evil force painfully depresses me and casts my heart down, that it may not be able to look up to God," writes Father John, in one of his comparatively early writings. The radiation of the evil forces of the devil is similar to poison that enters the body. The kingdom of life and the kingdom of death go together. And involuntarily the question arises: Why does the Lord allow the devil to exist, and even to act on good souls?

And in this Father John sees providential plans of God. "If you do not experience in yourself the influence of the evil spirit, you will not know and you will not value as you should the goodness shown to you by the benevolence of the Holy Spirit; not having known the spirit that destroys, you also will not know the Life-giving Spirit. Only because of contrary opposites of good and evil, of life and death, we understand one and the other... Glory to God, the Wise and All-Good, that He permits the spirit of evil and death to tempt us and cause us suffering. Otherwise, how could we begin to value the consolation of Grace, the consolation of the Holy Spirit, the Comforter and Life-giver!"

For this reason we have been given the Holy Church, Her Sacraments, and all of Her ordinances so that we might have the opportunity to remain under the constant influence of the all-conquering Grace of God.

The work of the Grace of God we see openly in life. If one had been proud, a lover of oneself, unkind, but became humble and gracious, he became so by the power of Grace. The unbeliever, a believer — by the power of Grace. The lover of money, no longer acquisitive, but honest and generous by the power of Grace. The glutton became moderate in eating from the conscious knowledge of high moral purpose, by the Grace of God. He who hated and was full of malice, a lover of his fellow man by the power of Grace. He who was cold toward God, toward the Church, was transformed, he became a fervent believer in God, by the act of Grace. "From this is is evident that many live without Grace, not knowing its importance and its need for themselves, and do not seek it... Many live in all kinds of abundance, and pleasure, but they have no Grace in their hearts, this most valuable treasure for the Christian without which the Christian cannot be a true Christian and inherit the kingdom of God."

"The sign of God's mercy and that of His Most Holy Mother of God toward us, after or during prayer, is peace within the heart, especially after the affect of some passion, which is the absence of peace of soul. By peace of soul and a certain holy inclination of the heart we can easily ascertain that our prayer is heard and the Grace asked for is received."

Take advantage then, Christian, of God's treasure of Grace! "When you pray to the Father and the Holy Spirit in the Trinity, the One God, do not seek Him outside yourself, but perceive Him within yourself as living in you, completely penetrating within you and knowing you. *Know ye not that ye are temples of God, and the Spirit of God dwelleth in you?*

Remember "that your soul is like some imprint of godliness and all the riches of the soul consist of God, as within a treasure (the treasure of Grace) from which we can draw every spiritual good, by the prayer of faith, and by patience, and by purifying oneself from all iniquity."

"As there is an overabundance of sources of water on earth, and all drink from them, come and draw freely, for the Lord is an ocean of spiritual waters; come and draw all the spiritual good with the dipper of true, firm, and unashamed faith. Only extend this hearty dipper and you will inevitably draw abundantly the water of life, the forgiveness of sins, and peace of conscience. But fear doubt; it deprives you of the means of drawing forth every mercy of God."

The waters from this source you will also find in communion with saints during prayer; they are in the graceful life of the Church. "The priesthood and in general, all the saints, are blessed water containers, from which the water of Grace is transmitted to other believers. Living waters will flow from the depths of rivers."

In such a manner Father John teaches us the fundamental truths of the Christian faith and life founded on these truths. The value of his theological teaching for us consists of the close connection between his theological thought, his words, and his life, and all his sanctified activity. The value is in this, that his personal life justified, proved, and realized his faith in action. "Experience!" — "Based on experience!" with this exclamation Father John often finishes his separate writings. "No matter how many times I prayed with faith, God always heard me and answered my prayers." What can be said stronger than these words?

The Liturgical Theology
of Father A. Schmemann

Throughout its history, Russian theological science is accused of falling too much under the influence of the non-Orthodox West. The influence of Latin scholasticism on Kievan theology lasted until the beginning of the 19th century. If later theological science freed itself from this influence, then reproaches were heard of another nature, i.e., that our theologians were not independent, that they were often limited by "copying the Germans," as Metropolitan Anthony expressed it. This characterization was unpleasant; but, since this dependency did not destroy the general Orthodox direction of theology, it did no real harm. What can one do if the historical and theological science of the West was extensively developed long ago while ours was still embryonic? Due to necessity we had to draw from these sources, and, having drawn from them, we obviously became dependent on them. More important is the fact that the study of sources concerning all facets of church history, even Eastern sources, predominantly belonged to and belongs to the West. In our tragic era when Russian theological science is nearly obliterated, the study of the Orthodox East has passed exclusively into the hands of Western theologians and historians. Their study is done carefully and, in the majority of cases, with love.

Nevertheless, one should never forget how unique genuine Orthodox consciousness is, how independent, and how full it is of its own inimitable spirit. *For what man knoweth the things of a man, save the spirit of man which is in him?* (I Cor. 2:11). The words of Apostle Paul can be applied to the Church. The Western man who is not a member of the Orthodox Church, even if scholarly, is in no position to penetrate the spirit of the Church, the spirit of Orthodoxy. This is to say nothing of those scholarly Western church historians who themselves have lost their Christian faith.

Even the scholarly believers of the West inevitably bear the imprint of denominationalism. Protestant scholars are subject to preconceived notions and opinions, long ago deeply rooted in the Protestant psyche. Their false understanding of the era of Constantine the Great is ample proof of this. From this proceeds their biased interpretation of the written sources of the first period of Church history. It would be a grave mistake to acknowledge in Christianity at the present time the presence of a unified, objective, historical-theological science. This would mean, in many circumstances, to accept such a treatment of the history of Christianity which contradicts the historical tradition of the Church and the Orthodox world-view, and undermines the dogmas of the Orthodox Faith. Such "theological ecumenism" would be a great temptation.

Before us is a work of Protopresbyter Alexander Schmemann, *Introduction to Liturgical Theology* (Paris, YMCA Press, 1961; English translation: The Faith Press, London, 1966). The book is offered as an "introduction" to a special course in liturgical theology planned by the author. In it are indicated the basics of a proposed new system of theology, after which is given an historical outline of the development of the Rule or Typicon of Divine services. This second, historical part has the nature of a scientific investigation.

The author views his book as the foundation for a new area of theological science — "Liturgical Theology," placing before this science, and consequently before himself, the extraordinary task, "to guard the purity of divine services... to preserve it from distortion and misinterpretation" (p. 10). This new theology should be the guide for the "reexamination of limitless liturgical material contained in the Menaion and Octoechoi" (for some reason the last word is in the plural). Together with this task concerning the services is another concerning theology: the historical-liturgical structure of our theology should be the touchstone in determining the worthiness and failings of our usual so-called academic theology. The author writes: we must "historically seek and discover the key to liturgical theology. We must restore the darkened ecclesiological, catholic consciousness of the Church by means of this theological research." These plans are extraordinarily serious, the responsibility is enormous, requiring absolute Orthodoxy in the structure of the proposed science in order that it truly could "stand in defense" of both Divine services as well as theology.

The fundamental part of the *Introduction to Liturgical Theology* — the history of the Typicon — is based primarily on Western scientific investigations in French, English, and German, and partially on Russian sources. The author is convinced that he has succeeded, as he expresses it, in "escaping Western captivity" while using non-Orthodox sources. He avoids the extreme affirmations of Protestant historians. He writes: "We categorically reject the understanding of the Peace of Constantine (i.e., the era of Constantine the Great) as a 'pseudo-victory' of Christianity — victory bought at the price of compromise" (p. 86). However, such affirmations are not enough in themselves, when we are speaking of a subject having so much significance as has been historically demonstrated. Therefore, disregarding the scholarly baggage in the book, passing over the structure of the work, we consider it our obligation to focus attention on the book's contents in one respect: has the author indeed escaped Western captivity? As many of his statements testify, he has in fact not escaped it.

The Orthodox Liturgical Order:
The Product of Historical Cause and Effect,
or Divine Inspiration and Guidance?

In investigating the main stages of development of the Rule of Divine services, or Typicon, the author looks upon them as an ordinary historical manifestation, formed as a result of the influence of changing historical circumstances. He writes: "Orthodox writers are usually inclined to 'absolutize' the history of worship, to consider the whole of it as divinely established and Providential" (p. 72). The author rejects such a view. He does not see "the value of principles" in the definitive formulation of the Typicon; in every case he acknowledges them as dubious. He rejects and even censures a "blind absolutization of the Typicon" when in practice this is joined, in his opinion, to a factual violation of it at every step. He sees "the restoration of the Typicon as hopeless"; the theological meaning of the daily cycle of services he finds "obscured and eclipsed by secondary strata in the Typicon" which have accumulated in the Divine services since the 4th century (pp. 161–2). The ecclesiological key to the understanding of the Typicon, according to the author, has been lost, and we are left to seek and find the key to liturgical theology by means of historical research.

Such a view of the Typicon is new to us. The Typicon, in the form which it has come down to our time in its two basic versions, is the realized idea of Christian worship; the worship of the first century was a kernel which has grown and matured to its present state, having now taken its finished form. We have in mind, of course, not the *content* of the services, not the hymns and prayers themselves, which often bear the stamp of the literary style of an era and are replaced one by another, but the very *system* of Divine services, their order, concord, harmony, consistency of principles and fullness of God's glory and communion with the Heavenly Church on the one hand, and on the other the fullness of their expression of the human soul — from the Paschal hymns to the Great Lenten lamentation over moral falls. The present Rule of Divine services was already contained in the idea of the Divine services of the first Christians in the same way that in the seed of a plant are already contained the forms of the plant's future growth up to the moment when it begins to bear mature fruits, or in the way that in the embryonic organism of a living creature its future form is already concealed. To the foreign eye, to the non-Orthodox West, the fact that our Rule has taken a static form is viewed as petrification, fossilization. For us this static form represents the finality of growth, the attainment of all possible fullness. Such finality of developed form we also observe in Eastern Church iconography, in church architecture, in the interior appearance of the best churches, in the traditional melodies of church singing. Further attempts at development in these spheres often leads to decadence, leading not up but down. One can draw only one conclusion: we are nearer to the end of history than to the beginning... Of course, as in other spheres of Church history, so also in this sphere of liturgics we should see a path established by God, Providence, and not only the logic of causes and effects.

The author approaches the history of the Typicon from another point of view; we shall call it the pragmatic point of view. In his exposition the fundamental apostolic, early Christian liturgical order has been overlaid by a series of strata which lie one upon the other, partially obscuring each other. These strata are: "mysteriological" worship, which arose not without the indirect influence of the pagan mysteries in the 4th century; then the influence of the liturgical order of desert monasticism; and finally the form adapted for the world from the monastic order. The scientific schema of the author is: the "thesis" of an extreme involvement of Christianity and its worship in the "world" during the Constantinian Era which evoked the "antithesis" of monastic repulsion from the new form of "liturgical piety," and this process concludes with the "synthesis" of the Byzantine period. Alone and without argumentation this phrase stands as a description of the stormy Constantinian Era: "But everything has its germination in the preceding epoch" (p. 73). The author pays tribute to the method that reigns totally in contemporary science: leaving aside the idea of an overshadowing by Divine Grace, the concept of the sanctity of those who established the liturgical order, he limits himself to a naked chain of causes and effects. Thus positivism intrudes now into Christian sciences, into the sphere of the Church's history in all its branches. If, however, the positivist method is acknowledged as a scientific working principle in *science*, in natural sciences, one can by no means apply it to living religion, nor to every sphere of the life of Christianity and the Church, insofar as we remain believers. And when the author in one place notes concerning this era: "The Church experienced her new freedom as a providential act destined to bring to Christ people then dwelling in the darkness and shadow of death" (p. 87), one wishes to ask: Why does the author himself not express his solidarity with the Church in acknowledging this providentialness?

They tell us: no one keeps the Typicon, and besides, the theological key to understanding it has been lost. We answer: the difficulty in fully keeping the Typicon is connected with the idea of maximalism inherent in the Orthodox understanding of Christianity. This maximalism is found in relation to the moral standards of the Gospel, the strictness of church canons, the area of ascetic practice, of prayer and services based on the commandment, *pray without ceasing*. Only in monasteries do the church services approach the norm of perfection, and at that only relatively. Life in the world and parishes force an unavoidable lessening of the norm, and therefore the parish practice cannot be viewed as the Orthodox model and ideal in the sphere of church services. Nonetheless, we cannot refer to the practice in parishes as a "distortion," in the theological sense, of the principles of Divine services. Even in the cases of "intolerable" shortening, the services retain a great amount of content and exalted meaning, and do not lose their intrinsic value. Such shortenings are "intolerable" because they bear witness to our self-indulgence, our laziness, our carelessness in our duty of prayer. One cannot objectively judge the value of the liturgical Rule according to the practice here in the diaspora. One cannot draw conclusions from this practice concerning the total loss of understanding of the spirit of the Rubrics.

Let us proceed to more substantial questions.

The Constantinian Era

We all know what an immense change occurred in the position of the Church with Constantine the Great's proclamation of freedom for the Church at the beginning of the 4th century. This outward act was also reflected everywhere in the inward life of the Church. Was there here a *break* in the inner structure of the Church's life, or was there a *development*? The consciousness of the Orthodox Church replies in one way, and Protestantism in another to this question. The main part of Fr. A. Schmemann's book is given over to the elucidation of this question.

The period of Constantine the Great and later is characterized by the author as the era of a profound "regeneration of liturgical piety." Therefore, the author sees in the Church of this time, not new forms of expressions of piety, flowing from the *breadth and liberty* of the Christian spirit in accord with the words of the Apostle: *Where the Spirit of the Lord is, there is liberty*, but rather a *regeneration* of the interpretation of worship and a deviation from the early Christian liturgical spirit. He develops a point of view inspired long ago by the prejudices of the Lutheran Reformation. Thus, the history of the structure of our services is being interpreted in the light of this "regeneration of liturgical piety."

A propos of this, it is also difficult to reconcile oneself to the term "liturgical piety." In the ordinary usage of words, piety is Christian faith, hope, and love, independent of the forms of their expression. Such an understanding is instilled in us by the Sacred Scriptures, which distinguish only authentic piety (*piety is profitable unto all things* — I Tim. 4:8) from false or empty piety (James 1:26; II Tim. 3:5). Piety is expressed in prayer, in Divine services, and the forms of its expression vary depending on circumstances: whether in church, at home, in prison, or in the catacombs. But we Orthodox scarcely need a special term like "liturgical piety" or "church piety," as if one were pious in a different manner in church than at home, and as if there existed two kinds of religiousness: "religiousness of faith" and "religiousness of cult." Both the language of the Holy Fathers and of theology have always done without such a concept. Therefore it is a new idea, foreign to us, of a special liturgical piety that the author instills when he writes: "It is in the profound regeneration of liturgical piety and not in new forms of cult, however striking these may seem to be at first glance, that we must see the basic change brought about in the Church's liturgical life by the Peace of Constantine" (p. 78). And in another place: "The center of attention is shifted from the living Church to the church building itself, which was until then a simple place of assembly... Now the temple becomes a sanctuary, a place for the habitation and residence of the sacred... This is the beginning of church piety" (pp. 89–90). The freedom of the Church under Constantine establishes, writes the author, "a new understanding of the cult, a new liturgical piety" (p. 80), a "mysteriological piety." In his usage of such terms one senses in the author something more than the replacement of one terminology by another more contemporary one; one senses something foreign to Orthodox consciousness. This fundamental point is decisively reflected in the author's views on the Mysteries, the hierarchy, and the veneration of saints, which we shall now examine.

The Mysteries and the Sanctifying Element
in Sacred Rites

The author adheres to the concept that the idea of "sanctification," of "mysteries," and in general of the sanctifying power of sacred rites was foreign to the ancient Church and arose only in the era after Constantine. Although the author denies a direct borrowing of the idea of "mysteries-sacraments" from the pagan mysteries, he nonetheless recognizes the "mysteriality-sacralization" in worship as a new element of "stratification" in this era. "The very word 'mystery,' " he writes, citing the Jesuit scholar (now Cardinal) J. Danielou, "did not originally have the meaning in Christianity that was subsequently given it, a mysteriological meaning; in the New Testament Scriptures it is used only in the singular and in accordance with the general significance of the economy of our salvation. The word 'mystery' (*mysterion*) in Paul and in early Christianity always signified the whole work of Christ, the whole of salvation"; thus, in the author's opinion, the application of this word even to separate aspects of the work of Christ belongs to the following era.

In vain, however, does the author cite a Western scholar concerning the word "mystery." If in Saint Paul we read the precise words: *Let a man so account of us, as of the ministers of Christ and stewards of the mysteries*

(Greek: μυστηρίων, genitive plural) *of God* (I Cor. 4:1). The Apostles were stewards of the Mysteries, and this apostolic stewardship was expressed concretely in the service of the Divine stewardship: a) in invocatory sermons, b) in joining to the Church through Baptism, c) in bringing down the Holy Spirit through the laying down of hands, d) in strengthening the union of the faithful with Christ in the Mystery of the Eucharist, e) in their further deepening in the mysteries of the Kingdom of God, concerning which the same Apostle says: *Howbeit we speak wisdom among them that are perfect. But we speak the wisdom of God in a mystery, even the hidden wisdom* (I Cor. 2:6–7). Thus the activity of the Apostles was full of sacramental* (μυστήριων, μυστηρίῳ) elements.

Basing himself on the ready conclusions of Western researchers in his judgments on the ancient Church, the author pays no attention to the direct evidence of apostolic writings, even though they have the primary significance as landmarks in the life of the early Christian Church. The New Testament Scriptures speak directly of "sanctification," sanctification by the Word of God and prayer. *Nothing is to be refused, if it be received with thanksgiving: For it is sanctified by the word of God and prayer* (I Tim. 4:4–5). And it is said of Baptism: *Ye are washed, ye are sanctified, ye are justified* (I Cor. 6:11). The very expression *cup of blessing* (I Cor. 10:16) is testimony of sanctification through blessing. The apostolic laying on of hands cannot be understood otherwise than as a sanctification.

A special place in the book is occupied by a commentary on the Mystery of the Eucharist. The author maintains the idea that in the early Church the Eucharist had a totally different meaning from the one it subsequently received. The Eucharist, he believes, was an expression of the ecclesiological union in an assembly of the faithful, the joyful banquet of the Lord. Its whole meaning was directed to the future, to eschatology, and therefore it presented itself as a "worship outside of time," not bound to history or remembrances, as eschatological worship, by which it was sharply distinct from the simple forms of worship, which are called in the book the "worship in time." In the 4th century, however, we are told there occurred an acute regeneration of the original character of the Eucharist. It was given an "individual-sanctifying" understanding, which was the

---

*The words "mystery" and "sacrament" are fully interchangeable, and either have been used in places where they make sense and provide clarity in this translation. Ed.

result of two stratifications: initially mysteriological, and then monastic-ascetic.

Notwithstanding the assertions of this historico-liturgical school, the individual-sanctifying significance of the Mystery of the Eucharist, i.e., the significance not only of a union of believers among themselves, but before anything else a union of each believer with Christ through partaking of His Body and Blood, is fully and definitely expressed by the Apostle in the tenth and eleventh chapters of the First Epistle to the Corinthians: *Whosoever shall eat this bread, and drink this cup of the Lord, unworthily, shall be guilty of the Body and Blood of the Lord. But let a man examine himself, and so let him eat of that bread, and drink of that cup. For he that eateth and drinketh unworthily, eateth and drinketh judgment to himself, not discerning the Lord's Body. For this cause many are weak and sickly among you, and many die* (I Cor. 11:27). These teachings of the Apostle are concerned with individual reception of the holy Mysteries and with individual responsibility. If unworthy reception of them is judged, it is clear that, according to the Apostle, a worthy reception of them is the cause for individual sanctification. It is absolutely clear that the Apostle understands the Eucharist as a mystery: *The cup of blessing which we bless, is it not the Communion of the Blood of Christ? The bread which we break, is it not the Communion of the Body of Christ?* (I Cor. 10:16) How can one say that the idea of "mystery" was not in the Church in apostolic times?

Maintaining the idea of the total "extra-temporality" of the Eucharist in the early Church, Fr. A. Schmemann considers as a violation of tradition the uniting of it with historical remembrances of the Gospel. He writes: "In the early Eucharist there was no idea of a ritual symbolization of the life of Christ and His Sacrifice. This is a theme which will appear later...under the influence of one theology and as the point of departure for another. The remembrance of Christ which He instituted (*This do in remembrance of Me*) is the affirmation of His 'Parousia,' of His presence; it is the actualization of His Kingdom... One may say without exaggeration that the early Church consciously and openly set herself in opposition to mysteriological piety and cults of the mysteries" (pp. 85–86).

Despite all the categoricalness of the author's commentary on the words: *This do in remembrance of Me*, it contradicts the directives of New Testament Scriptures. The Apostle says outright: *For as often as ye eat this bread, and drink this cup, ye do show the Lord's death till He come* (I Cor.

11:26). That is, until the very Second Coming of the Lord the Eucharist will be joined to the remembrance of Christ's death on the Cross. And how could the Apostles and Christians of the ancient Church omit the thought, while celebrating the Eucharist, of the sufferings of Christ, if the Saviour in establishing it, at the Last Supper, Himself spoke of the sufferings of His Body, of the shedding of His Blood (*which is broken for you, which is shed for you and for many*), and in Gethsemane prayed of the cup: *Let this cup pass from Me*? How could they not preface the joyful thought of the Resurrection and glory of the Lord with the thought of His Cross and death? Both Christ and the Apostles call upon us never to forget the Cross.

Concerning the later historical practice of serving the Eucharist, Fr. A. Schmemann writes, "the characteristically gradual development of interpreting the rituals of the Liturgy as a mystical depiction of the life of Christ… was a replacement of the ecclesiological understanding of the Eucharist with a depictive-symbolical one, and even more clearly expresses the mysteriological regeneration of liturgical piety. Together with this regeneration is connected the development of an entirely new part of the Eucharist — the Proskomedia, which is entirely and exclusively symbolical (?), and in this respect 'duplicates' the Eucharist (the symbolic sacrifice in cutting the bread and pouring the wine into the chalice, etc.). And finally, nothing exposes this transition to a 'sanctifying' understanding of the Mystery and service more than the change in the manner of communicating — changing [the practice of communicating] from the idea of a liturgical-community act, 'which seals' (?) the Eucharistic change of bread, to the idea of an individual sanctifying act having a relation to personal piety, and not to the ecclesiological status of the communicant. In reference to the practice of Communion we can truly speak here of a 'revolution' " (p. ?).

The thoughts cited above elicit a whole new series of objections. A) Proskomedia is "preparation." How can one proceed without preparation? Any meal, even the most simple meal, cannot take place without preparation. B) The Proskomedia is served by the priest within a closed altar and does not have the characteristic of a community service. C) What should the thoughts of the priest be directed towards during the Proskomedia if not to the recollection of our Saviour's crucifixion? The service book for the Divine Liturgy supports this thought by the words in chapter

53 of the Prophet Isaiah about the suffering Messiah. D) The Liturgy of the
Faithful is not duplicated in the recollections of the Proskomedia. In order
that the actions of the sacred celebrant not be soulless, in the secret prayers
at the Proskomedia, the Church directs him to recall the crucifixion and
death of the Saviour, and at the Liturgy of the Faithful, the taking down
from the Cross, placing in the tomb, descent into Hades, and His resurrection and ascent into Heaven. These recollections are not "depictions"
nor symbols. Concerning symbolism, it occupies a very modest part in the
service (we are not speaking here of authors who interpret the services). In
fact the service consists of various prayers, symbolism has nothing to do
with them, and has a connection only with some of the celebrant's actions.
These actions, in fact, have a *real* significance and are, consequently, only
given an extra, supplementary significance. E) The change from the
ancient form of communicating from the Chalice to the more contemporary practice of communicating laymen is a change of one practice of
communing to another, which does not change the essence of the Mystery.
To claim a "regeneration" or "revolution" in the celebration of the Mystery of Communion is a sin against the Orthodox Church.

The Hierarchy and the Mystery of the Priesthood

The author expresses the idea that only in the post-Constantinian era
did there occur a division into clergy and simple believers, which did not
exist in the early Church and occurred as the result of a "breakthrough of
mysteriological conceptions." The very idea of the "assembly of the
Church," he says, was reformed: "In the Byzantine era the emphasis is
gradually transferred…to the clergy as celebrants of the mystery" (p. 99).
"The early Church lived with the consciousness of herself as the people of
God, a royal priesthood, with the idea of the elect, but she did not apply
the principle of consecration either to entry into the Church or much less
to ordination to the various hierarchical orders" (p. 100). From the 4th
century on, he continues, there can be traced the "idea of sanctification,"
i.e., consecration to the hierarchical ranks. Now the baptized, the "consecrated," turn out to be not yet consecrated for the mysteries; "the true
mystery of consecration became now not Baptism, but the sacrament of
ordination." "The cult was removed from the unconsecrated not only
'psychologically,' but also in its external organization. The altar or sanctuary became its place, and access to the sanctuary was closed to the unini-

tiated" (p. 101); the division was furthered by the gradual raising of the iconostasis. "The mystery presupposes *theurgii*, consecrated celebrants; the sacralization of the clergy led in its turn to the 'secularization' of the laity." There fell aside "the understanding of all Christians as a 'royal priesthood'," expressed in the symbol of royal anointing, after which there is no "step by step elevation through the degrees of a sacred mystery" (p. 100). The author quotes Saint Dionysius the Areopagite, who warned against revealing the holy mysteries "to profane impurity," and likewise similar warnings of Saints Cyril of Jerusalem and Basil the Great.

In this description of the Constantinian era and thereafter, the Protestant treatment is evident. The golden age of Christian freedom and the age of the great hierarchs, the age of the flowering of Christian literature, is presented here as something negative, a supposed intrusion of pagan elements into the Church, rather than as something positive. But at any time in the Church have simple believers actually received the condemnatory appellation of "profane"? From the *Catechetical Lectures* of Saint Cyril of Jerusalem it is absolutely clear that he warns against communicating the mysteries of faith to pagans. Saint Basil the Great writes of the same thing: "What would be the propriety of writing to proclaim the teaching concerning that which the unbaptized are not permitted even to view?" (*On the Holy Spirit*, ch. 27) Do we really have to quote the numerous testimonies in the words of the Lord Himself and in the writings of the Apostles concerning the division into pastors and "flock," the warnings to pastors of their duty, their responsibility, their obligation to give an accounting for the souls entrusted to them, the strict admonitions of the angels to the Churches which are engraved in the Apocalypse? Do not the Acts of the Apostles and the pastoral Epistles of the Apostle Paul speak of a special consecration *through laying on of hands* into the hierarchical degrees?

The author of this book acknowledges that a closed altar separated the clergy from the faithful. But he gives an incorrect conception of the altar. One should know that the altar and its altar table in the Orthodox Church serve only for the offering of the Bloodless Sacrifice at the Liturgy. The remaining Divine services, according to the idea of the Typicon, are celebrated in the middle part of the church. An indication of this is the pontifical service. Even while celebrating the Liturgy the bishop enters the altar only at the "Small Entry" in order to listen to the Gospel and celebrate the Mystery of the Eucharist; all remaining Divine services the bishop celebrates in the middle of the church. The litanies are intoned by the deacon at all services, including the Liturgy, outside the altar; and the Typicon directs priests who celebrate Vespers and Matins without a deacon to intone the litanies before the Royal Doors. All services of the *Book of Needs* (*Trebnik*) and all mysteries of the Church, except for the Eucharist and Ordination, are celebrated outside the altar. Only to augment the solemnity of the services at feast-day Vespers and Matins it is accepted to open the doors of the altar for a short time, and that only for the exit of the celebrants at solemn moments to go to the middle of the church. During daily and lenten services the altar, one may say, is excluded from the sphere of the faithful's attention; and if the celebrant goes off into the altar even then, this is rather in order not to attract needless attention to himself, and not at all to emphasize his clerical prestige.

The idea of the appearance from the 4th century on of a new "church" piety is an obvious exaggeration. Christians who had been raised from the first days of the Church on images not only of the New Testament, but also of the Old Testament, especially the Psalter, could not have been totally deprived of a feeling of special reverence for the places of worship (the House of the Lord). They had the example of the Lord Himself, Who called the Temple of Jerusalem "the House of My Father"; they had the instruction of the Apostle: *If any man defile the Temple of God, him shall God destroy* (I Cor. 3:17), and although here in the Apostle the idea of temple is transferred to the soul of man, this does not destroy the acknowledgment by the Apostle of the sanctity of the material temple.

The Invocation and Glorification of Saints

Speaking of the intercession and glorification of saints in the form in which it was defined in the 4th to 5th centuries, Fr. A. Schmemann underlines [what he refers to as] the excessiveness of this glorification in the present structure of our Divine services, and he sees in this an indication of the "eclipse of catholic ecclesiological consciousness" in the Church (p. 166). Is not one real problem centered in the fact that *he himself* does not enter into the catholic fullness of the Orthodox view of the Church?

What is it in the Divine services, something significant and visible to everyone, that distinguishes the Orthodox Church from all other confessions of the Christian Faith? It is communion with the Heavenly Church. This is our pre-eminence, or primogeniture, our glory. The constant

remembrance of the Heavenly Church is our guiding star in difficult circumstances; we are strengthened by the awareness that we are surrounded by choirs of invisible comforters, co-sufferers, defenders, guides, examples of sanctity, from whose nearness we ourselves may receive a fragrance. How fully and how consistently we are reminded of this communion of the heavenly with the earthly by the content of our whole worship
— precisely that material from which Fr. A. Schmemann intends to build
his system of "liturgical theology"! How fully did Saint John of Kronstadt
live by this sense of the nearness to us of the saints of Heaven!

Is this awareness of the unity of the heavenly and the earthly proven
by the revelation of the New Testament? It is proven totally. Its firm foundation is found in the words of the Saviour: *God is not a God of the dead,
but of the living: for in Him all are living* (Luke 20:38). We are commanded by the Apostles to *remember them which have the rule over you, who
have spoken unto you the word of God: whose faith follow, considering the
end of their lives* (Heb. 13:7). Protestantism is completely without an
answer for the teaching of the Apostle found in Hebrews 12:22–23, where
it is said that Christians have entered into close communion with the Lord
Jesus Christ and with the Heavenly Church of angels and righteous men
who have attained perfection in Christ. What is more necessary and
important for us: to strive for ecumenical communion and union with
those who think differently and yet remain in their different opinion, or to
preserve catholic communion of spirit with those teachers of the Faith,
luminaries of one Faith, who by their life and by their death exhibited
faithfulness to Christ and His Church and entered into yet fuller union
with Her Head?

Let us hear how this side of the Church's life is understood by Fr. A.
Schmemann.

He affirms that there occurred an abrupt change in the Constantinian
era in that there appeared a new stratum in worship in the form of "the
extraordinary and rapid growth of the veneration of saints" (p. 141). As
the final result of this, "the monthly Menaion dominates in worship...
Historians of the Liturgy have for some time directed their attention to
this literal inundation of worship by the monthly calendar of saints' days"
(p. 141).

Concerning this supposed "inundation" of worship we shall note the
following. Serving of daily Vespers and Matins requires no less than three

hours, while a simple service to a saint takes up some four pages in the Menaion, occupying only a small part of the service. In the remaining services of the daily cycle (the Hours, Compline, Midnight Office) the remembrance of the saints is limited to a kontakion, sometimes a troparion also, or does not appear at all; and it occupies only a small place in the services of Great Lent. If the day of worship is lengthened by a polyeleos service to a saint, it is for this reason, it has acquired that "major key," the diminishing of which the author reproaches the contemporary Typicon.

Let us continue the description given in the book of the glorification of saints. The author writes: "In the broadest terms this change may be defined as follows. The 'emphasis' in the cult of saints shifted from the sacramentally eschatological to the sanctifying and intercessory meaning of veneration of the saints. The remains of the saint, and later even articles belonging to him or having once touched his body, came to be regarded as sacred objects having the effect of communicating their power to those who touched them… The early Church treated the relics of the martyrs with great honor — 'But there is no indication,' writes Fr. Delahaye, 'that any special power was ascribed to relics in this era, or that any special, supernatural result was expected by touching them! Toward the end of the fourth century, however, there is ample evidence to show that in the eyes of believers some special power flowed from the relics themselves' (quoted from Fr. Delahaye's book). This new faith helps to explain such facts of the new era as the invention of relics, their division into pieces, and their transfer or translation, as well as the whole development of the veneration of 'secondary holy objects' — objects which have touched relics and become in turn themselves sources of sanctifying power."

Let us note that from the pen of an Orthodox writer the above description exhibits a particular primitiveness and irreverence.

"At the same time," the author continues, "the intercessory character of the cult of saints was also developing. Again, this was rooted in the tradition of the early Church, in which prayers addressed to deceased members of the Church were very widespread, as evidenced by the inscriptions in the catacombs. But between this early practice and that which developed gradually from the 4th century on there is an essential difference. Originally the invocation of the departed was rooted in the faith in the 'communion of saints' — prayers were addressed to any departed person and not especially to martyrs… But a very substantial change took place when this invocation of the departed was narrowed down and began to be addressed only to a particular category of the departed."

Thus we logically conclude, according to the author, that if we appeal with the words 'pray for us' to the departed members of the Church without reference to whether they were devout in their faith or life or were Christians only in name, then this fully corresponds to the spirit of the Church; but if we appeal to those who by their whole ascetic life or martyr's death testified to their faith, then this is already a lowering of the spirit of the Church!

"From the 4th century onward," continues the excerpt from the book, "there appeared in the Church first an everyday and practical, but later a theoretical and theological concept of the saints as special intercessors before God, as intermediaries between men and God."

This is a completely Protestant approach, not to be expected from an Orthodox theologian. It is sufficient to read in the Apostle Paul how he asks those to whom he writes to be intercessors for him and intermediaries before God so that he might be returned to them from imprisonment and might visit them; in the Apostle James (5:16): *The prayer of a righteous man availeth much*; in the book of Job (42:8): *My servant Job shall pray for you; for him will I accept.*

The author continues: "The original Christocentric significance of the veneration of saints was altered in this intercessory concept. In the early tradition the martyr or saint was first and foremost a witness to the new life and therefore an image of Christ." The reading of the Acts of the Martyrs in the early Church had as its purpose "to show the presence and action of Christ in the martyr, i.e., the presence in him of the 'new life.' It was not meant to 'glorify' the saint himself... But in the new intercessory view of the saint the center of gravity shifted. The saint is now an intercessor and a helper... The honoring of saints fell into the category of a Feast Day," with the purpose of "the communication to the faithful of the sacred power of a particular saint, his special grace... The saint is present and as it were manifested in his relics or icon, and the meaning of his holy day lies in acquiring sanctification (?) by means of praising him or coming into contact with him, which is, as we know, the main element in mysteriological piety."

Likewise unfavorable is the literary appraisal by the author of the liturgical material referring to the veneration of saints. We read: "We know also how important in the development of Christian hagiography was the form of the panegyric... It was precisely this conventional, rhetorical form of solemn praise which almost wholly determined the liturgical texts dealing with the veneration of saints. One cannot fail to be struck by the rhetorical elements in our *Menaion*, and especially the 'impersonality' of the countless prayers to and readings about the saints. Indeed this impersonality is retained even when the saint's life is well known and a wealth of material could be offered as an inspired 'instruction.' While the lives of the saints are designed mainly to strike the reader's imagination with miracles, horrors, etc., the liturgical material consists almost exclusively of praises and petitions" (pp. 143–146).

We presume that there is no need to sort out in detail this whole long series of assertions made by the author, who so often exaggerates the forms of our veneration of saints. We are amazed that an Orthodox author takes his stand in the line of un-Orthodox reviewers of Orthodox piety who are incapable of entering into a psychology foreign to them. We shall make only a few short remarks.

The honoring of saints is included in the category of feasts because in them *Christ* is glorified, concerning which it is constantly and clearly stated in the hymns and other appeals to them; for in the saints is fulfilled the Apostle's testament: *That Christ may dwell in you* (Eph. 3:17).

We touch the icon of a saint or his relics guided not by the calculation of receiving a sanctification from them, or some kind of power, a special grace, but by the natural desire of expressing in action our veneration and love for the saint.

Besides, we receive the fragrance of sanctity, of fullness of Grace, in various forms. Everything material that reminds us of the sacred sphere, everything that diverts our consciousness, even if only for a moment, from the vanity of the world and directs it to the thought of the destination of our soul and acts beneficially on it, on our moral state — whether it be an icon, antidoron, sanctified water, a particle of relics, a part of a vestment that belonged to a saint, a blessing with the sign of the Cross — all this is sacred for us because, as we see in practice, it is capable of making one reverent and awakening the soul. For such a relationship to tangible objects we have a direct justification in Holy Scripture: in the accounts of the woman with a flow of blood who touched the garment of the Saviour, of the healing action of pieces of the garment of the Apostle Paul, and even of the shadow of the Apostle Peter.

The reasons for the seemingly stereotyped character of Church hymns, in particular hymns to saints, are to be found not in the intellectual poverty nor in the spiritual primitiveness of the hymnographers. We see that in all spheres of the Church's work there reigns a canon, a model: whether in sacred melodies, in the construction of hymns, or in iconography. Characteristic of hymns is a typification corresponding to the particular rank of saints to which the saint belongs: hierarchs, monk-saints, etc. But at the same time there is always the element of individualization, so that one cannot speak of the impersonality of the images of saints. Evidently the Church has sufficient psychological motives for such a representation.

As for petitions to saints, they have almost exclusively as object their prayers for our salvation. Is this reprehensible? Is there here a lowering of Church spirit? Thus did the Apostle Paul pray for his spiritual children: *I pray to God that ye do no evil; and for this also we pray, even for your perfection* (I Cor. 13:7). If in prayers, especially in molebens, we pray for protection from general disasters and for general needs, this is only natural; but these molebens do not even enter into the framework of the Typicon.

Church Feasts

We shall conclude our review with a question of secondary importance, namely, concerning Church feasts as they are presented in the book. The author agrees with a Western liturgical historian that for ancient Christians there was no distinction between Church feasts and ordinary days, and he says in the words of the historian (J. Danielou, S.J.): "Baptism introduced each person into the only Feast — the eternal Passover, the Eighth Day. There were no holidays — since everything had in fact become a holy day" (p. 133). But with the beginning of the mysteriological era this sense was lost. Feast days were multiplied, and together with them ordinary days were also multiplied. (So asserts the author; but in reality it is precisely according to the Typicon that there are no "ordinary days," since for every day there is prescribed a whole cycle of church services.) According to Fr. A. Schmemann, the bond with the liturgical self-awareness of the early Church was lost, and the element of *chance* was introduced in the uniting of feasts among themselves and to the "Christian year." The author gives examples: "The dating of the Feast of the Transfiguration of the Lord on August 6 has no explanation other than this was the date of consecration of three churches on Mount Tabor" (p. 136), whereas in antiquity, according to the author's assertion, this commemoration was bound up with Pascha, which is indicated also by the words of the kontakion: *that when they should see Thee crucified...* The dates of the feasts of the Mother of God, in the words of the author, are accidental. "The Feast of the Dormition, on August 15, originates in the consecration of a church to the Mother of God located between Bethlehem and Jerusalem, and the dates of September 8 (the Nativity of the Mother of God and November 21, Her Entry into the Temple) have a similar origin. Outside the Mariological cycle there appeared, for similar reasons, the Feast of the Exaltation of the Cross (connected with the consecration of the Holy Sepulcher), and the Feast of the Beheading of John the Baptist on August 29 (the consecration of the Church of Saint John the Baptist in Samaria at Sebaste)" (p. 137).

In these references of the author a characteristic sign is his trust of Western conclusions in contrast to, as we believe, the simple conclusion drawn from the order of the church-worship year. The Byzantine church year begins on September 1. The first feast in the year corresponds to the beginning of New Testament history: the Nativity of the Most-holy Mother of God; the last great feast of the church year is in its last month: the Dormition of the Mother of God. This is sequential and logical. The Feast of the Transfiguration of the Lord occurs at the beginning of August doubtless because the cycle of Gospel reading at about this time approaches the account of the Evangelist Matthew of the Lord's Transfiguration, and the commemoration of this significant Gospel event is apportioned to a special feast. As for the words of the kontakion of the Transfiguration: *that when they should see Thee crucified*, they correspond to the words of the Lord spoken to His disciples six days before His Transfiguration on the Mount and repeated immediately after the Transfiguration: *From that time forth began Jesus to show unto His disciples, how that He must go into Jerusalem, and suffer many things of the elders and chief priests and scribes, and be killed, and be raised again the third day* (Matt. 16:21, 17:9, 22). Therefore the Church, in accordance with the Gospel, six days before the Transfiguration begins the singing of the katavasia "Moses, inscribing the Cross" (it may be that the bringing out of the Cross on August 1 is bound up with this), and just forty days after the Feast of the Transfiguration is celebrated the commemoration of the Lord's sufferings on the Cross and death on the day of the Exaltation of the Precious Cross. And the designation of the time of this feast also is scarcely accidental: this time corresponds, like the time of the Feast of the Transfiguration, to the approach of the Gospel reading at the Liturgy of the Lord's suffering on the Cross and death. Here is one of the examples that indicate that the structure of Divine services in the Typicon is distinguished by proper sequence, harmony, and a sound basis.

If it is suggested that in the church calendar a strict sequentialness of the Gospel events is not observed, this is because the Gospel events take in many years and in the calendar they are arranged as it were in the form of a spiral embracing several years: it contains a series of nine-month periods (from the conception to the nativity of Saint John the Baptist, the Mother of God, the Saviour), two 40-day periods of the Gospel, etc.

In the concluding part of his book the author, not in entire agreement with what he has said up to that point, is ready to come closer, it would seem, to the historical Orthodox point of view; but just here he makes such reservations that they virtually conceal the basic position. He says: "The Byzantine synthesis must be accepted as the elaboration and revelation of the Church's original 'rule of prayer,' no matter how well developed in it are the elements which are alien (?) to this *lex orandi* (rule of prayer) and which have obscured it. Thus in spite of the strong influence of the mysteriological psychology (?) on the one hand and the ascetical-individualistic psychology on the other — an influence that affected above all the regeneration (?) of liturgical piety, the Typicon as such has remained organically connected with the 'worship of time' which, as we have tried to show, contained the original organizing principle. This worship of time, we repeat, was obscured and eclipsed by 'secondary' layers (?) in the Typicon, but it remained always as the foundation of its inner logic and the principle of its inner unity" (p. 162).

Such is the author's resume. It remains for one to be satisfied with little. It was too much to expect that our Typicon has preserved even the very principle of Christian worship!

Conclusion

We have dealt with the book of Father A. Schmemann in full detail because in the future a liturgical dogmatics text may be given to Orthodox readers based on the views presented in this book. If the foundation is so dubious, can we be convinced that the building erected on them will be sound? We do not at all negate the Western historico-liturgical and theo-logical science and its objective value. We cannot manage entirely without it. We acknowledge its merits. But we cannot blindly trust the conclusions of Western historians. If we speak of worship as members of the Orthodox Church, the principle of understanding the history of our worship and its current status by which the Church Herself lives should be present. This principle diverges fundamentally from Western Protestant attitudes. If we have not understood this principle, our efforts should be directed to dis-covering it, understanding it.

The logic of history tells us that in public life departures from a straight path occur as the consequence of changes in principles and ideas. If we maintain the Orthodox Symbol of Faith, if we confess that we stand on the right dogmatic path, we should not doubt that both the direction of Church life and the structure of worship which was erected on the foun-dation of our Orthodox confession of faith, are faultless and true. We can-not acknowledge that our "liturgical piety," after a series of regenerations, has gone far, far away from the spirit of Apostolic times. If we observe a decline in piety, a failure to understand the Divine services, the reason for this lies *outside the Church*: it is in the decline of faith in the masses, in the decline of morality, in the loss of Church consciousness. But where Church consciousness and piety are preserved, there is no rebirth in the understanding of Christianity. We accept the Gospel and Apostolic Scrip-tures not in a refraction through some kind of special prism, but in their immediate, straightforward sense. We are convinced that our public prayer is based on the very same dogmatic and psychological foundations on which it was made in Apostolic and ancient Christian times, notwith-standing the difference in forms of worship.

Is Father Alexander Schmemann prepared to acknowledge that in fact the character of *his* piety is different from the character of the piety of the ancient Church?

Liturgical Books:
From Manuscript to Print

(A page from the *History of Liturgical Texts*)

If at any time one had had occasion to visit an Old Believer church or chapel in old, pre-Revolutionary Russia, and then afterwards chanced to visit a Little Russian church in some remote corner of the Carpathian Mountains, would one not have heard something familiar in the Carpathian church chants? Would they not bring to mind certain peculiar expressions in chants heard some time before in the Old Believers' reading and singing? "Virgin Theotokos, rejoice! *Highly favored* Mary, the Lord is with thee..." Whence comes this similarity? Whence the similarity between the Great Russian Old Believers and the West Russian Uniates? Can one not hear in this Uniate voice the voice of venerable antiquity?

Yes, this is in fact the voice of antiquity, but it does not speak of the Unia, or in favor of the Unia. This preservation of antiquity takes us back to the period before the Unia (the Union of Brest was concluded at the end of the 16th century). This unexpected similarity between the Russian North and South-West, which though far removed from one another are yet one nationally, says only that in the western hinterlands there were reasons for holding firmly to their order of church services, rites and customs. To preserve unharmed their faith which was conveyed in the divine services through the long period of the forcibly imposed Unia, however long it lasted — such was the instinctive aspiration of the oppressed people; it inspired the people to hold fast to the "old rite," come what may. The people, if one may speak of the majority, preserved themselves in the course of the 300-year period of the Unia.

The agreement between the old liturgical forms of South-West Russia and the Russian North take us back to that era long ago, when Rus' presented itself as a single unit in the spiritual sense, although in political relations it was divided by the border which separated the Lithuanian-Polish realm from Muscovite Rus'. A single Russian people lived in different domains. The ancient Kievan metropolitan province was soon divided in two; each of the two parts laid claim to the title "Kievan"; they were not only estranged, but rivaled each other. Nevertheless, the spiritual, ecclesiastical life was held in common, similar, one in essence.

However, the divine services within each of the metropolitan provinces were not entirely uniform. From the beginnings of its Christianity, the Russian Church was under the influence of several neighboring Orthodox Church centers: Constantinople, Palestine, Athos and the Slavic West (Serbia). This disparity of influence was also reflected in the divine services. Pilgrims to Mount Athos and Palestine brought back Greek liturgical books of the Palestinian and Athonite types and their impressions of the services in those places. The hierarchs that arrived from Constantinople and persons sent there for ordination introduced Constantinopolitan usages. From the Slavic West came the already existing service books of the Serbo-Bulgarian edition. One should add that the churches of the Russian North and South-West were entirely similar to one another, not only in terms of a "standard," but also in their internal lack of coordination, i.e., in simultaneous implementation of various liturgical texts. The peculiarities of one part of Russia were characteristic of her other part.

The church books, as is well known, were in manuscript. The copying of books was considered a holy obedience and a labor of prime importance. From the life of St. Theodosius of the Kiev Caves it is known that he spun threads from "wool" to bind books, at the same time and in the same place where Hilarion copied the books and the elder Nikon bound them. The writing of books was conducted with special care and attention. In unrestricted sale, often for one book — a liturgicon, a euchologion — a sum was paid equal in value to an entire estate. One ought not to think that the copying of books led to a larger number of scribal errors and mistakes in the texts. There was always the possibility of checking one manuscript against another. The variant texts were due to the fact that the originals in circulation among the transcribers came from different sources. Variant readings did not give occasion to any sort of confusion. Thus was the case as long as the production of books was carried out manually. But an abrupt turn of events occurred when the goose quill gave way at last to the printing press. This transition, apparently so beneficial, gave rise to a series of questions and created serious complications in ecclesiastical affairs. The result of such complications for the Russian Church was, as is well known, the grievous affliction of the Old Believer Schism.

In the mid-15th century, printing was invented in the West. And in the West we see that the first steps at printing Orthodox ecclesiastical books, one must say, were quite successful. Already by the end of that century, in 1491, the first Orthodox liturgical book in Slavonic — the *Osmoglasnik* or *Octoechos* — appeared, which was very skillfully produced. It was printed in two colors in Cracow at the printing shop of Shvaipolt (Svyatopolk) Feol' (Fiyalka); in its wake followed other liturgical books (the Horologion, Lenten Triodion and Pentecostarion). It is important to note that in the edition of Feol' the peculiarities of the Russian edition of the liturgical books are encountered; in the menologion one finds the names of Russian saints. (Two fragmentary copies of this first Slavonic printing were located in the public libraries of St. Petersburg and Moscow, and a complete copy in a library in Silesia, Germany.) Two years passed, and the church books were produced at two other centers — at a little town in Montenegro and in Venice (the Horologion printed by Andreas Toresani).

The printing business did not reach Russian lands for yet some time. For a long time Venice remained the center where the printing of Orthodox liturgical books was concentrated, principally in Greek, and to a lesser degree, in Slavonic. Why did this honor belong to Venice? Venice was the mistress of the Adriatic Sea after its return to the Byzantine Empire following the Peace of 812. In the course of the entire second millennium of our era, before the French Revolution and Napoleon I, she constituted an independent realm linked only nominally, for the sake of mercantile interests, with Constantinople. She was always successful in warding off the attempts of the popes of Rome to annex her to the papal states; and of course, she became one of the main centers of refuge for the Greek emigration after the fall of Constantinople to the Turks in 1453. Venice was also a powerful center of university education in the Middle Ages, both Latin and Greek. In the 15th century, the century of the beginning of book printing, there were already two hundred and fifty printing presses in Venice. Greek ecclesiastical editions served the Greek East, and there were also Greek monasteries and communities in Italy; the Slavonic editions served the Slavic West. In 1619 and the years following it, the Serbian Voevode Bozhidar Bukovic had his own printing press there.

The work of Slavonic printing shifted nearer to us — to Prague and Vilno (the presses of Skorina). Finally, in the second half of the 16th century, it reached Moscow. In 1553, Tsar Ivan the Terrible issued a decree concerning the construction of a printing house in Moscow. The "first printer" there was the famous Ivan Fedorov. In 1564, the first printed book — the *Apostol* (Book of Epistles)— appeared, with Moscow designated as the place of its publication. In itself, the decade of delay in the appearance of this book gives us occasion to presuppose the arising of misunderstandings during the printing; indeed, for an unexplained reason, Fedorov was forced to flee Moscow for the border. He hid in Lithuania, in Zabludovo near Byelostok, at the home of the "most exalted Hetman" Khodkevich.

The personality of the printer Ivan Fedorov attracts attention because of the significance this fervent and, in all likelihood, self-sacrificing idealist was to have in the history of the Russian book. At that time there already existed in Poland several small Russo-Slavonic printing presses. Fedorov organized his great printing enterprise in Lvov. But he had no means of his own and, the printing press being mortgaged, he found himself at Prince Ostrozhsky's in the city of Ostrog. There, under his supervision, the famous Ostrog Bible saw the light of day in 1530, with a second printing in 1531. Fedorov continued to dream about his own business and returned to Lvov; but he was in no position to deal with promissory notes. He died a pauper, and after his death the community of Lvov tried to save his business and bought his press from his creditors. Thus, the founding of two presses came about, both of which were destined to carry on the work of ecclesiastical enlightenment in the Western borderlands until well into the twentieth century. The offspring of Fedorov's press were: a) the famous press of the Lvov Stavropegia, which was the center of Russian consciousness in Galicia until the late 19th century, and b) the press of the Kiev Caves Lavra, which also served the needs of the Church until the last days of the Russian Empire. Such a distribution of the inheritance of Fedorov occurred because the Lvov Stavropegia constituted only one part of the press; the other had been transferred to Striatin (a locality of Galicia, the estate of the Bishop of Lvov). There it was outfitted anew, and thence, in 1615, was handed over to Elisei Pletenetsky, the archimandrite of the Kiev Caves Lavra, and transferred by him to Kiev.

Another Muscovite printer, a colleague of Ivan Fedorov, Peter Mstislavets, who fled with him to Lithuania, established himself in Vilno and organized the afterwards well known Vilnian press of Mamonich.

The sojourn of the press in Striatin was remarkable, besides other publications, because of the issue of a new type of church book: this was the great *Complete Liturgicon* of 1604, which had been corrected in accordance with the Venetian Greek edition. Hence, with the production of this Liturgicon begins the history of the "correction" of the Russian liturgical books; here action was first taken to correct the books. The publishers explained what difficulty they had in choosing the original for the printed edition. The manuscript books did not agree with one another, and it was difficult to choose from among them that which, by rights, might be called the best. They had to turn to the Greek edition and make a new translation. The correction was done according to the Venetian edition. It is possible that the Venetian text of the Liturgicon preserved that form of the order of the liturgy which the famous liturgist and churchman Philotheos, Patriarch of Constantinople, gave it in the 14th century. The Striatin edition was in fact on the highest level. The explanatory directions first given in it for the actions of the celebrants have remained almost without alteration until the present day.

Thus, a principle was established: instead of local manuscripts that did not agree with one another, the text of the Venetian Greek edition was to be given in the publication of liturgical books.

When the work of publishing liturgical books developed in Kiev under metropolitans Job Boretsky and Peter Moghila in the first half of the 16th century, there were no variations in the choice of text: translating committees were organized, and books — horologia, the Octoechos, the sequential Psalter, the Lenten Triodion and the Pentecostarion, etc. — were reproduced according to the Greek printed edition. In this work much initiative and genius was shown, much labor invested. And one must say that the editions of Kiev, and later of Lvov, were models of scholarship and of external appearance. The ecclesio-historical and political circumstances of Western Russia were such that it was essential for churchmen to show the maximum concentration of effort for the defense of the Church. Only ten years before the Striatin edition was complete, the

Union of Brest was concluded. The Orthodox Church in Poland was then nearly deprived of bishops. The leadership of church life and the defense of Orthodoxy devolved upon the monasteries, who bore this task with honor, and also upon the brotherhoods which were the mainstay of the Church among the laity. In 1620, Patriarch Theophanes of Jerusalem, who was then passing through Kiev, performed a great secret consecration of bishops for the Western Russian Church, at the risk of his own life. The Orthodox hierarchy of that area dates from this journey. After the rights of the Church were restored to a considerable degree through great effort and struggle, a tremendous rise in spirit was experienced. Orthodox Kiev viewed itself as the outstanding center of all the Slavic peoples that shared the same faith. In the introduction to one of the books can be found the statement that it was intended not only for all of Russia, Little and Great, but also for the southern Slavs — the Serbs, Bulgarians, the Adriatic Slavs and, finally, for Moldavia, Wallachia and Semigradia.

However, in this work there appeared also several departures from the norm which were not entirely propitious: the books were supplied with amplified directions, and new synaxaria were composed for the Triodia. All this was good and proper; but in the rubrics, directions for the celebrants were given which already reflected the character of local peculiarities; a new Euchologion was compiled, the so-called Great Euchologion of Peter Moghila, very complete in its content, but departing far from the Orthodox tradition. In it many prayers for various occasions were introduced, composed deliberately for that edition, of which several are very close in content to prayers of the Roman Catholic *rituale*, and, furthermore, explanatory articles were inserted before the texts of the rites, which were entirely in the style of Western scholastic science of that time, in particular, with an indication of "intention, form and matter" of each of the Mysteries. All of this was not essentially an expression of latinization, but might only indicate an attempt to eliminate defects for which their opponents reproached them, and in certain cases to emphasize the difference between Orthodoxy and Roman Catholicism. Nevertheless, these devices set a distinctive seal upon the character of the Kievan editions, which subsequently proved to be a stumbling-block in the matter of the correction of the books in Moscow.

In those years at the outset of the 17th century, when Orthodox western Russia was experiencing a bitter, tumultuous era of suffering and conflict with the ecclesiastical union that had been promulgated, Muscovite Russia was groaning under the blows of the Time of Troubles. No sooner had Moscow recovered from the turmoil, than the question of the correction of the ecclesiastical books was placed before its hierarchy, and with it another question analogous to that experienced by western Russia: according to which books should this "correction" be made? The problem of correcting the books proceeded in a particularly acute and painful manner. Under Patriarchs Philaret, Joasaph and Joseph no solution was reached: corrections were carried out in an unorganized manner, according to the old manuscripts, in the course of half a century; the inadequacy of such an arrangement was clear to many. In Moscow the Kievan books were regarded with suspicion. At one point, books printed in Kiev were solemnly committed to the flames in one of Moscow's squares. The hope of receiving corrected books thus devolved upon the Greek East. For this particular purpose an embassy headed by Arsenius Sukhanov was twice equipped and sent to the Near East. On this second journey, Sukhanov purchased about five hundred manuscript books which are the adornment of the Moscow Synodal (now Patriarchal) Library. However, Sukhanov brought back a negative impression of the East under the Turkish Yoke — the impression that pure Orthodoxy had already been violated there. In particular, Arsenius Sukhanov conveyed the news that, not long before Nikon had ascended the patriarchal throne, the monks of all the Greek monasteries of Mount Athos had assembled in synod and condemned the making of the sign of the Cross with two fingers as heresy; furthermore, they had burned the old style Muscovite liturgical books then located in the Athonite monasteries. Thus, no irreproachable texts for the correction of the liturgical books were found, until Patriarch Nikon made his definitive statement. Under the influence of trustworthy hierarchs of the East, Patriarch Nikon ordered the correction to be made according to the Greek books. These books were all of the Venetian edition. Thus, for example, the Euchologion of Moscow was corrected in accordance with the Venetian Euchologion of 1602. It was found necessary to select Kievans as correctors, for only they had the necessary preparation for the task at hand and, of primary importance, knew Greek well enough. As it turns out, they merely, so to speak, duplicated the work that had already been done in Kiev. Naturally, the work was reduced to repetition, or even to simple transcription of the Kievan translations.

Patriarch Nikon's abrogation of the old hand-written books and old "unwritten" rites, such as the two-fingered sign of the Cross and clockwise procession around the church, provoked a tempest. Its result was a schism within the Russian Church — the schism of the Old Believers (or Old Ritualists). Despite this storm, all the changes and corrections did enter into the life of the Russian Church. We now use books of the edition made by Patriarch Nikon's correctors. The Old Ritualists remain with the old books and the old rites. The schism haunts us even to this very day.

How can one explain why one and the same reform elicited such diverse consequences? It proceeded peacefully in western Russia yet painfully in the North-East. Of course, here one must take into consideration historical circumstances and the psychology of both West and North, both being shaped by history. Western Russia was too absorbed with the fundamental battle for the preservation of the faith, so much so that questions of internal and particular character, in particular the selection of liturgical texts, were relegated to a secondary status. Muscovite Russia looked upon itself as the sole and unshaken depository of ancient piety, bound to remain faithful not only in great, but in little things, not only in primary, but also in *secondary* matters. But aside from this, can one say with certainty that the reform in the western borderlands proceeded without any opposition? The church books printed in the provinces of Lithuania-Poland provide us with a basis for thinking otherwise. There no such protest, revolt and schism took place, but there was, without doubt, a silent rebuff. These are its symptoms. On the western borderlands, besides the great printshops of Kiev, Lvov and Vilno, there was, in the 17th century, a great network of small printshops belonging to the monasteries and brotherhoods, which served local needs. In the 17th century, there were such printing presses in Ostrog, Derman, Ugortsy, Minsk, Chetverten, Striatin, Pochaev, Zabludov, Uniev, Yeviu, Kliros, and Suprasl; some of these became Uniate even in that century.* The expense entailed in obtaining type and a press for a book with octavo-sized pages, printed in one color was probably not considerable. On inspecting such a

---

Note: One of the best presses of this type, which survived until our time, was the ecclesiastical press of the Pochaev Lavra. It was founded by St. Job of Pochaev, Abbot of the Monastery of Pochaev, an ascetic, champion of the faith, participant in the Kievan Council of 1628, and co-worker with Prince Konstantin K. Ostrozhsky, during the period of struggle against the newly-introduced Unia. The book *The Mirror of Theology* by Kiril

book, the eye is struck by the lack of technical means or skill evinced in the production of the individual pages, e.g., the last words of the lower lines of pages are often deformed, and letters are pushed out of alignment. But the content of such editions shows that the printers strove to hold fast to the old forms. Texts of church books had come apart, Kiev and Lvov were distributing their new editions, but the lesser printshops all throughout that century continued to print the old texts, based on the manuscript books. In the euchologia, liturgicans, horologia and triodia of the local editions of the western borderlands, we find all or almost all of the characteristic peculiarities of the Old Believer books. This betokens the fact that the tradition was preserved, that it was cherished, that the new peculiarities in the liturgical books were not so readily accepted. Tradition was the mainstay of Orthodoxy. Later, when, under pressure from the governmental apparatus the Unia began to rule, it officially copied the books of the Moghilian model, only with corresponding alterations and additions peculiarly Uniate. But the parish clergy and the people, having nominally accepted the Union, were all the more strongly drawn to the old forms, and have partially carried these old forms up to our times. This is why not so long ago one could hear, and perhaps still can hear, in Carpathian churches such characteristic expressions as "by death He *tread upon* death" instead of "trampled down" in the paschal troparion, and "highly favored" instead of "full of Grace" in the troparion "Virgin Theotokos, rejoice" — chants which hearken back to the old hook-notation chants, unison recitative, *et al.* This is why, even on returning to Orthodoxy, these

---

Trankvillon remains the monument of the initial period of the work of this press. Later, the Monastery of Pochaev and its printing press were seized by the Uniates and the *typographia* [printshop] was made a supply house of liturgical books for Volhynia and the provinces adjacent to it. Thus it continued until the reunification of Volhynia with Russia at the end of the 18th century and the restoration of Orthodoxy. Then the Monastery of Pochaev and its press were returned to the Orthodox Church, and it was raised to the rank of a Lavra. A new flowering of this *typographia* in Orthodoxy occurred at the outset of the 20th century, thanks to the labors of Archimandrite Vitaly (later Archbishop of Eastern America). After the collapse of the Russian government, when the Lavra of Pochaev found itself within the borders of Poland, the printing brotherhood of Pochaev, headed by Archimandrite Vitaly, moved a portion of the printing stock across the border into Slovakia, to Vladimirova, and there founded the "Typographia of St. Job of Pochaev." After World War II this activity was transferred to Holy Trinity Monastery, Jordanville, NY, in the United States, and to Montreal. After all the buffeting of history these church presses alone have preserved a direct succession with the historical Russian Orthodox printing labor.

people often express the desire to preserve their local ritual and textual peculiarities.

Which side was right in this conflict of two currents within the Orthodox Church — the old or the new? Who is to blame? No one is to blame. The normal process of history is guilty — the process which inexorably accumulated for several centuries a certain sum of differences in comparison to the original form of the divine services. Geographical distance and political borders were guilty, as, of course, was the difference of language, thanks to which the liturgical services in various countries received their own nuances and distinctions. The tempo of alteration was quicker in the Greek East than in the Russo-Slavic North. The study of Greek liturgical manuscripts initiated by Professor A. A. Dimitrievsky has shown that one can find all the peculiarities of the pre-reform Russian services, beginning with the double Alleluia, in Greek manuscript books. But the Greek East managed to take new steps, while Muscovite and Western Russia remained with their own heritage. How should Orthodox Russia have reacted to the fact of the disparity between national antiquity and the Greek norm? To *spare* antiquity meant to discard the idea of the liturgical uniformity of the whole Church. On the other hand, to sacrifice its customs, its antiquity, for the sake of unity with other Churches at that time — did this not seem to be a break in its unity with its own past, a contempt for the holy Church of its homeland, a belittling of the dignity of the saints who had saved themselves within this heritage? But to remain only with its own, however, led to retreating within oneself, alienating oneself from the other Orthodox Churches, eliciting reproach for one's conceit. Which was preferable, what should have been sacrificed? There might be two replies to this dilemma, even in our own times. But there had to be an answer, the printing press urgently had to decide this question in the end. The choice was made in favor of unity with the whole Church in the liturgical system and rites. Thus the question stood in Muscovite Russia. Thus also in Western Europe — the same problem, and the same solution (only several decades earlier); and the same reaction (which one may observe even in our times) in the preservation of the ritual vestiges of a venerable antiquity, side by side with the basic, general liturgical-ritual system. The creation in Russia of churches of the "edinovyertsi" (Old Believers who had rejoined the Russian Orthodox Church), where the divine services were celebrated in accordance with the old ritual, witnessed that the Orthodox

Church made a distinction between the "Old Belief" and the schism; it did not condemn the old rituals, but condemned arbitrariness.

There was one accomplice, albeit unwilling, in the Muscovite schism, and that was Venice. Thus, in conclusion, there remains but to ask: where did Venice find its new edition of the Greek liturgical texts? From the point of view of loyalty to Orthodoxy, these texts were entirely without reproach, pure. But this is the source of the perplexity: insofar as one is able to rely on descriptions of Greek ecclesiastical manuscripts given in Russian liturgical science, there comes to light, even among the Greeks, a similar rift between the manuscript and printed books, such as we observe in Russia. The peculiarities of the Venetian printed text do not find precedent in the manuscripts. What is the reason for this? That there were not enough learned manuscripts? That by chance there appeared in the hands of the researchers books of very ancient origin and old type, and that they did not set their eyes on newer manuscripts? Or, finally, could Venice perhaps have had its own personal source from which it took its texts, apart from the Greek East? The latter is entirely plausible if we take into account that in southern Italy and in Venice itself there were Greek monasteries and an Orthodox population. Be that as it may, this question was not elucidated in Russian historico-liturgical science until the First World War. Another question arises, in and of itself: Was it so completely easy to attain uniformity among the Greeks themselves with the introduction of the printed editions? Were there not open and secret divisions between adherents of the old, manuscript type of church books and proponents of the new, printed books, or perhaps conflicts? Why, for example, do the Jerusalem Liturgicon of the Liturgy of St. John Chrysostom and the Liturgicon of the Venetian printing differ from each other so markedly that in liturgical science it is accepted practice to speak of the "Jerusalem edition" of the Liturgicon and the "Venetian"? These questions remain unanswered. It is possible that liturgists of the next generation shall find an answer.

A Luminary of the Russian Church

His Beatitude Metropolitan Anthony

Metropolitan Anthony, in the world Alexei Khrapovitsky, was born on March 17, 1863, in the village of Vatagino, Novgorod district. His father, belonging to an old aristocratic family, was active in local and governmental institutions. His mother, the daughter of a Kharkov landowner, was distinguished by her profound piety and maintained a religious way of life in the home. At age seven Alexei, the future bishop, moved from the village to Novgorod because of his father's work, and a year later on to St. Petersburg. Here he entered the St. Petersburg gymnasium No. 5, which he completed with honors. Guided by his heart he entered the St. Petersburg Theological Academy. Four days after completing the academy in 1885 he was tonsured a monk. Soon after, as a hieromonk he was appointed a teacher at the Kholm Theological Seminary. A year later he returned as a lecturer to the St. Petersburg Theological Academy where, in 1889, he was appointed, as an archimandrite, to be rector of the St. Petersburg Theological Seminary. Four months later he became rector of the Moscow Theological Academy. The latter appointment came when he was twenty-seven years old. His five-year tenure at this post was the height of his activities as an educator in a higher theological school. He captured the hearts of the students by his love of youth, by a charming character, by the strength of personal conviction, and by direct, open speech. He guided not by authority of the law, but by moral influence.

By this same disposition he distinguished his activities as rector of the Kazan Theological Academy where he was raised to the rank of bishop. Thus ended his fifteen year period as an educator. Bishop Anthony was appointed to the diocese of Ufa and two years later he was transferred to Volhynia. His archepiscopal ministry in the Volhynia diocese, from 1902 to 1914, manifested itself in tireless and diverse activity. In his pastoral letters, in lively interaction with the clergy, and in his personal example Vladyka instilled in the clergy an image of "a good shepherd, father of his people, and a reverent minister of Christ's Mysteries." He inspired a view of the priesthood as the highest calling on earth. He entered into direct contact with the people of Volhynia, especially through the Pochaev Lavra. He brought the intelligentsia into the Church, established charities, built great churches — Holy Trinity Cathedral of Pochaev, the Ovruch Cathedral. He wrote services to saints. Simultaneously he wielded more and more influence on the overall direction of Russian ecclesiastical life, especially after his being raised to the rank of archbishop and becoming a permanent member of the Holy Synod in 1912. In 1913 the Kazan Theological Academy conferred upon him an honorary doctorate of theology. Vladyka Anthony spent the years of the war, 1914–1917, as head of the Kharkov diocese. When, by demand of the revolutionary authorities, he left Kharkov and withdrew to the faraway Valaam Monastery, the Kharkov diocesan council almost unanimously again chose him to lead their diocese and succeeded in arranging his return. In that same year (1917) he attended the Moscow All-Russian Church Sobor and was one of the three candidates for patriarch. He was raised to the rank of metropolitan and appointed to the Kiev diocese which he headed for only six months. The development of revolutionary activities left him without a permanent residence. He was exiled for eight months to a Uniate Basilian monastery in Buchach. Following this came a short return to Kiev, departure to the south of Russia, Taganrog, Rostov-on-Don, Ekaterinograd, Novorossisk, later, Mount Athos, return to the Crimea, evacuation to Constantinople, finally in 1920, Serbia. Metropolitan Anthony spent the last period of his life in Sremsky-Karlovtsy, Yugoslavia, uniting, by virtue of his personality and as President of the Council of Bishops, the Russian Orthodox Church Abroad. From Sremsky-Karlovtsy the Metropolitan travelled to the Holy Land and to different cities and areas in Western Europe.

Metropolitan Anthony died on August 10, 1936 (new style), in the 73rd year of his life. This is a short summary of the biographical facts of this former Hierarch of the Russian Church. It is difficult to describe the spiritual qualities of the reposed archpastor and capture his activity in one article. Love for God, with the strength of feeling of the first Christians, and a living, active love toward people defined his whole life.

The direction of Metropolitan Anthony's deep piety was defined by himself in Dostoyevski's hero, the Elder Zosima, "bright and joyful asceticism." Religious compunction which manifested itself so brightly in his youth unceasingly accompanied him all his life. This compunction was expressed as tears during the Great Vespers on Pentecost when he read the kneeling prayers which were especially dear to him. Compunction is seen in his thoughts and work on "The Dogma of the Holy Trinity," and became his Graceful gift in old age when "tears of compunction flowed from his eyes in torrents."

Our mouth is open unto you, our heart is enlarged; ye are not straitened in us (II Cor.6:11–12) wrote Bishop Anthony to the students of the Kazan Theological Academy, using the words of the Apostle in answer to their farewell address. These words express his attitude not only toward his students, but toward all people. "I cannot but answer when people write me." Everybody wrote to him , people who met him only once, even those to whom he had spoken a few words wrote to him, and he answered in such a way that his words became a guideline for the rest of their lives.

When it came to charity his right hand did not know what his left hand did. Nobody knows how many countless college students, gymnasium students, and youth overall were recipients of his material support in the form of scholarships, tuition, or extraordinary help, not only among Russians, but also Greeks, Bulgarians, Serbs, when he occupied the "wealthy" Volhynia diocese. He did not give up charity even when he found himself in exile and poverty.

Our late Archpastor made an enormous contribution to Orthodox theological thought. His theological works reflect the same aspect of his personality, in which the "feeling of love" has become the "idea of love." The series of his published theological writings begins with his master's degree dissertation, "Psychological Data in Favor of Free Will and Moral Responsibility." After explaining this fundamental problem [free will and responsibility] of human personality, he speaks in his next work, "The Moral Idea of the Dogma of the Holy Trinity," of "love as the essence of Divine Life." In the work, "The Dogma of Redemption," he presents the meaning of redemption as the effect of "the co-suffering love of Christ." The number of Metropolitan Anthony's theological works is great. In his collected works there are twenty-one treatises on various theological subjects and twenty-four articles which make up the section, "Pastoral Theology," — the fruit of his academic lectures. His pastoral epistles, especially to the clergy of Volhynia, are famous.

A large section of his literary works is taken up by ecclesiastical commentary, in particular his criticism of the influential thinkers of pre-revolutionary Russian society — Leo Tolstoy, Renan, and others. On these subjects he wrote speeches and gave lectures; he also touched on them in his lively and energetic sermons.

The late Metropolitan knew the history of his native land and people. He valued Russian classical literature and was up-to-date on current literature. He particularly admired, as is well known, the genius of F. M. Dostoyevski. While yet a youth he listened "with bated breath" to Dostoyevski as he gave lectures at literary gatherings. After reading *The Brothers Karamazov* he "could not sleep for several nights." He maintained this attitude all his life, leaving a text concerning this in, " A Dictionary on the Works of Dostoyevski."

In foreign writings his attention was directed towards French literature. He singled out members of the "new school," such as Paul Burje, in whose writings he saw a turnabout towards the moral foundations of art.

All his life the late Metropolitan lived for the idea of restoring the patriarchate in the Russian Church and consciously worked toward its realization. This idea came to his consciousness when, as a little boy, he asked his father, "Why do we not have our own patriarch?" In connection with this idea he convincingly expressed a new view on the historical personality of Patriarch Nikon, considering him a selfless defender of the great idea of the independence of the Church. The latest objective historical scholarship has justified the correctness of this view.

Metropolitan Anthony took part in many glorifications of saints and was particularly influential in the canonizations of Saint John of Tobolsk, Saint Joasaph of Belgorod, and Saint Anna of Kashin. He wrote many services, among them, to the saints of Volhynia: St. Macarius of Ovruch, the Nun-martyr Anastasia, the service and akathist hymn to St. Job of Pochaev, and St. Theodore of Ostrog. He also wrote the services and akathist hymns to the Pochaev icon of the Mother of God and the Ozeriansk icon of the Mother of God. The services to Sts. Cyril and Methodius, St. Joasaph, and others, also came from his pen.

To understand what guided the late Metropolitan in his political aspi-
rations, one must understand that all his views, both political and nation-
alistic, were determined by his religious world-view.

He looked upon Russia as an undiscovered treasury of the great Christian idea. He loved his native land because in her he saw "the Gospel
embodied in the way of life and character of the people."

In general, he looked upon government from the point of view that it
could create conditions "most favorable for the development of moral
principles." In the people he sought to find the "precious characteristics of
a churchly way of life." Above all, he suffered deeply for his native land.

Being by nature a public person, Metropolitan Anthony established
communications with representatives of the civilized world and religious
life in the West. After the Revolution he appealed to them many times
with a call to defend the persecuted Russian Church, to fight against the
atheists, and with warnings concerning the dangers of militant Commu-
nism — and he received an immediate response. He united around his
personality a galaxy of devotees deeply devoted to the Church, devotees
who, until the end of their days, remained the spiritual leaders of the Russian Church Abroad and an authority for the whole Orthodox Church.
His works constitute a rich legacy, and his personality and life a lofty
example for imitation and edification.

The Old Testament and
Rationalistic Biblical Criticism

I.

THE NATURE OF CONTEMPORARY BIBLICAL CRITICISM

Western rationalistic biblical criticism is a phenomenon of long standing, dating back approximately 200 years. It flourished towards the end of the 19th century, and in our century has become only more widely popularized. It bears the title "scientific," but, we know how often — especially in the field of history — the personal, predetermined conceptions of a world-view are reflected in the conclusions of researchers who arrive at these conclusions ahead of time.

With what points of view do the people of this century approach the Bible, or, in this case, the Old Testament? For the intelligent Jew, it is his natural heritage, a source for the study of the ancient mode of life of his ancestors, his tradition, his history, instinctive thought patterns, his culture. For the non-believer, it is a book which elicits hostility and rejection. He is prepared to study this subject with the special intent of undermining belief in its very authenticity and, in general, in its truthfulness, its ideas, and its values. The inquisitive scholar, whose mind greedily seeks material for his work as the root of a plant seeks out moisture in the earth, approaches the Bible as a collection of literary monuments which is in need of an objective research in accordance with the principles of a scientific positivism which excludes from its field of vision the activity of the Providence of God. A person of faith, for whom the Bible is sacred, takes part in this work of criticism least of all, and if he does approach it, it is, as a matter of principle, with a different orientation which does not fit the methodological tracks of the exact sciences.

It must be admitted that the historical research of the distant past, whose sources are only incidental and incomplete historical and archaeological data, which are often indirect, should generally be approached with caution, no matter how "splendidly served up" this data may be (as the late Prof. A. Kartashev of the Paris Theological Institute, a scholar of biblical criticism, himself stated concerning its findings). Before us lies the rich ground of observations of non-biblical, literary-historical criticism which forces us to be alert to the learned conclusions of criticism. The "Slovo o Polku Igoreve", Lay of the Hosts of Igor was long subject to rejection or to doubts as to its authenticity, and in recent times its authenticity was subjected to criticism by the French scholar, Dr. Mason. Yet Russian archaeologists are even now determining the boundaries of ancient fortifications and other sites for excavation according to the information contained in the "Slovo o Polku Igoreve." We see also how much error is stubbornly held onto in the scholarly works of the West regarding the history of 19th century Russia, not to speak of the great difficulty with which a true portrayal of the causes of the Russian revolution is coming to light.

This so-called "scientific" biblical criticism is a product of the Protestant world. Such is the irony of fate — that the same religious movement in Christianity which rejected the living voice of the Church which is contained in its sacred Tradition, and recognized the Bible as the sole source of the teaching of the Faith, which saw divine inspiration in each letter of the Scriptures, specifically took upon themselves the task of dismantling of their own foundation. Feeling for the sanctity of the Scriptures grew cold among these theologians. It was left for them only to ponder: whence and when came each stone of the foundation, with what is it cemented, what renovations have been carried out on this mass, additions thereto, etc.? Hypothesis followed hypothesis. For the work to be accepted it was necessary to employ "scientific methods of research." But scientific methods are based on the principles of positivism, one of whose principles is the rejection of the supernatural element in the life of the world, and especially in historical events. Willingly or unwillingly, for Protestant theology, which was included as one of the faculties of university sciences, this meant accepting the methodological principles common to all the other sciences. Thus, for example, if in the sacred books one or another prophecy is given, and then the fulfillment of that prophecy is indicated, the researcher of the text feels he has every right to conclude that the prophecy was written after the event it concerns. This is one of a series of factors which have determined the direction of contemporary biblical criticism. Even one such detail in the methods of research should warn us ahead of time against completely trusting the conclusions of this criticism. For belief in the Providence and the foreknowledge of God is inherent in the Christian, and this means faith in the possibility of communications to people accounted worthy (the prophets), or knowledge of coming events, be they in the form of visible images, as clear premonitions, or as direct revelations.

The negative side of contemporary biblical criticism lies in its offhanded dissection of the text of the Bible, and in this way the Bible itself becomes lifeless matter for its critics and those who follow them. A feeling for the sanctity of the Bible has already been killed in them. By destroying the integrity of the text of the sacred books, they deprive the Bible of its soul. Dissecting its physiological side, they are no longer capable of seeing its psychological influence. Will a person studying the physiology of the eye discern during his investigation that the eyes are an expression of the soul? That the eyes of another person can pierce straight through you? That eyes can be kind, evil, soft, sharp, insolent, envious, frightening, mad? That eyes hypnotize? Just as a physiologist cannot discover these characteristics in studying the eyes, so too the positivist critic cannot find in the Bible the confirmation of faith, a consciousness of Divine Providence, moral nourishment for his soul. With what they themselves breathe [i.e., their attitude], people naturally contaminate others, destroying in them the capacity for faith. The scholars themselves feel exalted far above the material, as above the naive primitive. In fact, their own era is negatively reflected in this criticism. Living as they do in an age full of falsehood in the mutual relations between people and between governments, under the cover of cultural conventions, critics are prepared to find the same hidden characteristics in the Bible. In their statements the religious leaders of the people are passing off what is new as ancient, the works of their own hands as the writings of great authorities, that which they themselves have perceived as the foresight of prophets. In the eyes of criticism, all of these tactics of craftiness, forgery, falsification, deception, were supposed to help attain noble religious, moral and political goals; and no matter how surprising, how strange it might seem, they have produced, as admitted by the same scholars, the most futile results!?

The Bible itself does not present its soul and its body to us in this way. It impresses upon us that nothing remains hidden from the eyes of God, nor, sooner or later, from the people: *for there is nothing…hidden, that shall not be known* (Matt. 10:26). The Bible constantly calls us to think and live in truth, righteousness, justice, purity of mind and senses, and in holiness of deed. It brands every lie, deception, wickedness, hypocrisy: *A good tree cannot bring forth bad fruit, neither can a corrupt tree bring forth good fruit* (Matt. 7:18). It teaches that righteousness cannot be attained through falsehood, holiness through hypocrisy; that faith cannot be exalted or strengthened by deception. The sacred writers, in the depth of their own humility, never even thought of expressing their own thoughts or teachings: they transmitted only the will of God, believing that the voice of God spoke through their humility; and the compilers of their writings approached their own task with the consciousness that they were touching holy objects.

The critics' work of dissecting the Bible is very carefully divided. It comprises two levels — first, "lower criticism"; second, "higher criticism." The first concerns itself with philological aspects, the lexicon of the Bible, the material of comparative linguistics. The second concerns itself with researching the literary content of the Bible from the point of view of its sources, with questions as to the authorship of the books, with proposals of literary borrowing, with confirmation from the point of view of historical and archaeological data. Unfortunately, set on a ready-made track which leads in a particular direction, it rolls along without ever looking back.

We should not be troubled that the conclusions of scientific criticism are accepted by today's learned Protestant theologians, and that lately even Roman Catholic theology has bowed down before it, and that they have even been sanctioned by the highest authority of the Roman Catholic Church, with the Nihil Obstat stamp in the recently published *Catholic Encyclopedia of the Twentieth Century*. But we cannot remain silent, for these conclusions are already invading Orthodox theological schools. The Orthodox Theological Institute of Paris has already approved them in the speech which Professor Kartashev delivered at the graduation ceremonies of the Institute "Academy" in the presence of Metropolitan Evlogy and honored guests in 1944, (published in 1947). In Professor Kartashev's speech these conclusions cast a shadow over New Testament Scriptures as well. One cannot but sense in these manifestations the tendency towards general disintegration and mass leveling which is apparent in all of the trends of modern civilization, including decisive steps towards widespread religious equalization and merging in the contemporary world, which can be attained only through the rejection of many values and dogmas that have hitherto been considered inviolable.

The structure of biblical criticism is founded on a series of hypotheses, and up to now has in its details been continually rebuilt, leading ever further away from the truth. We believe that a time will come when one of its principal hypothetical supports will crumble and a long portion of the building will collapse. We do not say the whole building, as we do not deny that through research new historical data are found, to add to and to cast light on views on particular questions, and perhaps in some cases to replace inaccurate views on the period of time or the authorship of one or another of the books of the Old Testament.

New opinions on determining the time of the writing of the various books of the Sacred Scriptures, or even, in some cases, the authorship, do not yet necessarily betoken the undermining of the sacred authority of a book of the Old Testament. The Church accepted the canon of the books of the Old Testament from the Old Testament Church as it was compiled and confirmed around the time of Ezra, without investigating the history of each book. What was important was that each book contained valuable material which teaches doctrine and morality and, most important, each confirmed the chosen people's expectation of the Messiah. As is known, in the greater part of the books of the Old Testament the author is not named in the text itself, and several books are called simply by the names of the individuals with whom they primarily deal. In the books of the holy writers there are chapters written by other people, in which we are told, for example, about the final testament, the death and the burial of the holy writer of the given book. As for what concerns the divine inspiration of the sacred books, their content itself bears witness to it. For us one thing is important: that these books were written by "holy men of God."

In connection with what has been said, we trust it will not be superfluous first to outline briefly the Orthodox Christian attitude towards the Old Testament, then to put forth the content and character of rationalistic criticism, and afterwards to give an answer thereto which is governed by an Orthodox consciousness, derived from logical and psychological considerations and archaeological data.

The Christian's Attitude Toward the Old Testament

The Christian's attitude towards the Old Testament is determined by the teachings of the Saviour. In the Old Testament books, lost, as it were, among the Mosaic books that set forth the Law and determined the standards of everyday life, Christ has shown us a higher, unexcelled, eternal commandment: *Thou shalt love the Lord thy God with all thy heart, and with all thy soul, and with all thy mind*...and the second is like it: *Thou shalt love thy neighbor as thyself* (Matt. 22:37, 39). He also said: *Search the Scriptures; for in them ye think ye have eternal life: and they are they which testify of Me* (John 5:39). The unquestionable value of these Scriptures, for us Christians, even more than for the Jews, is determined by this testimony concerning Christ. As to individual books of the Old Testament, they acquire significance for us depending upon their relative worth as *school masters which bring us unto Christ* (Gal. 3:24), i.e., teachers who lead to Christ the chosen portion of humanity, as the Apostle Paul puts it. Some aspects of the Old Testament remained relevant only until *the time of reformation*, i.e., until the coming of the Saviour (Heb. 9:8–10). The Apostle Paul writes that the establishment of the New Testament *made the first old* (Heb. 8:13). We find the limitations of the Old Testament conception of God especially in those passages in the Old Testament books where, for example, God's allowing the cruel slaughter of foreigners by the people of Israel *is taken* as a command of God, as we read for example, in the book of Joshua. The weakness, the relativity of religious and moral conceptions corresponding to the infantile and youthful state of humanity and ancient Judaism, damaged moreover by sin from time immemorial, are frequently expressed there, even in those cases when they are sanctioned by the name of God.

Nevertheless, even these facts do not mean that the Old Testament loses its value in Christianity. This can be seen by all in the way that the Church treasures the texts of the books of the Old Testament, how it guards their every letter. Two thousand years have passed since the Old Testament period came to an end. Yet still, unchangingly, the Psalter is read at all the divine services in Orthodox churches, and just as unchangingly, it would seem, are preserved words which are foreign to us — Israel, Sion, tribe of Judah, tribe of Ephraim, the names of various ancient peoples: Ammonites, Moabites and others, and also, expressions which one might think of as not being essentially Christian, such as, *In the morning I slew all the sinners of the land* (Ps. 100:8). However, the words and the expressions have remained, but their meaning has changed. Such expressions have acquired a new meaning — the spiritual Israel, the heavenly Sion, the battle against the spiritual foe, spirits of wickedness in high places. It can be said that the Psalter has become the model for Christian prayer, and all of our divine services are saturated with excerpts from it and other books.

The content of the Old Testament Scriptures was Christianized by the Church. Within the Church the Old Testament Scriptures have been filled with the thought of Christ, of the Cross, of the Mother of God. "Having made the sign of the Cross with his staff, Moses straightway divided the Red Sea...," "Horse and rider did Christ cast down in the Red Sea..."; and the three youths of Babylon were saved by Christ from the fire in the furnace: "...Christ spread a spiritual dew upon the children that revered God..." And the Prophet Jonah was saved through the Cross: "In the belly of the beast of the waters Jonah stretched out his hands in the form of a cross..." Only for the childish mind is the Old Testament set forth as "sacred history," as if "history" comprises its essence for a Christian. However, for us adults, especially through the content of the hymnography of the divine services, a more lofty understanding of it is revealed, shadowy and prefigurative. Many of the Fathers of the Church teach us to prefer the spiritual aspect of the Bible to literal interpretation. Saint Maximus the Confessor teaches that: "In Sacred Scripture it is possible to distinguish between flesh and spirit, as if it were a person of sorts. And he that would say that the letter of the Scripture is its flesh, and its meaning its spirit or soul, would not sin against the truth. It is plain, then, that wise is he who, leaving the flesh as something corruptible, cleaveth wholly to the spirit, as something that doth not decay." And Saint Maximus himself, in his interpretations of the Sacred Scriptures, emphasizes its mystical-kerygmatic meaning, leaving aside its narrative aspect as "flesh." And the Canon of Saint Andrew of Crete chanted during the Great Fast provides us with an example of how persons and events of the Old Testament become symbols of the spiritual falls and rebirths of the Christian. However, if one does not know the contents of biblical history, one will not receive the intended edification from the elevated content of the Canon.

Sacred Scripture is divinely inspired. But divine inspiration is not the same as omniscience. The authors of the sacred books were men who were raised above the common religious-moral level, capable of sensing and of absorbing the inspiration of the forces of Grace, and, especially at certain moments, of rising to spiritual heights, of experiencing the illumination of mystical light, and, finally, were capable of reaching moments when they could hear *unspeakable words, which it is not lawful for a man to utter* (II Cor. 12:4), which were transmitted through them, or at other times remained unexpressed and inexpressible by words. But these same Scriptures contain an abundance of ordinary material: sacred and popular traditions, genealogies, religious and civil law, historical events, pictures of everyday life — in a word, that which the authors considered worthy of preservation in the memory of future generations as a support for their faith and spirit. In their entirety, the Sacred Scriptures are sanctified, overshadowed by the Holy Spirit, and each of their component parts corresponds to the sacred contents and holy aim of the whole, as, let us say, a bird's feather to the bodily structure of the whole bird, or as every sacred object accepted for use in a church, for they serve for the greater glory of God.

We are guided by these basic conditions when we approach the theories of so-called "scientific" biblical criticism of modern times.

A Short Outline of the Conclusions of Rationalistic Criticism of the Old Testament

To give a picture of the character of biblical criticism of the Old Testament, we will present a general outline of it, as it is presented in popular Protestant works, and lately in Roman Catholic ones as well; and then we will concentrate our attention on the Pentateuch [Genesis, Exodus, Leviticus. Numbers and Deuteronomy] of Moses, since criticism of the Pentateuch is in essence the foundation of a series of critical theories regarding the Old Testament.

A general outline of criticism which has arisen out of the Protestant-university sphere, is here set forth according to the following basic surveys:

Old Testament History, by Iswar Perits, Ph.D., Harvard. (NY: 1915–16).

The Growth and Contents of the Old Testament, by Charles Foster Kent, Ph.D., Litt.D., Yale University. (NY: 1925).

The beginnings of Hebrew literary works, adapted later in literary monuments, comprise popular vocal musical compositions as, for example, the Song of Deborah, which became part of the fifth chapter of the book of Judges, the Song of Miriam in the fifteenth chapter of Exodus, and the songs mentioned in the twenty-first chapter of the book of Numbers.

1. During the reign of David the first official *historical records* were made, giving an account of events preceding the establishment of the monarchy, forming the basis of the book of Judges and of the second chapter of the first book of Kings.

2. In the ninth century B.C., about the year 850 — nearly six hundred years after the death of Moses — oral prophecies and the rudimentary records of the laws of the Jewish people were compiled by a certain individual, a type of the ancient prophets, which later became material for the first four Mosaic books.

3. About fifty to a hundred years later, in the eighth century B.C., a parallel work on the same sort of material was carried out by another person who belonged to a group of priests. In this manner, two versions of the narrative arose.

The fairly frequent repetitions of what with slight variations was said previously were the initial stimulus for suggesting two versions in the first books of the Bible. The fact that the name of God "Elohim" is used in some parts or chapters of the Hebrew text of the Pentateuch, and Yahweh in others, brought attention to the possibility of two versions. Though both of these names frequently appear together, this did not hinder the conclusion that the text which we have today represents a union of the writing of two persons who lived at different times and different places; and that subsequently these two records, two versions, were combined conscientiously,often by verse, and even by lines, and interwoven with each other into a single text, with, however, new additions from the "editors." In conjunction with the characteristics indicated, one version was branded "Y" (Yahwist), for the compiler of this version, and the other was branded "E" (Elohist), for the compiler of the other version.

However, more detailed study of the text brought critics to the realization that differentiating by the characteristics of the name of God was not exact; it did not always agree with the contents of each version. But then the opportunity arose to ascribe to them a different meaning, without changing the names of "Y" and "E": meaning the representation of two geographical areas, where, as it is proposed, each version was compiled. Now "Y" is usually assumed to be the version of the tribe and kingdom of "Judah" (*Yooda*), and "E" as the version of "Ephraim," in other words, of the Northern or Israelite Kingdom which after the death of Solomon was formed out of the ten tribes of Israel by Jeroboam, who belonged to the tribe of Ephraim.

Critics find two accounts of the creation of the world in the book of Genesis; one is the Yahwist, from 2:4 to 3:24, and the other is Elohist, from 1:1 to 2:4. The story of the Flood is also spread between two versions, on the basis of the repetitions found there, and is divided into twenty-eight parts, fourteen for each version. An even more conscientious separation of verses into parts can be found in one critic's investigation of the fourteenth chapter of Exodus, in the story of the crossing of the Red Sea. This theory is not called the "scissors and paste theory" in vain. The Yahwist version is characterized by a more earthly character, more picturesque, poetic. In it God is presented in human form, with human understanding and actions. The Elohist version is cleverly presented as being more elevated: God is the ruler of the world and creates by the word of His mouth, but it is poorer in images, drier.

4. Next in order, according to the time of the compiling of the Old Testament books, comes the historian "D" — the Deuteronomist, author of Deuteronomy. The first through the eleventh, the twenty-seventh, twenty-ninth, and the successive chapters up to the end of the book are attributed to him. It is thought that he lived in approximately the seventh century; that means almost ten centuries after Moses. He wrote from the point of view of the great prophets, namely that the rise of faith leads to the prosperity of the people, and the decline of faith to tribulation. At about the same time, with the same aim, the history of the conquest of Canaan was written, which later became known as the book of Joshua and the first and second books of Kings.

The compilation of Deuteronomy is ascribed to a time of religious renewal in the Kingdom of Judah, after the death of the Prophet Isaiah, among a prophetical faction, for use in the struggle against idolatry and other apostasies tolerated during the reigns of the Kings Manasseh and Amon (698–643–631 B.C.). The account contained in the book of Kings concerning the finding of a "Book of the Law" (621 B.C.) by the High Priest Hilkiah during the reign of King Josiah, by common assumption, refers to Deuteronomy. Some critics think that it was actually hidden for a time to prevent it being stolen, and was then uncovered, while others presume that it was compiled by Hilkiah and only put forth by him as a Mosaic book (the opinion of Prof. Kartashev). The announcement to the people of the discovery of this book and the reading of it throughout the nation brought about a great religious reformation in the Kingdom of Judah.

5. The historian "P" (for "priest") gave final shape to the entire Pentateuch and also to the book of Joshua. He combined the "Y" and "E" accounts into one narrative, choosing from each version (due to the similarity of the stories) that text which agreed more closely with his own ideas and, yet more often, including both versions, amalgamating them. When necessary for the continuity of thought, he connected texts of different origin with his own words. He wrote from the point of view of the priests of his time, emphasizing the ritualistic element of the laws, which had in fact evolved, as it were, in the course of eight centuries of the national-political life of Israel (during the era of the Judges), but which were attributed to the Prophet Moses.

Complete agreement among the critics as to when the amalgam of the two versions was achieved has not yet been forthcoming. Some presume that it was carried out immediately after the fall of the Kingdom of Israel, when the Israelite priests, escaping thence in 722 B.C., brought with them to Jerusalem the version of the first four books of the Pentateuch that they had, and after the validity of the Ephraimite legends was recognized, the combining of the two versions was carried out in Jerusalem. According to another suggestion, the combining was achieved only after the return of the Jews from the Babylonian captivity during the reign of Cyrus the Persian.

6. The "Ecclesiastical," or church historian, who labored at about 300 B.C., again edited legal and historical books, from Genesis to the book of Kings, and continued history to approximately his own time. Then the Bible included First and Second Chronicles, and also Ezra and Nehemiah.

He used an already established method of historical research, citing a series of sources from which he himself drew information (see II Chronicles). He used the personal journals of Ezra and Nehemiah, and Aramaic documents (without translation). He introduced a new approach to the history of the Old Testament — the approach of a cleric. His own work can be called a "church chronicle of Jerusalem."

Criticism places the origin of the Psalms, with the possible exception of several psalms from the time of David, in the time of Persian rule following the Babylonian captivity; this is the "Book of Psalms of the Second Temple."

A whole series of books is ascribed to this same period: Judith, Esther, Ruth, Tobit, the Story of Susannah, the Story of Bel and the Dragon, and the third and fourth books of the Maccabees. Also included among these is the book of Job.

7. The final period is that of Hellenization. It includes the time of the Maccabees (175–63 B.C.). It is considered to be the time of the final shaping of previous writings of the Prophets, also of the books of Chronicles, Ezra and Nehemiah. The "wisdom literature" appeared. The impetus for it allegedly originated in contact with Greek philosophical thought; however, it is agreed that here Jewish thought followed its own path. The books of Proverbs, Ecclesiastes and the Wisdom of Joshua, Son of Sirach, are attributed to this time. A fragment of the Wisdom of Joshua, Son of Sirach, almost half of the book in the original Hebrew text, was found in Egypt. The first and second books of the Maccabees were compiled at that time. The book of the Prophet Daniel is ascribed to this period, the language of which contains many Persian and Greek words. Consequently, they attribute the prophecy concerning the seventy weeks to the time of Antiochus Epiphanes, seeing in it a "reflection, directed towards an event which had already taken place," in the same manner as criticism reacts towards other prophecies.

Roman Catholic Scholarship on the Derivation of the Canon of the Sacred Books of the Old Testament

It is especially interesting for us to see how Roman Catholic theology approaches the conclusions of the new biblical criticism. Among Christians of other confessions the Roman Church of the second millennium had and has a more complete and, in its own way, a more fully developed theological and church-historical science, in consequence of which its system of corresponding alterations found for themselves a visible reflection in Russian theology of the most recent centuries. But how far has it now departed from its own traditions!

The basic tendency of Roman Catholic ecclesiastical thought has usually been conservative. This can be said of the leadership of the Vatican to an even greater degree. Until the last several decades it has always restrained tendencies towards liberal leanings. During the time of the religious reformation of Luther, the Pope, supported by the Council of Trent, forbade lay people to read the Bible. Now Roman theologians explain that this prohibition referred to "free translations which were not sanctioned by the Church."

How has the See of Rome reacted to the conclusions of biblical criticism?

In the first decades of our century, they were subject to condemnation. Subsequently, however, voices were raised proclaiming the necessity of making a wide opening into the sphere of Catholic thought and worldview for the achievements of the natural sciences in their various forms to enter. Along with this, a reversal took place in theological thought itself with the acceptance of new views on the content of the Bible and the origin of the Scriptures, in the spirit of the new biblical criticism. *The Twentieth Century Encyclopedia of Catholicism,* projected at 150 volumes, with headings in 16 series, first began to see print in 1956, in French, English and other languages. The series "Nature and Man" included such headings as: "The Origin of Man," "Evolution," "What is Man?," "What is Life?," the aim of which was to reconcile the findings of contemporary natural sciences with basic Roman Catholic dogma. The sixth series of volumes deals with the subject of the "Word of God," in other words, the Bible as a whole, its parts and aspects, and it must be said that the conclusions of contemporary biblical criticism have been completely accepted. All of the volumes of the Encyclopedia bear the authorization and approval of the Roman Catholic censorship: the Imprimatur and Nihil Obstat.

Here we see an agreement of views on the Old Testament of leftist-Protestant criticism and Roman Catholic theology on the main points. Are the foundations of these new views solid? Actually, they are completely hypothetical, and are rooted in their own sort of passion for discovery, for innovation and, at the same time, in a suspicious, skeptical attitude towards that which in the past was elevated, pure, and holy. These new views not only lessen the merit of the *schoolmasters that lead men to Christ*, i.e. those of the Old Testament Church, but also cast a shadow over the New Testament, over the writings of the apostles. The content of the Pentateuch is cited in the Psalms, by the prophets, in the preaching of the apostles, in the book of Acts (see the sermon of the Apostle Paul in ch. 13), and by the Saviour Himself, when, while instructing the Jews, He left these words for us as well: *For had ye believed Moses, ye would have believed Me; for he wrote of Me. But if ye believe not his writings, how shall ye believe My words?* (John 5:46–47).

II.
The Sacred Value of the Pentateuch

Among the questions raised by biblical criticism of the Old Testament based on the principles of positivism, the question of the Pentateuch and by whom it was compiled becomes, of course, the basic, or key issue. Of course it would be naive to draw a picture of the labor of the compiler of what is acknowledged as the most ancient of mankind's literary monuments in such a way as to portray it as taking place under the conditions of contemporary literary work, a developed technology of writing, and the other comforts of culture. It is not necessary to insist on ascribing the Pentateuch solely and literally to the hand of the Prophet Moses the God-seer. What is important is the recognition that all of it proceeds from the Prophet himself. For us and, in general, for people who approach reading the Bible without a preconceived suspicion, there can be no doubt as to its Mosaic authorship. Both textual and psychological reasons confirm this beyond a doubt.

We will make use of the voice of learned researchers who have not accepted and do not accept the conclusions of criticism on the given question. Yet, even if one were not to resort to learned authorities, a whole series of simple considerations, which turn us away from the conclusions of this criticism, occurs of its own accord to the ordinary reader of Scripture. The same thing could happen to the critics of the text who are enamored of their own hypothetical concepts, as occurs when one is in the thick of a forest for a long time; one can lose that spontaneous impression of a picture of the forest, which is received when viewed from a particular perspective.

The Names of God: Yahweh and Elohim

It is sufficient to recognize, or at least assume, that both names, Yahweh and Elohim, were current in the time of Moses, to understand the impossibility for a writer completely to ignore one name of God, as if it were unworthy of being included in the book, and use the other exclusively. Thus, in their epistles the apostles call our Saviour either Lord, or Christ, or just Jesus, or they use all three names together. We see the same thing in our prayerful appeals to God: the appellations "God" and "Lord" are constantly interchanged.

Criticism does not seem to make any effort to pause and consider what it was that must have motivated the Prophet Moses to use two names of God in turn. The name of God "Elohim" is exalted, primordial, ancestral, and at the same time deeply mystical. Its grammatical form in the plural (the singular form is Eloah), was obviously an expression of reverence with the Hebrews, as in Russian "вы" (you — polite form) shows respect for a person. However, on becoming part of the common speech of the people, this mystical plural form, which for Christians is a sign of the dogma of the All-holy Trinity, could then turn the thought of the Hebrew people in the direction of polytheism. It was important to make room for another name of God which would not even have a grammatical plural form. Evidently, it was not then foreign to Hebrew speech. In the revelation to Moses in the burning bush, God revealed Himself under the name of Yahweh — "I am He Who is." And Moses records the exalted meaning of the name in his book.

Is Yahweh presented in the Pentateuch as the national God of the Hebrews? No; for in the book of Genesis Yahweh creates man not as the ancestor of the Hebrew nation alone, but as the ancestor of *all* mankind. Gradually Moses introduced this name into the narrative of the book of Genesis, and from the book of Exodus on it is used predominantly; undoubtedly it was introduced into the oral speech of the people to the same extent.

Is There a Difference in Style?

The critics see a radical difference between the first and second chapters of the book of Genesis. However, in over two hundred years criticism has not reached any agreement as to when the first chapter was written: at the beginning of the era of the kings, or after the Babylonian captivity?

Nevertheless, it is possible to indicate a convenient clue in the text which points to the antiquity and unity of origin of both chapters. This clue is the "giving of names." In the first chapter: "And God called the light day, and the darkness He called night," "And God called the firmament Heaven," "And God called the dry land earth, and the gatherings of the waters He called seas..." In the second chapter: "And God formed...all the wild beasts of the field, and all the birds of the sky, and He brought them to Adam, to see what he would call them, and whatever Adam called any living creature, that was the name of it. And Adam gave names to all the cattle and to all the birds of the sky, and to all the wild beasts of the field..." After woman was created for him, Adam said: "She shall be called woman, because she was taken out of her husband." It would seem that such details, e.g., the giving of names, indicated in the history of the creation of the world, are unessential. But we encounter them in both chapters, and this indicates a unity of thought, a tendency. What language for this name-giving did the author of Genesis have in mind? If we attribute the writing of these chapters to the most ancient times, to the age of Moses, then the author of Genesis obviously had in mind a time when the *original unity of language was still sensed*, when the traditions of the time before the construction of the Tower of Babel and the confusion of tongues, were kept — traditions which were brought from Mesopotamia by the Patriarch Abraham.

How exactly is the unity of thought in both chapters demonstrated here, where in the first God gives the names; in the second, Adam? We answer: the unity is evident in the concept of the value of the word, the value of human speech, as a gift of God. Originally, in the first chapter, the naming of God's creations proceeded from the mouth of God Himself; and later, in the second chapter, the gift of speech is communicated by God to man. He is left to create names for the creations of God, but under the direction of God Himself. The form of the providential actions of God changes, but the thought of the author of Genesis concerning them continues according to a *single, harmonious plan*. This is no mechanical amalgam of two texts.

We see the same close bond of concepts, not accidental but organic, between the first and third chapters of the book of Genesis. The problem of evil already arises in the first chapter. If, as we read there, everything left the hands of the Creator perfect; if "God saw that...they were very good," then from whence do evil, illness, suffering, death, arise? The answer is given immediately: the account of the fall into sin at the end of the second and in all of the third chapter.

The difference of styles between the "two versions" is determined by the critics in the following manner: the "E" version is dry, but more elevated and intellectual; the "Y" version, while livelier and more concrete, is naive and worldly in spirit. But this absence of uniformity can be explained naturally. It is sufficient to assume that Moses had two sources for his narratives. One was oral traditions, more picturesque, the material for "Y"; the other sources were genealogical, ancient cuneiform inscriptions on tablets, legends about events of the past that might have been preserved in the family of Abraham and brought with them out of Mesopotamia, comprising the material designated by critics as "E." Besides which, is it at all possible to call simplistic or primitive the profound content that is hidden, for example, in the expression "the tree of knowledge of good and evil," considered to be part of the "Y" version? This expression has retained its vividness for ages and millennia. All of mankind's culture which always carries within itself two opposing elements — good and evil — can be defined by it, when access to the Tree of Life is so difficult and when the fruits of culture are so readily capable of leading to death, both spiritual and physical.

On the Repetitions in the Pentateuch

People repeat themselves for various reasons. The compiler of the Pentateuch need not have had only a single reason for his repetitions. If, because of the presence of repetition, the conclusion is drawn that later compilers of the present text had before them two sources, two versions, then why not assume that at times Moses had before his eyes parallel, fragmentary one, two or even three sources of Canaanite or Chaldean origin, since at that time ancient Chaldea, like Egypt, had its own writing? This is one possible reason for the repetitions indicated. Another reason could be the difficult technique of ancient writing: inscriptions on individual clay or wood tablets, on sheets of papyrus, which could later be transferred twice to parchment scrolls; then also the slowness of writing, during which the continuity of the narrative was broken, necessitating the return to details of an event already recorded.

It is essential also to consider the psychological bases for repetition. The ancient writer, not having at his disposal either a sufficient variety of terms or force of expression due to the meager content of the vocabulary of an ancient language, resorted to the device of repetition to concentrate attention on his thought or on the importance of an event, emphasizing thereby the importance of the given statement. But the scrupulous critic, failing to take this into account, could possibly infer, for instance, while reading the title of the Russian *Primary Chronicle*, "This is the chronicle of past years, from whence came the Russian land, who first began to rule in Kiev, and from whence the Russian land came to be," that two versions are hidden in this heading, since it contains two subordinate clauses, of one and the same content. Repetitions for expressing the importance of an action are frequent in the Bible. Such are "And God said" in the description of the creation of the world; in the Psalms, *With patience I waited patiently for the Lord* (Ps. 39:2), and others.

Let us here benefit from the thoughts of Metropolitan Macarius of Moscow, written more than one hundred years ago concerning the very same arguments which criticism uses today. He writes: "In it [the Pentateuch] repetitions of the same thought and sometimes seeming contradictions are encountered...; very frequently narratives are interrupted by long speeches and other digressions; laws are laid down in the context of events, and not at all with the order and strictness that is found in exact codices. In general, no purposeful attention to the skillful arrangement and exposition of subjects is in evidence. And all of this should be in the Pentateuch if its author is Moses. He has described events as the events occurred. Therefore, it is natural, that when narrating something, he suddenly breaks off the story and inserts his speech to the people, as it was in reality; in the book he makes the same repetitions which really took place and, speaking about some event, then and there sets forth the law to which that event gave rise. Moses had no need to set down skillful transitions in his book... Frequent repetitions of the same statements, forceful discourses with the people, fatherly admonitions, reproaches and threats — all of this was in actuality quite characteristic of Moses in his relations with the Hebrews and, naturally, in his books as well." (*Introduction to Orthodoxy Theology*, Macarius, Archbishop of Lithuania and Vilno, DD, 4th ed. [St. Petersburg, 1871], p. 365)

What Does the Terseness of the pre-Abrahamic Narratives in the Book of Genesis Signify?

If the story of the fall of Adam and Eve and the history of Noah and the flood are set aside, the brevity of the narratives of the first chapters of the book of Genesis attracts our attention. Subtracting the period of 2000 years from Abraham to the New Testament from the conventional Old Testament chronology which determines the period from the creation of the first man to the birth of Christ to be 5508 years, we are left with a period of 3500 years, which is dealt with in eleven chapters of the Bible; and if we bypass the chapters which contain the accounts of the fall and Noah and the flood, we have only seven chapters. Three and a half thousand years in seven chapters which contain little more than genealogical tables and the story of the construction of the Tower of Babel and the dispersion of the nations. This is the sort of caution, the sort of strictness in selecting sources for the narrative that we observe in the compiler. Would it be the same if he had taken to including current popular legends, heroic epic and popular, oral or recorded religious myths? We do not have the facts to judge how the names of the ancient patriarchs could have been preserved in Mesopotamia, escaping oblivion in the days of the flood, and how far we can today construct a chronology of the antediluvian era according to them; but undoubtedly these names acquired a fixed form somewhere in one way or another (perhaps they were not as difficult to assimilate orally as they are for us; perhaps they were recorded at burial sites; perhaps their preservation was, as it were, a religious responsibility of the heads of families — the patriarchs themselves; these are complex and independent questions which belong to the domain of archaeology). But these Chaldean genealogical records were available for the early inclusion in the first pages of Hebrew literature. The other accounts of the first chapters of Genesis are of similar origin, of course, but through the illumination of the Holy Spirit in the consciousness of the sacred writer they were cleansed of the dross of polytheism which constitutes the essence of myths. And we have no right to speak of myths in the Bible; we have full license to speak only of demythologization, of a return of the myth's content to the original, monotheistic, holy traditions. The divine inspiration of the sacred author, the God-seer Moses, worthy of a series of direct revelations from God, lies in this very selection, purification, examination of oral material and material written in cuneiform; in this labor carried out in the fear of

God, with the constant elevation of thought to God, with the immediate awareness of the Providence of God which is unceasingly active in the world. Could the compilers of the legends, songs and laws of the people in the period around 800 or 1000 years after Moses have carried out such a task and, moreover, nearly simultaneously in two kingdoms? Why would the compilers who, as the critics insist, belonged to the class of priests and prophets, even begin to include in the book of Genesis elements of Jewish traditions which in their time would already appear to be temptations, if the reason for this work was for them the moral elevation of the people?

Concerning the understanding of "myth," let us make use of the words of the outstanding French Roman Catholic exegete, F. Vigourue. He writes: "The meaning of myth has been contrived by rationalists to deny miracles and to deface the true character of revelation. The word "myth," contrary to actual history, is a type of fictional and imaginary history, a sort of fable that is used as a cloak to cover the expression of religious and metaphysical ideas and theories, or even physical phenomena. Nothing is as contrary to myth as Holy Scripture. One of the immediate goals of the Old Testament was the establishment of a barrier against a mythical trend which drew all of the peoples of antiquity to polytheism and its fables. As for the New Testament, the tendency towards mythicism, after the age of Augustus, when these books were written, came to an end among all pagan peoples of the civilized world, not to mention the Jews." (*Instructions for Reading the Bible, vol. I*, F. Vigourue, [Trans. from the 9th French ed., Moscow, 1897], pp. 176–177) Unfortunately, those French exegetes who collaborated in the *Catholic Encyclopedia of the Twentieth Century* have departed far from the position of their authoritative compatriot, F. Vigourue, one of the oldest laborers in the scientific study of Holy Scripture.

"De-mythologization" means that the revelation of God, drawn from mankind's common tradition but already dimmed by political additions, was re-established in its original purity of monotheistic truth; however, in verbal expression the truth continues to remain represented figuratively, the actions of God being depicted as human actions. All of this is because of the paucity of words in primitive language, which correspond to elevated and abstract concepts. Even in contemporary, highly developed languages we observe a similar insufficiency of words.

Could the Hebrews have been Acquainted with a Culture
as Technical and Intellectual as is Presented in the Book of Genesis
and the Rest of the Books of the Pentateuch?

Even if animal husbandry was the ancient basis of the way of life of the forefathers of the Jews, this does not provide sufficient grounds for calling the Jews a herding, wandering tribe, or nomads who were unacquainted with the interests of a more settled people. The emigration of Jacob and his sons to Egypt in and of itself already acquainted them and their descendants with Egyptian culture, especially while they enjoyed freedom and even concessions. The elevation of Joseph to his influential position in Egypt put him personally, and perhaps the Jewish people closest to him, on the same level as educated Egyptians. The interest of the Egyptians in their past, which we know of, even then served as an example to the emigrants to Egypt, and provided them with the possibility of returning to memories of both their near and distant past, of life in Palestine, and of trying to preserve those memories for their descendants. Such memories could have been put into writing in part even before Moses' time.

One cannot presume that Moses, the leader of Israel, limited himself to leading his people out of Egypt, and then left them to the mercy of fate thereafter. Can one permit the presupposition that he did not elaborate some sort of political plan for his people; that he did not give any thought to what might await them in the future; that he did not outline those means that would be necessary to unify his people, nationally and religiously? This would not have been difficult for him to accomplish, because a) he had a complete understanding of Egyptian culture; otherwise he would not have won the trust of the people; b) in compiling special laws for Israel, he had before him a parallel in the laws, customs, and methods of influence of the Egyptian state upon his people which he discarded in some instances, and in others used as ready examples. He could not have done otherwise. Living in the desert with his father-in-law Jethro, Moses was wholly immersed, mind and heart, in the plan with which God inspired him, and which, according to human reasoning, was extremely uncertain. When it was necessary to overcome by the strength of his spirit and the strength of his faith both the stubbornness of Pharaoh and of his own people, he had to consider everything which would be necessary in the future for his people's homeless wandering, and then for the Hebrew nation, the territory of which would have to be paid for with their own blood. Yet, it was difficult for him to foresee how the life of the nation would be established on that territory. The Hebrew people, while despising the Egyptians as their oppressors, nevertheless observed and assimilated their customs; they saw the Egyptian religious cult, the multiplicity of their priests, temples, and sacrifices, and because of this, in their exodus from Egypt, they zealously applied themselves to the formation of their own national-religious cult.

"Criticism" considers the Pentateuch a late work, and thus, Moses, "magnified" and "glorified" with the passage of time; i.e., invested it with an exaggerated greatness and glory. But the writings of Moses do not present such an image; they do not hide his failings, his moments of near despair, the fact that he did not expect the wandering to be so very long; neither do they hide his physical defects, his being a man "slow of speech and a stammerer," as the church hymn puts it.

Was it necessary to wait 800 or 1000 years after Moses to compile all the particulars of the precepts and directions and the minutest details of the journey, going so far as not to forget the decree that each participant in the exodus was to take his own little shovel along for his personal hygienic needs?

Arising out of the customs of antiquity, when education and, specifically, the keeping of chronicles were to be found in the hands of those serving religion, it is natural to think that it was established as the duty of Aaron, the brother of Moses, as the high priest, and his sons as the first priests, both to keep the chronicles of events, and also to make a record of laws and orders promulgated by Moses during the forty years of wandering. One need not understand the authorship of the Mosaic books as a record from his own hand. Side by side with his personal manuscript his dictation to scribes had its place. As for current events, they were more likely to have been recorded in response to directions or assignments given to trusted persons to carry out. The birth of Moses and his upbringing at Pharaoh's court were most likely to have been described to his brother. The record of Moses' deathbed instructions and the description of his repose must have become the moral obligation of Joshua, whom Moses had chosen as the leader of the people after him. Thus do the exegetes also depict this labor. For a leader of the people, such as Moses remained to the last days of his life, the most difficult task was that of compiling the first book, Genesis, and it could have been carried out only sporadically, just as a feast day falls among regular days. Thereafter, repetition could have appeared, and at times, certain discrepancies could have begun to creep into the records.

Moses, a Historical Novel by Sholom Ashe

Among recent creative literature there has been a successful attempt at retelling the story of Moses, the exodus and the wandering in the desert of the Jewish people, by Sholom Ashe, a twentieth century Jewish writer. The name of this writer is well known because of the part he took in several Russian periodicals of the pre-revolutionary period, and now, from a whole series of novels dealing with American life, written in English. The long work *Moses* (comprising some 500 pages) merits our attention because it shows the naturalness and the quite viable possibility of the entire course of events which are set forth in the books of Moses. The value of this work lies in that the author does not depart from the text of the Bible but fully preserves the idea of God leading the people of Israel in those days, concerning himself only with enlivening the narrative with a picturesque rendering of events which are given in compressed form in the sacred account in the Bible. In particular the author sets before the reader a method for the technical organization of notes for the future Pentateuch which was feasible at that time: the preparation of solid material for writing, the obtaining of inks from seaweed or shells; further — the collection of sacred traditions from the lips of the elders of Israel, the selection of scribes. In like manner, described on a large scale, is the possible picture of the preparations for equipping the tabernacle during the people's annual sojourn at the foot of Sinai, and the works of the equipping itself: how Moses, ascending Sinai, amid the outcroppings of copper ore, discovers an area covered by thick vegetation which has a wonderful aroma and a thicket of huge acacias; how later this costly wooden material is fashioned into parts of the tabernacle, and the aromatic plants into fragrant incense for the services; how the collection of gold and silver objects is conducted so that they may be worked into utensils for the services of the tabernacle; the temple — a free labor, not carried out under the whips of overseers, a labor for their own people, not for their oppressors; with what diligence master craftsmen took to their specialities which they had acquired in Egypt — some men took to the dry reworking of metal, beating gold into sheets with stone hammers, others to smelting sil-

ver, having obtained it locally on Sinai, and to smelting copper; others
were masters of woodworking and of the tooling and cleaning of leather;
women, according to their skill, labored in preparing and dying wool, in
spinning thread, and those skilled in fine work were found as well, for
embroidering designs after the spinning, for preparing vestments and
objects for the services. Everything took place under the observation of
directors of labor who were chosen by Moses and the council of elders.
Later comes the description of the sanctification of the tabernacle and the
organization and consecration of the Aaronic priesthood, etc. In a word,
all that which has been considered unfeasible in those far-away times and
under those conditions by some critics of the Bible is not disregarded. The
testament and vows of Moses, and his death, as they are set forth in the
book of Deuteronomy, end the account.

About Works of Science and Scientific Data Which Confirm the Authenticity of the Pentateuch of Moses

The defense of the sacred value of biblical criticism was worked out at
the same time as the destructive, and in general, criticial theory reached its
full development at the end of the 19th century. It is not possible for us at
the present time to delve deeply into the vast scientific fields of philological and other research. We will point out only the previously mentioned
work by the French biblical exegete F. Vigourue, which belongs to the
same final years of the last century: *A Guide to Reading and Studying the
Bible*, which went through a long series of printings in France and was
translated into Russian. In it is given a bibliography of Western negative
criticism and positive anti-criticism of the Old Testament before the twentieth century. The author sorts out all of the arguments advanced in his
time by rationalistic criticism. He proves the authenticity of the Mosaic
books by evidence contained in the Bible itself, by the parallel "Samaritan"
Pentateuch discovered in modern times, by the evidence of Egyptian
monuments, from which it is clear that the author of the Pentateuch was
well acquainted with Egypt, even down to various trivial details, namely
Egypt as it was under Ramses and even earlier, and finally, it is confirmed
by an analysis of the language of the books themselves. In particular, F.
Vigourue points out that there are no grounds for separating the Pentateuch into two versions corresponding to the names of Yahweh and Elohim, citing all of the passages where they are used apart and together, and

he investigates the question of "discrepancies" in the Pentateuch, and of the possibility of later individual additions to the text to explain certain historical, geographical, and other names and indications.

Since critical reviewers of the text of the Bible see great exaggeration in its description of the tabernacle (A. Kartashev speaks of its "fairy-tale splendor"), and also point out the exaggeration of numbers (in the census of the people, the number of sacrificial animals, the amount of gold and silver collected for decorating the tabernacle), and see in this proof of the later origin of biblical stories, we here provide some scientific information.

From the article "Gold" by A. Miklashevsky (in the *Brokhaus and Efron Encyclopedic Dictionary*): "Judging from the results of excavations and archaeological research, gold was one of the first metals which mankind turned to its own use. Easily found and processed, it was from ancient times used in fashioning all sorts of objects. Excavations of extremely ancient burial mounds in Denmark have shown that arms and objects for domestic use were made principally of gold; only certain parts were of iron" (in one museum, for example, one can see the entire shaft of a spear made of gold, and only the spearhead of iron). Under "Mining" in Vol. XVII of the same work we read: "Mining had developed up to the year 3000 B.C. in Upper Egypt; it reached its height under the Ptolemies. According to the testimony of Strabo and Pliny, the Phoenicians (Phoenicia was a neighbor of Palestine) were able to smelt ores and organized the mining of gold and copper in Thrace (an area in what is now Greece), and around 1100 B.C., in southern Spain as well." — Gold is always found in its natural state: in powdered form in sand or in the veins of quartz. For this reason it is comparatively easy to obtain. Let us add a note from the contemporary press: In Erevan (in Georgia), on the mound of Mestsamor, a very large metal-working center dating to 3000 years before our era was disclosed. Excavations on this mound began some years ago. Archaeologists, astrophysicists and art historians worked together there. Besides smelting furnaces, foundry areas were found, approximately fourteen types of bronze workshops, and innumerable foundries carved in the basalt.

Concerning the numbers and calculations in the Bible, in some cases it is very natural to consider the possibility of an incorrect reading by the copiers of the original text, and mistakes in copying, especially when the text was transferred from one type of writing to another. The cuneiform of Mesopotamia, the hieroglyphics of Egypt, the circular writing of the Phoenicians, and the square Aramaic script all had their peculiarities in rendering numbers, and this could have paved the way for unintentional mistakes. By way of comparison, for example, let us recall that in our written Church Slavonic, it is sufficient to add the symbol "҂" to the sign for one, "а", and thus one becomes one thousand.* The Babylonian cuneiform system of symbols is curious. "One wedge meant one, two wedges two, etc., up to ten, which was expressed by joining two wedges in an angle, "<"; twenty — two such angles, thirty — three, etc. One hundred was expressed by means of two wedges — a vertical and next to it a horizontal, "I —"; one thousand by the symbol of ten before the symbol of one hundred, "< I —". An example of abbreviation: instead of writing the numeral 90 by means of nine signs (10 by 9), it was possible to write one special symbol in large calculations meaning 60, and with it three symbols for ten ("Babylonia," an article by A. Lopukhin. *Encyclopedic Dictionary of Brokhaus and Efron*). This system was convenient; however, it was quite easy for a person not familiar with it to become lost in it!

F. Vigourue cites several examples which support the possibility of the presence of mistakes in the contemporary text of the Bible, no matter how carefully throughout the history of the Bible the text was guarded after copies had been made from the only copy left after the Babylonian captivity. Thus, according to the Hebrew text of II Chronicles, Solomon had *4000* pairs of horses (in the Slavonic version: mares; in the Russian: stallions); but according to III Kings, he had 40,000. According to I Kings, David demanded 700 Syrian horsemen, but according to II Chronicles, 7,000. II Chronicles says that Jehoiachim was eight years old when he ascended the throne, but IV Kings says eighteen (Vigourue, *A Guide to Reading and Studying the Bible*, Vol. I, p. 109). It is clear that these disparate calculations are a result of scribal errors of translation.

The critics point out that the Hebrews wandering in the desert could not have had with them certain materials necessary for equipping themselves. But there are grounds for suggesting that they could have obtained these materials by means of trade or purchase from passing caravans trav-

---

*Compare the Greek numerical system and Church Slavonic system which was borrowed from it in total: they are identical, but the numbers from 11 to 19, the tens, and the units are in reverse order; for example, the number fifteen is "ιε" in Greek, but in Church Slavonic is "ѣ"

elling from the East to Egypt. In such a way Joseph became a slave in Egypt, when he was sold by his brothers to the merchants of a caravan, as we read in Genesis: *And they* [the brethren] *sat down to eat bread; and having lifted up their eyes they beheld, and lo, Ishmaelitish travellers came from Galaad, and their camels were heavily loaded with spices, and resin, and stacte; and they went to bring them to Egypt* (Gen. 37:25).

New Horizons in Biblical Research

A book by this title was published W. F. Albright, one of the foremost biblical archaeologists, and contains a series of popular accounts related to new findings in the realm of biblical archaeology.*

The information presented by this author is valuable for us in that in its principal tenets it runs in opposition to the theory of rationalistic criticism. Also important is the fact that the author writes as a representative of "free science," and in keeping with this does not overstep the boundaries of the method of scientific realism, i.e., of the method that perhaps does not deny the divine inspiration of Scripture, but leaves it aside, so as not to violate methodological principle.

In the above-mentioned book, in the account "Archaeology and the Tradition of Israel," the author firmly states his view of the book of Genesis on the basis of written materials of antiquity, newly discovered at excavations at four sites outside of Palestine: namely, two in Mesopotamia and two in Syria.

"Mari" (today Tell-El-Harim), situated half-way up the Euphrates, was excavated in 1933 by M. Andre Parrot. There the remains of a palace were found, dating from the period between 1730 and 1695 B.C., i.e., the period of the post-deluvian Patriarchs of the Bible. Many thousands of cuneiform tablets were found there, written by the king and those close to

---

*In the introduction by the English publishers of the book we read: "William Albright is one of the most outstanding biblical archaeologists, a world-renowned scholar, whose works are read and studied wherever the history of the Holy Land is studied. He is the author of more than 800 articles and books and has received more than 20 scholarly awards. His knowledge of languages, both modern and ancient, the solidity and variety of his scholarly credential, make him an important participant in the study of the Bible and all its aspects. He was the first among scholars with a theoretical knowledge of the Aramaic language to recognize the value of the Dead Sea scrolls, and pointed out their importance in resolving a number of disputed Biblical questions.

him, and also by the rulers of neighboring provinces, most of which were settled by north-western Semites who spoke a language almost identical to the biblical language of the time of the Patriarchs — in terms of vocabulary, expressions, syntax and personal names. Thus, a great amount of material is available which casts light on the life of the ancestors of Israel in the first half of the second millennium B.C. Biblical archaeology, as our author stresses, is not limited to excavations in Palestine, but is broadened by archaeological discoveries in lands far removed from Palestine.

Another site, even farther to the East, is Nuzi, where those who carry on the search, mostly Americans, have found the remains of estates and the citadel of an ancient city. There in the ruins many thousands of tablets with cuneiform writing were preserved, illustrating customs so similar to those found in Genesis that one can speak of them as being identical. All of the obscure passages in Genesis which have not yet been explained in the Hebrew text as it has come down to us, began to disclose their meaning from 1925 on, with the help of the studies of the tablets from Nuzi.

The location Alalakh in northern Syria was excavated by the late Leonard Woolley in the course of scientific expeditions. Now the name of this site is not Semitic and it belongs, apparently, to one of the ancient languages which was neither Semitic nor Indo-European, whose type has yet to be determined. However, cuneiform tablets of great value were found there which describe the theory and practice of laws among the Canaanites and their neighbors in the seventeenth, sixteenth and fifteenth centuries B.C.

More important than these sites in northern Syria, however, is Port Ugarit, now Ras Shamra. There, from 1929 to the present day, work is being carried out by Claude Schaeffer, and it has yielded rich material of various sorts: art objects, architectural works, and special inscriptions in a half-dozen languages, as well as much writing, predominantly in Babylonian cuneiform script and in the local Canaanite alphabet. Things were found here that were not dreamed of before 1931: more than a thousand whole and fragmented tablets inscribed in the ancient cuneiform alphabet of twenty-seven letters (plus three others not comparable to any of the ancient linear alphabets), representing the ancient northwestern Semitic dialect, i.e., essentially the pre-Phoenician Canaanite language which was very close to the most ancient poetic forms of the Bible, not to mention grammar and vocabulary.

Of course, all of this material is fully accessible only to a few persons who are quite knowledgeable in the field of history, archaeology, philology and linguistics, in their historical perspective.

The comparative study of ancient languages according to ancient sources provides us with an opportunity to understand the most ancient traditions of the Jews. It shows that a clear line has to be drawn between Hebrew cosmogony and popular traditions in Genesis on one hand, and the same sort of material from Canaan, Phoenicia, and Egypt on the other. Comparison reveals that religious traditions here and there had nothing or very little in common, though at the same time both traditions undoubtedly arose from a certain single Mesopotamian tradition of great antiquity. In particular, the story of the Flood according to Genesis has its parallel in the Sumerian-Akkadian histories of Mesopotamia. The author of the above-mentioned survey gives his personal opinion on the contents of the book of Genesis as follows.

The first eleven chapters of the book are political in character, enveloped by a religious spirit; the next part presents history, but history which has been preserved in the form of oral traditions. As for the first chapter of Genesis, the author confesses that he is awed by the fact that it is in several respects a great improvement over everything that was said about the origin of the world in written form prior to the beginning of the nineteenth century.

The author of the survey gives as examples a series of obscure passages of the Bible that have been clarified as a result of excavations. Thus, in Genesis 15:2 we encounter a certain Eliezer of Damascus, about whom Abraham complains he will be forced to leave him his whole estate at death, not having a son as his heir (this was before the birth of Ishmael and Isaac). We now know, writes Professor Albright, that according to the ancient practice of the Patriarchs, property was not supposed to leave the family, but a legal "loophole" was devised. If someone was forced to mortgage his property to a creditor because of a bad harvest or for any other reason, he had to adopt his creditor, and the latter became the heir to his property. Such circumstances obviously arose in this case: Eliezer, a rich merchant from Damascus, who, like other merchants of Damascus, lent money to the surrounding landholders and cattle breeders, became a great creditor of Abraham, and could have become his direct heir through adoption. Another story, related in Genesis 21, describes the occasion when Rachel, the daughter of Laban and the wife of Jacob, before leaving the house of her father, stole the images of his household deities, the "teraphim," and succeeded in hiding them despite the search conducted by her father. In the texts of Nuzi there is a law that when doubt arises as to the rights of inheritance, for example, if there is no formal will, possession of idols of the household deities is considered to be the primary evidence to the right of inheritance. Hitherto it was not clear what purpose this theft served, and why this trivial event was included in the history, but the scribal copyists preserved this story, keeping in mind that it must have had some real significance. The meaning of Rachel's actions is now explained. There are a number of other examples where mysterious passages in Genesis are made clear thanks to the findings at Nuzi and other sites. Because of this, almost all learned biblicists now acknowledge that the book of Genesis constitutes a written narrative of factual events which were preserved by the Hebrew people in the form of oral traditions. Furthermore, the religious, educational, and literary value of the narratives of the Bible is much greater than if the wars of those days, the migrations of tribal groups, etc., had been described there.

If, as we said, the legal customs of the book of Genesis present an authentic reflection of the laws of society at that time, if the social and juridical practices described in the book of Genesis correspond exactly to those of the age of the Patriarchs and not to the post-Mosaic period, then it follows, writes Professor Albright, that we have no right *a priori* to relegate the patriarchal chronicles to a later date. One cannot call them the result of retrospective points of view which were current during the time of the Prophets, but should consider them to be actual oral traditions, only slightly modified with the passage of time as regards the removal of mythical elements from the traditions, the emphasizing of certain points, which were held to be significant, etc.; but on the whole, one should see their value as an authentic chronicle of the distant past. The attempts of certain critics of the biblical text to transfer the time of the life of Abraham and the time of the Exodus of the Jews out of Egypt to later centuries are unjustified, writes the author.

Keeping to the point of view of a scholar who obviously accepts biblical material as one of the phenomena of human culture, namely religious culture, Professor Albright does not deny the possibility of any sort of additions or deletions made in the course of the centuries of the Bible's history, just as he does not express himself opposed to the designation of such phenomena by the signs Y, E, P, etc. But he does definitively state that "attempts to break up the text of the Bible into small pieces, sometimes dividing up the text into individual verses or lines ascribed to three different sources [as rationalistic criticism does] are quite futile — empty, groundless; persons holding to the principles of higher criticism are completely mistaken in their assumptions. "From this," he writes, "it does not necessarily follow that the hypothesis of the documents is false in principle, but it must be treated with much greater critical caution than has hitherto been done" (pp. 14–15).

What place does Moses occupy in history? Comparing the cultic, ritual, and civil prescriptions in the Pentateuch with both earlier and later developments, one can fix the final prescriptions of the Pentateuch close to the period between the fourteenth and eleventh centuries B.C. In the same way we have ground for stating that the religion of the Pentateuch stands between the patriarchal religion on one hand and the religion of the epoch of the Kingdoms on the other, and that it can be called monotheistic in the broad sense of the word. As for details, and mainly those of the construction of the Tabernacle as described in the Pentateuch, the author thinks that its appearance was perfected gradually, and parallel to this, a series of corresponding additions could have been inserted into the text comparable, for example, to the way in which the original American Constitution of 1789 was amended, "though it lost neither its original unity, nor the wholeness of its character." Let us leave these opinions of the author as his personal ones.

Professor Albright is decidedly opposed to the application of the understanding of "myth" to the narratives of the Bible. To him, in fact, belongs the introduction of the term "demythologization" in its proper understanding into the language of modern exegesis. He writes:

In Genesis and in several poetic images of the Bible there are a number of passages where a clearly mythological element was demythologized. For example, in Canaanite mythology there is a huge creature called 'tanin,' which is rendered in the Authorized Bible by the word 'whale.' 'Tanin' was a prehistoric monster which existed even before the gods, and was destroyed by the great god Baal, or his sister Anat, or by another Canaanite deity. But in Genesis it says that on the fifth day of Creation God created 'Taninim gedolim,' the first gigantic creations out of chaos [in the Slavonic and in the Authorized version: "great whales"]. They were not the predecessors of the gods, they were creations of God: this is the process of demythologization at first hand. It is also impossible to consider correct the proposition, for example, that 'tekhom' — 'the great deep' — in the first chapter of Genesis is a monster such as 'tekhmatu' was in early Canaanite mythology. Such allusions to Canaanite mythology also show little indication of belief in the reality of the original bearers of these names, just as our use of the word 'cereal' scarcely expresses our faith in the goddess Ceres. The Bible uses a number of names of ancient gods and goddesses as ordinary names: the name Astarte took on the meaning of shepherd; Shumen, the god of health, became 'to your health'; one divinity lent its name to the oak tree, another to the turpentine tree; yet another to wine. All of these are examples of demythologization.

(W.F. Albright, "The Ancient Israelite Mind,'
from a survey in *New Horizons in Biblical Research*)

In actuality, in essence, it is quite clear that the task of Moses consisted in rejecting pagan mythical legends of gods and goddesses, and confirming a monotheistic world view among his own people, as the one intentionally called to preserve and preach faith in the One God, the Omniscient Creator.

A General View of the Results of So-Called Scholarly Biblical Criticism

Limiting this survey to the subject of the Pentateuch, let us in conclusion express our principal ideas regarding the character of the work of biblical criticism and its goals.

For the early Christian Church all of the rabbinical determinations relative to the books of the Old Testament Scriptures were, apparently, not dogmatically necessary. However, it did preserve them to a great degree. But why? This springs from an understanding of the spirit, the religiosity of Old Testament man, in whose consciousness the "righteousness of

God" had preeminence, for the Lord Himself *is righteous and hath loved righteousness; upon righteousness hath His countenance looked* (Ps. 10:7). Hence, the religious Jew had a dread of any falsehood, deceit, injustice, and whatever else elicits the disclamation: *If in my heart I regarded unrighteousness, let the Lord not hear me. Wherefore God hath hearkened unto me, He hath been attentive to the voice of my supplication* (Ps. 65:18–19). *Fret not thyself so as to do evil. For evil doers shall utterly perish* (Ps. 36:8–9). *Set not your hopes on injustice* (Ps. 61:11). *I have hated the congregation of evildoers* (Ps. 25:5). *I have hated every way of unrighteousness* (Ps. 118:104). The principle of righteousness was so bound up with the understanding of "faith" for the Old Testament Jew that it was in fact Old Testament religion that developed the idea of "a righteous person," and "a righteous one," to signify a religious man, and this it passed on to Christianity.

"Scholarly criticism" all but constructs its hypotheses on a contradictory supposition: it is inclined to see the falsification, the forgery, and the artificial creation of ancient authorities and the deceitful utilization of these authorities everywhere among the collectors and preservers of the books of the Bible, the spiritual leaders of Israel. If this were so, then whole series of misunderstandings arise.

How could this artificial, untruthful approach to the matter coincide with the personal, lofty, spiritual animation, with the great enthusiasm in the souls of the directors of the Hebrew people — and finally, simply with the thought of the fear of God? From whence was the zeal for their religion, and their boldness, those "scourges" directed to the people, the readiness for self-denial, for self sacrifice generated in them? The same contradiction is met in passages about the people.

Let us pass on to a specific occurrence. How could a forgery, alleged to have been produced by the High Priest Hilkiah,* even if he had passed off a new work as an ancient one, have produced that religious revival among the Hebrew people which in the history of the Jews is called the

---

*We read in Prof. Kartashev's article, "How can we accept with a clear conscience the completely incredible story (chps. 22–23 of IV Kings) of the supposedly chance discovery of the 'Book of the Law' or 'Book of the Covenant,' found during the renovation of the Temple of Jerusalem — a book totally unknown both to the High Priest Hilkiah who found it, to the righteous King Josiah, who was faithful to Yahweh, and to the whole nation? And this was barely one thousand years after Moses. It took place in the year 621, thirty-six years before Jerusalem was

"first rebirth"? A similar question arises concerning the activity of Ezra. If Ezra, calling upon the blinded people *to walk in the law of God, which was given by the hand of Moses, the servant of God* (Neh. 10:29), basing himself upon the authority of Moses, was either hiding the truth or was himself led into error, was it that the people did not suspect this possibility, but gave the oath demanded by him which compelled them to such great sacrifices and self-restraint as, for example, the mass removal of those of their wives who were of non-Jewish blood? Could a "second rebirth" have take place in history on such dubious grounds?

Criticism maintains that from the time of the Babylonian captivity in the religious sphere the Jewish people fell increasingly under the influence of foreign peoples — the Babylonians, Persians, Greeks — and that this influence is reflected, on one hand, in the appearance of a great number of books of the Bible which have hitherto been accepted as dating from an earlier period, and, on the other hand, in the borrowing of a number of religious beliefs from the peoples that oppressed them. Thus criticism sees an instability and mutability in Old Testament Jewish beliefs. Are there sufficient grounds to confirm this? Does not oppression create an opposing tendency in the ideological response of a nation? Does it not incline more towards rejection [of the oppressors] and self-determination than to borrowing from foreign peoples? An indication of the type of reaction that involuntary subjection elicits in a nation can be seen in Psalm 136: *By the waters of Babylon.* An enslaved people can to a certain degree forget its language, but this comes about independently of its own will. On the other hand, in the area of religion, a sense of national self-preservation inspires the oppressed to fear especially the intrusion of an alien spirit in the spiritual domain. We have examples from a time nearer to our own. The Greeks and Western Slavic peoples, throughout many centuries of Turkish suzerainty, preserved Orthodoxy unchanged; those that did not remain faithful to it became denationalized. The Russian people preserved their faith just as strictly under the Tatar yoke. But the victorious ancient

---

taken by Nebuchadnezzar. No, this can only be comprehensible by admitting that it was not a new, strangely forgotten, neglected book that was found at the time of King Josiah, but a totally new one. The delusion that the Pentateuch existed from time immemorial thus goes up in smoke. Indeed, the Pentateuch did not yet exist" (this means from Kartashev's point of view, that a crude and extremely dangerous forgery was made).

Roman Empire created within itself a religious eclecticism which assimilated the various religions of the subject nations of which it was comprised. What is characteristic of a people applies to its leaders as well.

The autonomy, stability, and independence of biblical religious understanding and even of corresponding terminology is gradually being confirmed by the study of the ancient Hebrew manuscripts, found in our times, in Palestine, and particularly by the "Dead Sea Scrolls." This refers not only to the books of the Old Testament, but, to a lesser degree, to the Sacred Scriptures of the New Testament as well. Here again let us refer to the testimony of archaeology, according to the information of Professor Albright:

> They maintain that Greek philosophical thought had a marked influence on a portion of the Old Testament, especially on the books of Job and Ecclesiastes. I date the book of Job to approximately the seventh century B.C. The more deeply that its problems are studied, the clearer it becomes that there is no trace of a Greek philosophical treatment of these problems. As for Ecclesiastes, one can now more or less definitely date it towards the end of the fifth century B.C. Though I recognize the similarity of thought between the writings of the Prophets and that of many Greek thinkers of the sixth century B.C. and also the Phoenician written material we have from this same general period, I cannot see a trace of the influence of Greek philosophical thought, as many have once done, myself included. Hebrew literature is as old as Greek literature and is comparable to it in content. Generally speaking, nowhere before the sixth century — not in the pagan writings of the Near East, or in the Old Testament, or in Homer, Hesiod, or the early Greek poets — is it possible to find traces of authentic philosophical thought.
>
> (W.F. Albright, "The Ancient Israelite Mind")

The same author writes about the independence of biblical understanding from Greek influence, on the basis of research done on the Dead Sea Scrolls. But this material pertains to the New Testament.

Sophianism and Trends in Russian Intellectual Theology

The Question of Dogmatic Development

The theme of dogmatic development long ago became a subject of discussion in theological literature: can one accept, from the Church's point of view, the development of dogmas, or not? In the majority of cases, an argument about words ensues: a divergence comes about because a different connotation is applied to the term "development." Is "development" to be understood as a setting forth of what is already known, or as the disclosure of something new?

The common view of theological thought acknowledges that the Church conscience, being guided by the Holy Spirit, is the one and the same in its essence from the Apostles to the end of the (earthly pilgrimage) of the Church. The Christian teaching, the extent and comprehension of Divine Revelation, is unchanged. The doctrine of the Church does not develop and Church self-consciousness does not become any richer, deeper and wider with the passing of the centuries, than it was with the Apostles. The content of the Faith delivered by the Apostles is not subject to supplement. Although the Church is always led by the Holy Spirit, we do not see and do not expect new dogmatic revelations in the history of the Church.

The above understanding of the question about dogmatic development was generally present in Russian theology in the 19th century. What appeared to be a difference in the opinions of various persons on this question was really only a point of discussion. In discussions with Protestants, it was natural to defend the right of the Church to have set forth dogmas, in the sense that the Councils had the right to pronounce and sanction dogmatic positions. In discussions with Latins, it was necessary to refute arbitrary dogmatic novelties created by the Roman Church in later times, and thus to speak against the principle of the creation of new dogmas not delivered by the Church in ancient times. In particular, the Old Catholics, nearer to Orthodoxy, with both sides rejecting the Vatican dogma of papal infallibility — strengthened in Russian theological thought the conservative point of view on the question of dogmatic development, the view which does not approve of the establishment of new dogmatic definitions.

In the 1880's we meet with another approach to this given question. V. S. Soloviev, who was inclined toward a union of Orthodoxy with the Roman Church, wished to justify the dogmatic development of the Latins, and he defended the idea of the development of the dogmatic conscience of the Church. "The Body of Christ," he argued, "changes and becomes complete like any organism"; the original "testament" of Faith in the history of Christianity is being uncovered and elucidated; "Orthodoxy stands not merely by antiquity, but by the eternally living Spirit of God."

Not only Soloviev's sympathy for the Latins, but also his own personal religious-philosophical make-up impelled him to defend the point of view of (this type of) development. This included his idea about *Sophia* — God's Wisdom, about Theanthropism as an historical process, and others. In the 1890's, Soloviev, captivated by his own metaphysical system, began to spread the teaching of the "eternal Feminine Principle" which, he says,

> Is not only an inert image in God's mind, but a living spiritual being, possessing all the fullness of power and action. The whole world and historical process is a process of its realization and incarnation in a great diversity of forms and degrees... The heavenly object of our love is only one, always and for everyone one and the same — the eternal Feminine Principle of God...

Thus, a series of new conceptions began to enter into Russian religious thought. These concepts did not evoke special rebuttals in Russian theological studies because they were emitted more as philosophical thought rather than theological.

By means of his literary and oratorical skills, Soloviev was able to inspire an interest in religious problems among wide circles of Russian intellectual society. Nevertheless, this interest became merged with a turning away from the authentic Orthodox system of thought. This was expressed, for example, at the Petersburg "Religious-Philosophical Meetings" of 1901–1903. Here the questions were raised: "Can one consider the dogmatic teaching of the Church to be complete? Can one not expect new revelations? In what can the new religious-creative genius in Christianity be expressed and by what means can it remain in accord with Holy Scripture and with the Tradition of the Church, with the definitions of the Ecumenical Councils and with the teachings of the Holy Fathers?" Especially characteristic were discussions about "dogmatic development."

In the beginning of the present century, there appeared in Russian religious-social thought, the expectation of an awakening of a "new religious conscience" on Orthodox soil. Thoughts began to germinate that theology must not fear new revelations, that dogmatics must make wider use of a rational basis, that it cannot completely ignore contemporary personal prophetic inspiration, that the circle of basic dogmatic problems is subject to expansion, so that dogmatics must come to present itself as a full philosophical-theological system of the contemplation of the world. The original ideas put forth by Soloviev, first among them the matter of Sophianism, were developed into a second phase. The eminent representatives of the new current were the priest Paul Florensky (*The Pillar and Ground of Truth*, etc.) and Serge N. Bulgakov, later Archpriest (his later Sophianistic compositions include *The Undimming Light, The Unburning Bush, Hypostasis and Hypostasity, Friend of the Bridegroom, God's Lamb, The Comforter, John's Revelation*, etc.

In connection with these propositions, it is natural for us to raise the question: does dogmatic science, in its accepted structure, satisfy the need of a Christian to form a complete world outlook? If dogmatics refuses to acknowledge the principle of development, does it not remain a lifeless collection of incomplete dogmas?

It must be said with all conviction that the circle of revealed truths which compose the (Orthodox) system of dogmatic theology provides a complete opportunity to form a high and, simultaneously, a clear and simple world-view. Dogmatic theology, built on the foundation of solid dogmatic truths, speaks of a Personal God inexpressibly close to us, Who does not need a mediator between Himself and His creature, about God in Holy Trinity (Eph. 4:6) — above us (i.e., our Sovereign) with us and in us; about God Who loves His creation, loves man, and condescends to our infirmities, not depriving His creatures of freedom. It speaks of man and mankind, his lofty destiny and high spiritual possibilities, and, at the same time, it speaks of his pitiful real moral level, his fall. It presents paths and means for a return to the lost paradise, paths and means which were revealed by the Incarnation and death on the Cross of the Son of God, and a path to the attainment of eternal blessed life. All this is vitally necessary truth. Here, faith and life, knowledge and the application of it in action are undivided.

Dogmatic science does not claim to satisfy every aspect of the searching of the human mind. There is no doubt that Divine Revelation has revealed to our spiritual eyes only a small part of the knowledge of God and the spiritual world. We see, as the Apostle Paul says, *through a glass, darkly*. An immeasurable expanse of the mysteries of God remains unknown to us.

It is necessary to point out that the attempts to widen the boundaries of theology on a mystical or on a rational basis, which have appeared both in ancient and modern times, do not bring about a fuller knowledge of God and the world. These devices lead into the forest of narrow mental speculations and set new difficulties before the mind. The main one is the nebulous deliberations about the internal life in God. We witness them (these deliberations) in certain theologians who, having embarked upon the path of philosophizing in theology, do not enter into a direct feeling of reverence, an awareness and feeling of the nearness and holiness of God, and, in fact, they stifle this feeling.

These considerations do not mean that all development in the area of dogmatics is negative. What is subject to development?

The history of the Church shows that there has never been an increase in the quantity of dogmas in the most precise meaning of the word. It was not dogmas that were developed, but the area of dogmatics opened up until it reached its limits, given by the Holy Scripture.

In other words, an increasing number of the truths of the Faith received an exact formulation at the Ecumenical Councils, or in general have been confirmed by Ecumenical Councils. The work of the Church in this direction consisted in defining dogmatic issues, drawing their explanations from God's word, confirming them by Sacred Tradition and proclaiming them to all believers. In this work of the Church, the quantity and extent of dogmatic truths always remains one and the same. In view of the invasion of non-Orthodox opinions and teachings, the Church sanctions one dogmatic thesis — Orthodox, and rejects others — heretical. We cannot negate the fact that, thanks to the defining of dogmas, the content of the Faith became clearer in the conscience of the members of the Church and in the Church hierarchy itself.

Dogmatic science is subject, moreover, to development. Dogmatic science can become diverse in method, be completed with study material, used more broadly or more narrowly with exegetical material, scriptural philology, Church history, writings of the Holy Fathers and can also be used with rational considerations. It can more strongly or moderately respond to a heresy, false teaching, and various currents of contemporary religious thought. But theological science is an external subject in relationship to the spiritual life of the Church. It only studies the work of the Church and Her dogmatic and other definitions. Dogmatic theology, like science, can be developed itself, but it cannot develop and perfect the teaching of the Church. The blossoming or decline of theological science may or may not coincide with the general level of the spiritual life within the Church at any given historical period. The development of theological science can be halted without any loss to spiritual life. Theological science is not called upon to guide the Church: rather, it is obligated to seek for and strictly adhere to the guidance of the Church conscience.

We have been permitted to know what is necessary for the good of our souls. Knowledge about God, Divine life, and Divine Providence is given to people in the measure in which it has a direct moral, vital application. We are taught this by the Apostle Peter when he writes:

> *According as His divine power hath given unto us all things that pertain unto life and godliness…giving all diligence, add to your faith virtue, and to virtue knowledge, and to knowledge temperance, and to temperance patience, and to patience godliness, and to godliness brotherly kindness, and to brotherly kindness charity.*
> —II Peter 1:3–7

For the Christian, the essential thing is moral perfection. All the rest, which God's Word and the Church give, is a means to this basic aim.

Philosophy and Theology

Contemporary theological thought has become penetrated with the notion that Christian dogmatic theology must be "fertilized," enlightened by philosophical principles, and must assimilate philosophical understanding.

Vladimir Soloviev defines his task, in the first lines of his works (*History and the Future Theocracy*), thus: "To justify the faith of our fathers, to raise it to a new step of intelligent conscience..." There would be nothing reprehensible in a task such as the one formulated here. Nevertheless, it is necessary to be cautious of any mixing of two fields — dogmatic science and philosophy — a mixing which is ready to bring about an entanglement and obscurement of them, their content, and their methods.

In the first centuries of Christianity, Church writers and the Fathers of the Church generally responded to the challenge of their time regarding philosophical ideas, and made use of concepts which had been worked out by philosophy. Why? By this they were building a bridge from Greek philosophy to Christianity. Christianity appeared as a world-view which must replace the philosophical views of the classical world, being above them. Then, having become in the fourth century the official religion of the state, it was called by the state itself to take the place of all systems of world-views which had existed up to that time. This is demonstrated by the fact that at the First Ecumenical Council, a dispute took place between Christian teachers of the Faith and a "Philosopher." But more than a "replacement" was needed. Christian apologetics took up the task of taking hold of pagan philosophical thought and directing its understanding into the channel of Christianity. The ideas of Plato stood before Christian writers as a stage in paganism preparatory to Divine Revelation. Moreover, by the force of things, Orthodoxy had to struggle with Arianism not so much on the ground of Holy Scripture as against a philosophical path, since Arianism took its basic error from Greek philosophy, namely, the teaching about the Logos as being a mediating principle between God and the world, but a principle which stands lower than the Divinity Itself. In all this, however, the thought of the Holy Fathers was such that all truths of the Christian Faith are based on the foundation of Divine Revelation and not on rational abstract reasonings. St. Basil the Great, in his treatise, "What Benefit Can Be Drawn from Pagan Works," gives examples of how to use the instructive material contained in these writings. With the universal spread of Christian concepts, the reference toward Greek philosophy was gradually extinguished in the writing of the Holy Fathers.

This is understandable. Theology and philosophy differ first of all in their content. The Saviour's teaching on earth proclaimed to people not abstract ideas, but a new life for God's kingdom. The Apostles' preaching was a preaching of salvation in Christ. Thus, Christian dogmatic theology has as its central goal a complete examination of the teaching about salvation, about its necessity, and about the path to it. According to its basic content, theology is soteriological (from the Greek: σωτηρία — salvation). Dogmatic theology treats questions of ontology (the essence of existence) — about God in Himself, about the essence of the world and the nature of man — in a more limited aspect. This occurs not only because they are given to us in such a limited aspect in the Holy Scripture, but also according to [limited] psychological principles. Silence concerning the internal life in God is an expression of the vital feeling of God's omnipresence, reverence before God, and awe of God. In the Old Testament this feeling led to an awe of saying God's name. Only in the ascent of reverent feeling did the thought of the Fathers of the Church rise, in individual moments, to the contemplation of the inner Divine Life. The main area of their contemplation is the truth of the Holy Trinity which is revealed in the New Testament. The whole of Orthodox Christian theology also proceeds along this line.

Philosophy sets out along a different path. It is mainly interested in the questions of ontology: the essence of existence, about the unity of existence, about the relationship between absolute fundamentals and the world in its concrete phenomena, etc. Philosophy, by its nature, proceeds from skepticism, from doubt in what has been received, even including faith in God…it examines God "objectively," as with an object of cold, indifferent knowledge, an object which is subject to a rational examination, definition, and explanation of its essence, its relationship, as an absolute existence, to the world of phenomena.

These two areas — dogmatic theology and philosophy — also differ in their sources and methods.

The source for theological work is Divine Revelation which is contained in the Holy Scripture and Sacred Tradition. The fundamental character of Sacred Scripture and Tradition depends on our faith in their truth. Theology gathers and studies material which is found in these sources, systematizes it, assesses it, using in its work those very processes which experienced sciences use.

Philosophy is rational, abstract. It proceeds not from faith, as with theology, but seeks to be based either on undebatable intellectual theses, reaching further conclusions from them, or on scientific data or common human knowledge. Thus, it can hardly be said that philosophy is capable of raising the religion of the Fathers to the degree of knowledge.

Nevertheless, the differences indicated do not fundamentally reject the possible collaboration of the two given fields. Philosophy itself arrives at the deduction that there are boundaries which the human mind, because of its nature, is not in a condition to cross over. The fact that the history of philosophy reveals two currents — idealistic and materialistic — indicates that the construction (of philosophy) depends upon the personal predisposition of the mind and heart. In other words, (philosophy) leans upon fundamentals which lie beyond the boundary of proof. That which lies beyond the boundary of proof is the realm of faith: of negative, non-religious faith, or of positive, religious faith. For the religious mind, that which is "beyond the boundary" is the sphere of Divine Revelation.

It would appear, at this point, that there is a possibility for cooperation in the two areas of inquiry: theology and philosophy. This is the way religious philosophy is created; and in Christianity, this means Christian philosophy.

There is, however, a difficult path in Christian religious philosophy: to unite the freedom of the mind, as a principle of philosophy, with faithfulness to dogmas and all the teachings of the Church. "Go along the open road, whither the mind attracts you," calls the duty of philosophers. "Be faithful to Divine Truth," the duty of a Christian says. Therefore, one must always expect that in a practical realization, the composers of Christian philosophical systems will be forced to sacrifice, voluntarily or involuntarily, the principles of the one area for the use of the other. Church conscience greets sincere experiments in the creation of a harmonious philosophical-Christian contemplation of the world. But, the Church looks upon them as private, personal creations and does not sanction them with its authority. In any case, a clear delineation between dogmatic theology and Christian philosophy is necessary, and all attempts to transform dogmatics into Christian philosophy must be decisively rejected.

Observations About the Religious-Philosophical System
of Vladimir Soloviev

The thrust toward new currents in Russian philosophical-theological thought was given, as we said, by Vladimir S. Soloviev, who set forth as his task "to justify the Faith of the fathers" before the reason of his contemporaries. Unfortunately, he entered into a series of direct diversions from an Orthodox Christian pattern of thought — and many of those diversions are accepted and developed by his followers.

Below are series of points in Soloviev's thinking which differ from, and even directly turn away from, confessed Church doctrines.

1. He represents Christianity as a higher stage in the successive development of religion.

According to Soloviev, all religions are true, but one-sided; Christianity synthesizes the positive sides of preceding religions. He writes, "Just as eternal nature is only gradually revealed to the mind of man and mankind, and as a result of this we must also speak of the development of experimental or natural science, so also the divine basis is gradually revealed to the conscience of mankind, and we must speak of the development of religious experience and of religious thinking... Religious development is a positive and objective process, it is a real reciprocal action of God and man — a God-man process. It is clear," continues Soloviev, "that...neither any one of its steps, nor any one of the moments of the religious process can be in itself a lie or an error. 'False religion' is a contradiction in terms."

2. The teaching about the salvation of the world, in the form that it was given by the Apostles, is set aside. According to Soloviev, Christ came to earth not in order "to save the human race, but in order to raise it to a higher level in the order of a successive revelation of the divine basis in the world — of the ascent and deification of mankind and the world. Christ is the highest link in a series of theophanies, the crowning link of former theophanies."

3. Soloviev focuses theological attention directly on the ontological aspect of existence, i.e., on the life of God within Himself and, because of an insufficiency of data in the Holy Scripture, the mind runs into an arbitrary conclusion, either rational or founded on fantasy.

4. He introduced into the Divine Life a creature called *Sophia* (Wisdom), which stands on the boundary between Divinity and the created world.

5. A differentiation between masculine and feminine principles (or, bases) is introduced into the Divine Life. With Soloviev, it is somewhat subdued. Father Paul Florensky, following Soloviev, presents Sophia thus: "This is a great, reigning and feminine Being, which, being neither God nor the eternal Son of God, nor angel, nor a holy person, receives honor from both the concluder of the Old Testament and founder of the New" (*Pillar and Ground of Truth*).

6. There is introduced into Divine Life an elementary principle of striving which is compelled by the God-Logos Himself to participate in a definite process, which submits Him to that process — to raise the world from the condition of pure materiality and stagnation to the higher, most perfect form of existence.

7. God, as absolute, is God the Father, presented as distant and inaccessible to the world and to man. He is withdrawn from the world, despite God's word, into an inaccessible region of existence. As absolute existence, He has no contact with relative existence, with the world of phenomena. Thus, according to Soloviev, a Mediator is necessary between the Absolute and the world. Such a Mediator is the "Logos," Who was made incarnate in Christ.

8. According to Soloviev, the first Adam united in himself a divine and human nature similar to their correlation in the theanthropic nature of the Incarnate Word. Only, he violated this correlation. If this were so then the deification of man is not only a Graceful consecration of man, but is a restoration in him of theanthropicness, a restoration of two natures. This is not, however, in accord with the teaching of the Church, which understands deification solely as Grace-endowed. "There has never been and will never be," says Saint John of Damascus, "another person consisting of Divinity and humanity" aside from Jesus Christ.

9. Soloviev writes, "God is the All-mighty Creator and the Almighty, but not the ruler over the earth and the creatures which come from it... Divinity is incommensurable with earthly creation and can have a moral-practical relationship (of authority, domination, direction) toward them only under the mediation of a man who, as a demigod, is commensurable with both Divinity and with material nature. Thus, man is a necessary subject of the true sovereignty of God" (*Truth and the Future of Theocracy*).

This statement is unacceptable from the point of view of the glory and power of God and, as we said, it contradicts God's word. Moreover, it does not even withstand a simple observation. Man submits himself to nature not in God's name, as a mediator between God and the world, but for his personal egoistic aims and needs.

The several points of diversion of the views of Soloviev from the teachings of the Church, as noted here, indicate that, for the Orthodox conscience, the religious system of Soloviev is inadmissible in its entirety.

God's Wisdom (Sophia) in Scripture

We encounter the word "wisdom" (*sophia*) in the sacred books of both the Old and New Testaments.

In the New Testament Holy Scripture, it is used in three senses:

1. In the ordinary broad sense of wisdom, sapience: *Jesus increased in wisdom and stature and grace* (Luke 2:25); *But wisdom is justified of all her children* (Luke 7:35).

2. In the sense of God's wise economy which is expressed in the creation of the world, in the providence of God to the world, and in the salvation of the world from sin: *O the depth of the riches both of the wisdom and knowledge of God! For who hath known the mind of the Lord, or who hath been His counselor?* (Rom. 11:33–34). *We speak of the wisdom of God in a mystery, even the hidden wisdom, which God ordained before the world unto our glory* (I Cor. 2:7).

3. In relationship to the Son of God, as the Personal (hypostatic) Wisdom of God: *But we preach Christ crucified… Christ the power of God, and the wisdom of God* (I Cor. 1:23–24); *Who of God is made unto us wisdom* (I Cor. 1:30).

In the Old Testament Holy Scripture, we find wisdom spoken of in many places. Here, too, the term has three meanings. Wisdom is especially spoken of in the Book of Proverbs and in two of the deutero-canonical books: The Wisdom of Solomon and Ecclesiasticus (Wisdom of Sirach).

a. In the majority of cases, these works present human wisdom as a gift from God, which must be greatly valued. The names of the books themselves, *Wisdom of Solomon, Wisdom of Sirach* indicate that we must understand the word in the sense of human wisdom. In other Old Testament books separate episodes are cited which specially depict human wisdom — for example, the famous judgement of Solomon.

These books introduce us to the direction of thought of divinely inspired teachers of the Jewish nation. These teachers inspire the people to be guided by their minds and not by blind inclinations and passions, and to be diligent in ordering their lives with prudence, sound judgment, moral law, and a firm foundation of duty in personal, family, and social life. A significant part of the Book of Proverbs is dedicated to this theme. The title of this book, *Book of Proverbs,* informs the reader that he will encounter in it a figurative, metaphorical, and allegorical means of exposition. In the introduction to the book, after indicating its purpose, which is to give "understanding, wisdom, and instruction," the author expresses the assurance that *a wise man...will understand a parable, and a dark speech, the sayings of the wise also, and riddles* (Prov. 1:6, *Septuagint*), that is, he will understand the imagery and similitudes of poetically woven speech, its "hard sayings" (Prov. 1:3), not accepting all the images in the literal sense.

In truth, on further examination, one finds an abundance of images and personifications in the application of *the wisdom that man can possess. Acquire wisdom, acquire understanding... Say unto wisdom, thou art my sister; and call understanding thy kinswoman* (Prov. 7:4).*Forsake it not, and it shall cleave to thee; love it, and it shall keep thee... Secure it, and it shall exalt thee; honor it, that it may embrace thee; that it may give unto thy head a crown of graces, and may cover thee with a crown of delight* (Prov. 4:6,8,9 *Septuagint*). *For she sitteth by the gates of princes, and singeth in the entrances* (Prov. 8:3, *Septuagint*). The book, *Wisdom of Solomon,* also contains similar thoughts about human wisdom.

Of course, none of these discourses on wisdom can in any manner be construed to teach of a hypostatic Wisdom, of a "soul of the world" in the sophianistic sense. One possesses wisdom, acquires it, loses it, it serves him, its beginning is termed as being *the fear of the Lord,* and we find "reason," "justice," and "knowledge" placed on the same level with it.

b. And where does wisdom come from? Like everything else in the world, it has a single source: God. *For the Lord giveth wisdom, and from His presence come knowledge and understanding* (Prov. 2:6). God is *the guide even of wisdom and the corrector of the wise* (Wisdom of Solomon 7:15).

A second group of utterances in Holy Scripture refer to this wisdom of God, which is *the wisdom in God Himself.* Ideas of the wisdom in God are interspaced with ideas of the wisdom in man.

If dignity of understanding and wisdom are so exalted, then how majestic are they in God Himself! The writer uses the most majestic expressions possible in order to present the power and grandeur of *Divine Wisdom*. Here also he makes broad use of personification. He speaks of the grandeur of the Divine plan which, according to our human conceptions, seem to have proceeded the creation: because the wisdom of God lies at the foundation of all that exists. *The Lord made me the beginning of His ways for His works. He established me before time was in the beginning, before He made the earth, even before He made the depths... Before all hills, He begetteth me... When He prepared the heaven, I was present with Him* (Prov. 8:22–25, 27, Septuagint). The author speaks of the beauty of the world, expressing in images what was said of the creation in the book of Genesis (*it was very good*). He says on behalf of wisdom: *I was by Him. I was that wherein He took delight: and daily I rejoiced in His presence continually* (Prov. 8:30).

In all the above-cited images of wisdom, and other similar ones, there are no grounds for seeing in a direct sense any personal spiritual being, distinct from God Himself, a soul of the world or an idea of the world. This does not correspond to the images given here: an ideal "essence of the world" could not be called "present" at the creation of the world (see the Wisdom of Solomon 9:9); only something outside both the Creator and the creation could be "present." Likewise, it could not be an "implement" of the creation if it itself is the soul of the created world. Therefore, in the above-cited expressions it is natural to see personifications (a literary device), even though they are so expressive as to be nearly an hypostases or actual person.

c. Finally, the writer of the book of Proverbs is prophetically exalted in thought to the prefiguration of the *New Testament economy of God* which is to be revealed in the preaching of the Saviour of the world, in the salvation of the world and mankind, and in the creation of the New Testament Church. This prefiguration is to be found in the first verses of the ninth chapter of Proverbs: *Wisdom hath built a house for herself, and set up seven pillars. She hath killed her beasts: she hath mingled her wine in a bowl...* (Prov. 9:1–6, *Septuagint*). This magnificent image is equal in power to the prophecies of the Saviour in the Old Testament prophets.

Since the economy of salvation was performed by the Son of God, the Holy Fathers of the Church, and following them the Orthodox interpreters of the book of Proverbs in general, refer to the name "wisdom of God," which essentially belongs to the Holy Trinity as a whole, to the Second Person of the Holy Trinity, the Son of God, as the Fulfiller of the Counsel of the Holy Trinity.

By analogy with this prophetic passage, the images in the book of Proverbs which were indicated above as referring to the wisdom in God (in chapter 8) are also interpreted as applying to the Son of God. When the Old Testament writers, to whom the mystery of the Most Holy Trinity was not entirely revealed, say *In wisdom hath He made them all* — for a New Testament believer, a Christian, in the name "Word" and in the name "Wisdom" is revealed the Second Person of the Holy Trinity, the Son of God.

The Son of God, as a Hypostasis of the Holy Trinity, contains in Himself all the Divine attributes in the same fullness as do the Father and the Holy Spirit. However, as having manifested these attributes to the world in its creation and its salvation, He is called the Hypostatic Wisdom of God. On the same grounds, the Son of God can also be called the Hypostatic Love (see St. Symeon the New Theologian, Homily 53); the Hypostatic Light (*walk* [in the light] *while ye have light* — John 12:35); the Hypostatic Life ("Thou hast given birth to the Hypostatic Life" — Canon of the Annunciation, Ode 8); and the Hypostatic Power of God (*We preach...Christ the power of God* — I Cor. 1:24).

The Old Testament
in the New Testament Church

Adistance of many centuries separates us from the time when the books of the Old Testament were written, especially the first ones. And it is no longer easy for us to transfer our thoughts back to the state of soul and the conditions of life in which the books were first written, and which are described in the books themselves. This has given birth to many perplexities which confuse the thought of modern man. Such perplexities arise especially when people wish to find an agreement between contemporary, scientific views and the simplicity of the biblical ideas about the world. General questions also arise as to how many of the Old Testament views correspond to the New Testament outlook. And often people ask: "Why the Old Testament? Are not the teachings and scriptures of the New Testament sufficient?"

Concerning the enemies of Christianity, long ago their polemics against the Christian faith began with attacks on the Old Testament. Contemporary militant atheism considers Old Testament accounts the easiest material to suit its purpose. Those who have passed through a period of religious doubt, and perhaps denial of religion (especially those who have been through the Soviet school system with its anti-religious propaganda), usually say that the first stumbling block for their faith arose in this area.

This brief review of the Old Testament Scriptures cannot answer all the questions which arise in this regard; but will try to indicate some guiding principles, with the help of which many perplexities can be avoided.

In Accordance with the Saviour's and the Apostles' Commandment

The early Christian Church constantly dwelt in spirit in the Heavenly City, seeking the things to come, but she also organized the earthly aspect of her existence; in particular, she accumulated and took great care of the material treasures of the Faith. First among these treasures were the written documents concerning the Faith. The most important of the Scriptures were the Gospels, the sacred record of the earthly life and the teachings of the Lord Jesus Christ, the Son of God. Next came all the other writings of the Apostles. After them came the holy books of the Hebrews. The Church also treasures them as sacred writings.

What makes the Old Testament Scriptures valuable to the Church? The fact that a) they teach belief in the one, true God, and the fulfillment of God's commandments and b) they speak about the Saviour. Christ Himself points this out. *Search the scriptures; for in them ye think ye have eternal life and they are they which testify of Me,* He said to the Jewish scribes. In the parable about the Rich Man and Lazarus, the Saviour puts these words about the Rich Man's brothers into the mouth of Abraham: *They have Moses and the prophets; let them hear them.* "Moses" means the first five books of the Old Testament; "the prophets" — the last sixteen books. Speaking with His disciples, the Saviour mentioned the Psalter in addition to these books: *...all things must be fulfilled, which were written in the law of Moses, and in the prophets, and in the psalms, concerning Me.* After the Mystical Supper, *when they chanted a hymn, they went out into the Mount of Olives,* says the Evangelist Matthew. This refers to the chanting of psalms. The Saviour's words and examples are sufficient to make the Church esteem these books — the Law of Moses, the prophets and the psalms — to make her preserve them and learn from them.

In the Hebrew canon, the cycle of books recognized as sacred by the Hebrews, there were and still remain two more categories of books besides the Law and the Prophets: the didactic books, of which only the Psalter has been mentioned, and the historical books. The Church has accepted them, because the Apostles so ordained. Saint Paul writes to Timothy: *From a child thou hast known the holy scriptures, which are able to make thee wise unto salvation through faith which is in Christ Jesus.* This means: if one reads them wisely, then one will find in them the path which leads to strengthening in Christianity. The Apostle had in mind all the books of the Old Testament, as is evident from what he says next: *All scripture is given by inspiration of God, and is profitable for doctrine, for reproof, for correction, for instruction in righteousness* (II Tim. 3:15–16).

The Church has received the sacred Hebrew books in the Greek translation of the *Septuagint,* which was made long before the Nativity of

Christ. This translation was used by the Apostles, as they wrote their own epistles in Greek. The canon also contained sacred books of Hebraic origin, which however were extant only in Greek. The Orthodox Christian Church includes them in the collection of Old Testament books (in the biblical science of the West they are called the "deuterocanonical" books). From the time of their Council in Jamnia in 90 A.D., the Jews ceased to make use of these books in their religious life.

In accepting the Old Testament sacred scriptures, the Church has shown that she is the heir of the Old Testament Church — not of the national aspect of Judaism, but of the religious content of the Old Testament. In this heritage, some things have an eternal significance and value, but others have ceased to exist and are significant only as recollections of the past and for edification as prototypes, as, for example, the regulations concerning the tabernacle and the sacrifices, and the prescriptions for the Israelites' daily conduct. Therefore, the Church makes use of her Old Testament heritage quite authoritatively, in accordance with her understanding of the world, which is more complete than and superior to that of ancient Israel.

The Extent to Which the
Old Testament Has Been Used in the Church

While in principle fully recognizing the merit of the Old Testament books, the Christian Church has not, in practice, had the opportunity to make use of them everywhere, always, and to their full extent. This is clear from the fact that the Old Testament Scriptures occupy four times as many pages in the Bible as the New. Before books were printed, that is to say, during the first 1500 years of the Christian era, copying the books, collecting them, and acquiring them was, in itself, a difficult matter. Only a few families could have had a complete collection of them, and certainly not every Church community did. As a source of instruction in the Faith, as a guide for Christian life in the Church, the New Testament, of course, occupies the first place. It can be said only of the Old Testament Psalter that the Church has constantly used it, and still uses it, in its complete form. From the time of the Apostles until our day, she has used it in her services and as the companion of each Christian, and she will continue to use it until the end of the world. From the other books of the Old Testament, she has been satisfied with select readings, and these not even from all the books. In particular, we know of the Russian Church that although she had already shone forth resplendently in the 11th–12th centuries, before the Tatar invasion (this fullness of her life was expressed in the writing of Church services, in iconography and church architecture, and reflected in the literary monuments of ancient Russia) she nevertheless did not have a complete collection of the Old Testament books. Only at the end of the 15th century did Archbishop Gennadius of Novgorod manage, with great difficulty, to gather Slavonic translations of the books of the Old Testament. And even this was just for one archdiocese, for one bishop's cathedra! Only the printing press gave the Russian people the first complete Bible, published at the end of the 16th century and known as the Ostrog Bible. In our time, the Bible has become readily available. However, in practice the purely liturgical use of the books of the Old Testament has remained the same as always, as it was originally established by the Church.

Understandest Thou What Thou Readest?

According to the account in the Acts of the Apostles, when the Apostle Philip met one of Queen Candace's eunuchs on the road and saw the book of the Prophet Isaiah in his hands, he asked the eunuch, *Understandest thou what thou readest?* He replied, *How can I except some man should guide me?* (Acts 8:39). Philip instructed him in the Christian understanding of what he had been reading, with the result that this reading from the Old Testament was followed immediately, there on the road itself, by the eunuch's baptism. As the Apostle interpreted in the light of the Christian faith what the eunuch had been reading so we also must approach reading the Old Testament from the standpoint of the Christian Faith. It needs to be understood in a New Testament way, in the light which proceeds from the Church. For this purpose the Church offers us the patristic commentaries on the Holy Scriptures, preferring that we should assimilate the contents of the sacred books through them. It is necessary to bear in mind that the Old Testament is the *shadow of good things to come* (Heb. 10:1). If the reader forgets this, he may not receive the edification he should, as the Apostle Paul warns. Concerning the Jews he writes that *even unto this day, when Moses is read, the veil is upon their hearts*: with them it *remaineth untaken away in the reading of the Old Testament,* that is to say, they are not spiritually enlightened unto faith. Nevertheless, when they *shall turn to the Lord,* the Apostle concludes his thought, *the veil shall be taken away* (II Cor. 3:14–15). So we must also read these books from a Christian point of view. This means to read them while remembering the Lord's words: *...They* [the Scriptures] *are they which testify of Me.* They require not simply reading, but searching. In them are contained the preparation for the coming of Christ, promises, prophecies, and types or antitypes of Christ. It is according to this principle that the Old Testament readings are chosen for use in the church services. Furthermore, if the Church offers us moral edification in them, she chooses such passages as are written, as it were, in the light of the Gospel, which speak, for example, of the "eternal life" of the righteous ones, of "righteousness according to faith," and of Grace. If we Christians approach the books of the Old Testament in this light, then we find in them an enormous wealth of edification. Even as drops of dew on plants shine with all the colors of the rainbow when the sunlight falls on them, even as twigs of trees that are covered with ice are iridescent with all the tints of color as they reflect the sun, so these scriptures reflect that which was foreordained to appear later: the events, deeds, and teaching of the Gospel. But when the sun has set, those dew drops and the icy covering on the trees will no longer caress our eyes, although they themselves remain the same as they were when the sun was shining. It is the same with the Old Testament Scriptures. Without the sunlight of the Gospel they remain old and decaying, as the Apostle said of them, as the Church has also called them, and *that which decayeth and waxeth old is ready to vanish away,* as the Apostle expresses it (Heb. 8:13). The Kingdom of the chosen people of old has come to an end, the Kingdom of Christ has come: *the law and the prophets were until John; from henceforth the Kingdom of God is proclaimed* (Luke 16:16).

Why It Is Necessary to Know the Old Testament

We listen to the hymns and readings in Church, and two series of events are revealed before us: the Old Testament — and the New, as the type and the fulfillment, as the shadow and the truth, as the fall and the rising, as the loss and the gain. In the patristic writings and the hymns in the church services the Old and New Testaments are constantly being contrasted: Adam and Christ, Eve and the Mother of God. There, the earthly paradise; here, the Heavenly paradise. Through the woman came sin;

through the Virgin, salvation. The eating of the fruit unto death; the partaking of the Holy Gifts unto life. There, the forbidden tree; here, the saving Cross. There it is said, *Ye shall die the death*; here, *today shalt thou be with Me in paradise*. There, the serpent, the deceiver; here, Gabriel, the preacher of good tidings. There, the woman is told, *In sorrow shalt thou bring forth children*; here, the women at the tomb are told, *Rejoice*. The parallel is made throughout the entirety of the two Testaments. Salvation from the flood in the ark; salvation in the Church. The three strangers with Abraham; the Gospel truth of the Holy Trinity. The offering of Isaac as sacrifice; the Saviour's death on the Cross. The ladder which Jacob saw as in a dream; the Mother of God, the ladder of the Son of God's descent to earth. The sale of Joseph by his brothers; the betrayal of Christ by Judas. Slavery in Egypt; the spiritual slavery of mankind to the devil. The departure from Egypt; salvation in Christ. Crossing the Red Sea; Holy Baptism. The unconsumed bush; the perpetual virginity of the Mother of God. The Sabbath; the day of Resurrection. The ritual of circumcision; the Mystery of Baptism. Manna; the Lord's Supper of the New Testament. The Law of Moses; the Law of the Gospel. Sinai; the Sermon on the Mount. The tabernacle; the New Testament Church. The Ark of the Covenant; the Mother of God. The serpent on the staff; the nailing of Christ to the Cross. Aaron's rod which blossomed; the rebirth in Christ. We could continue with such comparisons even further.

The New Testament understanding, which is expressed in our hymns, makes the meaning of the Old Testament events even more profound. With what power did Moses divide the sea? — with the sign of the Cross. "Inscribing the invincible weapon of the Cross upon the waters, Moses marked a straight line before him with his staff and divided the Red Sea." Who led the Jews through the Red Sea? — Christ. Christ "hath thrown the horse and rider into the Red Sea,... and He hath saved Israel." The return of the sea to its former state after the Israelites had crossed was a prototype of the incorrupt purity of the Mother of God. "In the Red Sea there was once depicted an image of the Unwedded Bride..." (Dogmatic Theotokion, 5th Tone).

During the first and fifth weeks of Great Lent, we gather in church for the compunctionate and penitential canon of Saint Andrew of Crete. From the beginning of the Old Testament to the end, examples of righteousness and examples of transgressions pass before us in a long sequence, and then give place to New Testament ones; but only if we know the sacred history of the Old are we able to profit fully from the contents of the canon.

This is why a knowledge of Biblical history is necessary not only for adults; by giving our children lessons from the Old Testament we also prepare them to take part intelligently in the services, and understand them. But there are other, still more important reasons.

In the Saviour's preaching, and in the Apostles' writings, there are many references to people, events and texts from the Old Testament: to Moses, Elias, Jonah, to the testimony of the Prophet Isaiah, and so on.

In the Old Testament the *reasons* are given why salvation through the coming of the Son of God was essential for humanity.

Nor must we lose sight of the purely *moral edification* which the Old Testament contains. *The time would fail me*, writes the Apostle Paul, *to tell of Gideon, and of Barak, and of Sampson, and of Jephthae, of David also, and Samuel, and of the prophets: who through faith subdued kingdoms, wrought righteousness, obtained promises, stopped the mouths of lions, quenched the violence of fire, escaped the edge of the sword, out of weakness were made strong, waxed valiant in fight, turned to flight the armies of the aliens...of whom the world was not worthy: they wandered in deserts, and in mountains, and in dens and caves of the earth...*(Heb. 11:32–34, 38). We too can profit from this edification. The Church constantly places before our mind's eye the image of the Three Children in the Babylonian furnace.

Under the Church's Guidance and
Without the Church's Guidance

In the Church, everything is in its proper place. In the Church everything has its own tone and correct illumination. This applies as well to the Old Testament Scriptures. We know by heart the Ten Commandments that were given on Sinai, but we understand them far more profoundly than the Jews did, because for us they are illuminated and deepened by the Saviour's Sermon on the Mount. Much moral and ritual legislation passes before us throughout the Mosaic Law, but the words, *Thou shalt love the Lord thy God with all thy heart and with all thy soul and with all thy mind* and *Thou shalt love thy neighbor as thyself*, which are to be found amid the mass of Moses' other instructions, have *only through the Gospel* begun to shine for us with their full brilliance.

Neither the tabernacle, nor Solomon's temple exist any more; yet we study their construction because many symbols of the New Testament are contained in their ordinances. In church we hear readings from the prophets; but they are not offered to us so that we may know the fate of the peoples who surrounded Palestine, but because in these readings prophecies are made of Christ and the events of the Gospel.

But then it happened (in the 16th century, in Western Europe) that an enormous group of "Christians" who refused to be guided by ecclesiastical tradition (in over-reaction, of course, against the Roman distortion of the true Tradition), threw aside all the wealth of the Tradition of the ancient Church, deciding to keep, as the source and guide of faith, only the Holy Scriptures: the Bible in its two parts: the Old and the New Testaments. This is how Protestantism acted. Let us give it its due: it had become inflamed with thirst for the living word of God, it had come to love the Bible. But it did not learn that the Sacred Scriptures were collected by the Church and belong to the Church in her historical, apostolic succession. It did not take into account that the Church's Faith is illuminated by the Bible, just as, in its turn, the Bible is illuminated by the Church's Faith; one requires the other, each rests on the other. Left with the Holy Scriptures only, these "Christians" frenziedly began studying it, in the hope that, following its path closely, they would see this path so clearly that no longer would there be any cause for disagreements about faith. The Bible, three quarters of which, in terms of its overall volume, consists of the Old Testament, became a constant reference book. They investigated it in its minutest details, compared it with ancient Hebrew texts, counted how many times certain words are used in the Holy Scriptures. However, in doing this they began to lose a sense of proportion; they thought of the Old and New Testaments as two equivalent sources of the same Faith, as mutually supplementing each other, as two completely equal aspects of it. And with certain groups of Protestants, the predominance in quantity of the Old Testament and the fact that it occupies first place in order in the Bible gave rise to the view that the Old Testament also occupies first place in significance. Thus the Judaizing sects made their appearance. They began to place the monotheism (which they considered to be belief in simply one God) of the Old Testament higher than the New Testament monotheism with its divinely revealed truth of the one God in the Holy Trinity; the commandments given on Sinai became more important than the Gospel teaching; the Sabbath more important than Sunday, the day of the Resurrection.

Others, who may not have taken this Judaizing path, are yet unable to distinguish between the spirit of the Old Testament and that of the New, the spirit of slavery and the spirit of sonship, the spirit of the law and the spirit of freedom. Under the influence of certain passages of the Old Testament, they have rejected that fullness of worship which is expressed in the Christian Church in various forms of worship involving both the spirit and the body, they have rejected external methods of expressing it and, in particular, have disdained the symbol of Christianity — the Cross — and other sacred images, thereby bringing themselves under the Apostle's condemnation: *Thou that abhorrest idols, dost thou commit sacrilege?* (Rom. 2:22).

A third group of people (more humanistically oriented) confused either by the simplicity with which the ancient accounts are told, or by the severe character of antiquity (especially as it manifested itself in war), or by Hebrew ethnicism or by other features of the pre-Christian era, began to take a negative attitude towards these accounts, and then to the Bible itself in its entirety.

Even as it is impossible to eat bread alone without water, even though bread is essential for the organism, so it is impossible to be nourished spiritually by the Scriptures alone, without the refreshment of Grace provided by life in the Church. Protestant theological faculties, which purport to guard Christianity and its sources, and work on the study of the Bible, are, as it were, left with a bitter taste in their mouths. They were carried away with the critical analysis of scriptural texts, initially of the Old Testament, and later, of the New. As they gradually ceased to feel its spiritual power, they began to approach the sacred books like the ordinary documents of antiquity, using the methods and techniques of nineteenth century positivism. Some of these theologians sought to outdo each other in contriving theories for the origin of various books, contrary to the sacred tradition of antiquity. In order to explain instances of the foreknowledge of future events in the sacred books, they began to say that these books were, in fact, written at a later date, at the time of the actual events. The theories have changed, but the method itself has, for them, dealt a blow to the authority of Holy Scripture and the Christian Faith. It is true that simple Protestant believers ignored this so-called "Biblical criticism," and to a degree continue to do so.[1] But in so far as the pastors have attended modernist theological schools, they themselves not infrequently have been transmitters of this critical thought in their communities. The period of Biblical criticism is now on the wane, but this upheaval has led a large number of sects to the loss of dogmatic faith; they have begun to recognize only the moral teaching of the Gospel, forgetting that it is inseparable from its dogmatic doctrine.

It often happens that even good undertakings have their dark side.

Thus, the translation of the Bible into all contemporary languages was a great event in the field of Christian culture. We must admit that to a great degree this task has been fulfilled by Protestantism. However, it must also be admitted that it is more difficult to feel the breath of deep and sacred antiquity of the Old Testament Scriptures in our contemporary languages. When reading the Scriptures in these languages, not everyone will take into account the immense distance which separates the two epochs, the apostolic and our own, and hence, there arises an inability to understand and value the simplicity of the Biblical accounts. Not without reason some Jews carefully preserve the ancient Hebrew language of the Scriptures, and even avoid using a printed Bible for prayers and readings in the synagogues, but use manuscript copies of the Old Testament written on parchment.

Propagating the Bible over the face of the earth in editions of many millions was also certainly a great deed. But even here, has not the mass distribution made people take a less reverent attitude towards the Book of books?

What we have just said relates to activities within "Christendom." But to this were joined other circumstances from without. The Bible found itself face to face with scientific research: with geology, paleontology, archaeology. From beneath the earth appeared the world of the past, hitherto almost unknown. Contemporary science gave antiquity a span which extended back over an enormous number of millennia. The enemies of religion did not hesitate to use scientific data as evidence against the Bible,

---

1) But they have fallen into the other extreme of chiliastic fundamentalism, rejecting the metaphorical interpretations of the Holy Fathers.

which they placed on the judgement seat, saying to it in the words of Pilate: *Behold how many things they witness against Thee* (Mark 15:4).

Under these new conditions, we must confirm ourselves in a sure consciousness of the sanctity of the Bible, of its truth, of its value, of its exceptional nature and its grandeur, as the Book of books, the authentic record of mankind. Our task is to protect ourselves from confusion and doubts. It is chiefly the Holy Scriptures of the Old Testament which are contested by contemporary scientific theories. Therefore, let us approach the Old Testament more closely. Let us look into their very essence. As far as science is concerned, we may be quite sure that objective, unprejudiced, authentic science will always testify in its conclusions to the truth of the Bible. Saint John of Kronstadt advises:

> When you doubt in the truth of any person or any event described in Holy Scripture, then remember that *all Scripture is given by inspiration of God* (II Tim. 3:16), as the Apostle says, and is therefore true, and does not contain any imaginary persons, fables, and tales, although it includes parables which everyone can see are not actual narratives, but are written in figurative language. The whole of the Word of God is one, entire, indivisible truth; and if you assert that any narrative, sentence or word is untrue, then you sin against the truth of the whole of Holy Scripture and its primordial Truth, which is God Himself.
>
> —*My Life in Christ*, Saint John of Kronstadt, p. 70.

The Divine Inspiration of the Scriptures

We usually qualify "Scripture" with the word "sacred" (in Greek: ἱερός, ἱερά). "Sacred" means "sanctified," "having Grace in itself," "reflecting the wafting of the Holy Spirit." Only to the Gospels is the word "holy" always applied (in Greek: ἅγιος, αγία, ἅγιον), and, before the reading of the Gospel, we are called upon to pray that we will be worthy to hear it: "And that we may be vouchsafed to hear the Holy Gospel let us ask of the Lord God"; and we are obliged to listen to it standing: "Wisdom; aright; let us hear the Holy Gospel," while when listening to the Old Testament readings, the parables, the Orthodox Church allows us to sit. Even while the Psalms are being read, not so much as prayers, but rather offered for meditation, for edification, as for example, the kathismas at Matins, we are allowed to sit. Thus in relation to the sacred books we can also say, in the word of the Apostle Paul, that *one star differeth from another star in glory* (I Cor. 15:41). All of Scripture is divinely inspired, but its very subject matter elevates some books above others; there, the Israelites and the Old Testament law; here (in the New Testament) Christ the Saviour and His divine teaching. What constitutes the divinely inspired nature of Scripture? The sacred authors were invested or guided by that which, in supreme spiritual moments, becomes illumination and God's direct revelation. Concerning this latter state, they usually say of themselves, "I received revelation from the Lord," as we read in the prophets and in the Apostles Paul and John in the New Testament.[2] Together with all this, however, the writers use the usual means of acquiring knowledge. Thus, for information about the past, they turn to oral tradition. *Even those things that we have heard and have known and which our fathers have told us; they were not hid from their children, in another generation. They declared the praises of the Lord and His mighty acts and His wonders...*(Ps. 43:1). *O God, with our ears have we heard, for our fathers have told us the work which Thou hadst wrought in their days, in the days of old...*(Ps. 77:2-3). The Apostle Luke, who was not one of the twelve Apostles, describes the Gospel events as one *having had perfect understanding of all things from the very first* (Luke 1:3). The sacred authors use written documents, censuses of people, family genealogies; they state accounts with indications of building expenses, quantities of material, weights, prices, etc. In the historical books of the Old Testament, we find references to other books as sources; for example, in the books of Kings and Chronicles, *And the rest of the acts of Ahaziah which he did, behold, are they not written in the book of the chronicles of the kings of Israel? And the rest of the words of Joatham, and all that he did, behold, are not these written in the book of the chronicles of the kings of Judah?* (II Kings 1:18; 15:36; II Chron. 12:15; 13:22 and other places). Original documents are also quoted: the first book of Esdras reproduces word for word a whole series of orders and reports con-

2) According to Saint Andrew of Caesarea (in his commentary on Revelation), revelations occur during the illumination of the mind, either in visions sent by God in sleep, or in the waking state by means of divine illumination (Bp. Dimitry: *The Book of Revelation From a Twentieth Century Perspective*, Harbin, 1935, p. 11).

nected with the restoration of the Temple at Jerusalem. We must not think that the sacred authors were omniscient. That quality is not given even to the angels; it belongs to God alone. But these writers were holy. *The children of Israel could not steadfastly behold the face of Moses for the glory of his countenance* (II Cor. 3:7), recalls Saint Paul. This sanctity of the writers, their purity of mind, and heart, their consciousness of the loftiness of their calling and of their responsibility for fulfilling it, were directly expressed in their writings: in the sanctity, purity and righteousness of their thoughts, in the truth of their words, in the clear distinction of the true from the false. They began their records with inspiration from above and being thus inspired, they completed them. At certain moments, their spirit was enlightened by special Grace filled revelations from on high and by mystical insight into the past, as with the Prophet Moses in the book of Genesis, or into the future, as with the later prophets and Christ's Apostles. It is natural for us to imagine a vision as in a mist, like seeing behind a curtain for a moment. *Now we see through a glass darkly; but then* [in the age to come we shall see] *face to face* (I Cor. 13:15), testifies Saint Paul. Whether the attention is directed towards the past or the future, no account of time is made in this vision; the prophets see "things that are afar off as if they were near." This is why the Evangelists depict two future events, foretold by the Lord, the destruction of Jerusalem and the end of the world in such a way that they almost merge into one future perspective. *It is not for you to know the times or the seasons, which the Father hath put in His own authority* (Acts 1:7), said the Lord.

Divine inspiration belongs not only to Holy Scripture. As we know, the Holy Orthodox Church recognizes Holy Tradition as a source of faith equal to Holy Scripture. For Tradition, which expresses the voice of the whole Church, is also the voice of the Holy Spirit living in the Church. All our church services are also divinely inspired, as the Holy Church sings, "Let us worthily honor the witnesses of truth and heralds of piety in divinely inspired hymns (Kontakion to Sts. Zenobius and Zenobia, Oct. 30); and in particular, the Liturgy of the Holy Mysteries is called by the more elevated name of "Divine Liturgy," since it is divinely inspired.

The Grandeur of the Account of the Creation of the World

Let us open the book of Genesis. The first place in it is occupied by the origin of the world.

Moses, the seer of God, speaks briefly about the creation of the world. His account occupies about one page of the Bible. But at the same time he took in everything with a single glance. This brevity displays profound wisdom, for what loquacity could embrace the greatness of God's work? In essence this page is an entire book, which required great spiritual stature on the part of the sacred author and enlightenment from above. It is not without reason that Moses concludes his account of the creation as if he were concluding a large and long work: *This is the book of the generations of the heavens and the earth, when they were made, in the day in which the Lord God made the heavens and the earth* (Gen. 2:4).

This was a mighty task — to speak of how the world and all that is in the world came to be. A large enterprise in the realm of thought requires a correspondingly large store of means of expression, a technical and philosophical vocabulary. But what did Moses have? At his disposal was an almost primitive language, the entire vocabulary of which numbered only several hundred words. This language had almost none of those abstract concepts which now make it much easier for us to express our thoughts. The thinking of antiquity is almost entirely expressed in images, and all its words denote what the eyes and ears perceive of the visible world. Because of this, Moses uses the words of his time with care, so as not to immerse the idea of God in the crudeness of purely earthly perceptions. He has to say "God made," "God took," "God saw," "God said," and even — "God walked"; but the first words of Genesis, *In the beginning God made*, and then, *The Spirit of God moved over the water*, already speak clearly of God as a spirit, and consequently of the metaphorical nature of the anthropomorphic expressions we quoted above. In a later book, the Psalter, when the metaphorical nature of such expressions about the Spirit became generally understood, we encounter many more such expressions, and ones which are more vivid. In it we read about God's face, about the hands, eyes, steps, shoulders of God, of God's belly. *Take hold of weapon and shield, and arise unto my help* (Ps. 34:2), the psalmist appeals to God. In his homilies on the book of Genesis, commenting on the words, *And they heard the voice of the Lord God walking in the garden in the afternoon*, Saint John Chrysostom says:

> Let us not, beloved, inattentively pass over what is said by Divine Scripture, and let us not stumble over the words, but

reflect that such simple words are used because of our infirmity, and everything is accomplished fittingly for our salvation. Indeed, tell me, if we wish to accept the words in their literal meaning, and will not understand what we are told at the very beginning of the present reading. *And they heard*, it is said, *the voice of the Lord God walking in the garden in the afternoon.* What are you saying? God walks? Surely we are not ascribing feet to Him? And shall we not understand anything higher by this? No, God does not walk — quite the contrary! How, in fact, can He Who is everywhere and fills all things, Whose throne is heaven and the earth His footstool, really walk in paradise? What foolish man will say this? What then does it mean, *They heard the voice of the Lord God walking in the garden in the afternoon?* He wanted to awaken in them such a feeling (of His nearness), that it would cast them into anxiety, which is what actually happened: they felt this, trying to hide themselves from God Who was approaching them. Sin happened — and the crime — and shame fell upon them. The impartial judge, the conscience, rose up, cried out with a loud voice, reproached them, exposed them and, as it were, exhibited before their eyes, the seriousness of the crimes. In the beginning, the Master created man and placed the conscience in him, as an inexorable accuser, which cannot be deceived or flattered...[3]

In our era of geological and paleontological research and discoveries, the world of the past is depicted on an immeasurably vast time scale; the appearance of humanity itself is ascribed to immensely distant millennia. In questions of the origin and development of the world, science follows

---

3) Chrysostom, *Homilies on the Book of Genesis* (Vol. 4, pt. 1, p. 138). In the same place, in connection with the words *God formed the man of dust of the earth, and breathed...*, we read, "These words require the eyes of faith, and are spoken thus out of great condescension to our infirmity because the very expression "*God formed*" (in Greek: ἔπλασεν — as a sculptor forms a statue) *the man and breathed* are unworthy of God. But the Divine Scripture recounts this in this way for our sake and our infirmity, condescending to us, so that we, having become worthy of such condescension, should be able to ascend to the heights (of true understanding)" (Loc. cit., p. 98).

Here it is appropriate to take note of Chrysostom's warning as to how the words *and breathed upon his face the breath of life* should be understood. He says: "Certain foolish

its own path, but it is not essential for us to make efforts to bring the Biblical account into congruence and harmony in all points with the voice of contemporary science. We have no need to plunge ourselves into geology and paleontology to support the Biblical account. In principle we are convinced that the words of the Bible and scientific data will not prove to be in contradiction, even if at any given time their agreement in one respect or another is still not clear to us. In some cases scientific data can show us how we should understand the facts in the Bible. In some respects these two fields are not comparable; they have different purposes, to the extent that they have contrasting points of view from which they see the world.

Moses' task was not the study of the physical world. However, we agree in recognizing and honoring Moses for giving mankind the first elementary natural history; for being the first person in the world to give the history of early humanity; and, finally, for giving a beginning to the history of nations in the book of Genesis. All this only emphasizes his greatness. He presents the creation of the world and its history, in the small space of a single page of the Bible; hence it is already clear, from this brevity, why he does not draw the thread of the world's history through the deep abyss of the past, but rather presents it simply as one general picture. Moses' immediate aim in the account of the creation was to instill basic religious truths into his people and, through them, into other peoples.

The principal truth is that God is the one spiritual Being independent of the world. This truth was preserved in that branch of humanity which the fifth and sixth chapters of the book of Genesis call the "sons of God," and from them faith in the one God was passed on to Abraham and his descendants. By the time of Moses, the other peoples had already lost this truth for some time. It was even becoming darkened among the Hebrew people, surrounded as they were by polytheistic nations, and threatened to die out during their captivity in Egypt. For Moses himself the greatness of

---

people, carried away by their own considerations and not thinking about anything in a way that is fitting to God, do not take into account the fact that the expressions of Scripture are adapted (to our understanding), and dare to say that the soul proceeded from the essence of God. O madness! O folly! How many paths of perdition the devil has opened to those who wish to serve him! And in order to understand this, look how these people proceed down contrary paths! Seizing on the expression 'breathed,' some of them say that the soul proceeds from the essence of God; others, on the contrary, assert that it is changed into the essence of even the very lowest of the dumb beasts. What can be worse than such folly?" (*Loc. cit.*, p. 103).

the one, divine Spirit was revealed by the unconsumed, burning bush in the wilderness. He asked in perplexity: *Behold, I shall go forth to the children of Israel, and shall say to them, "The God of our fathers has sent me to you"; and they will ask of me, "What is His name?" What shall I say to them? Then, Moses heard a mystical voice give the name of the very essence of God: And God spoke to Moses, saying, I am the Being. Thus shall ye say to the children of Israel, the Being has sent me to you* (Ex. 3:13–14). Such is the lofty conception of God that Moses is expounding in the first words of the book of Genesis: *In the beginning God made the heaven and the earth.* Even when nothing material existed, there was the one Spirit, God, Who transcends time, transcends space, Whose existence is not limited to heaven, since heaven was made together with time and the earth. In the first line of the book of Genesis the name of God is given without any definitions or limitations: for the only thing that can be said about God is that He is, that He is the one, true, eternal Being, the Source of all being, He is the Being.

A series of other truths about God, the world, and man, are bound up with this truth and follow directly from the account of the creation. These are:

- God did not separate a part of Himself, was in no way diminished, nor was He augmented in creating the world.
- God created the world of His free will, and was not compelled by any necessity.
- The world does not, of itself, have a divine nature; it is neither the offspring of the Deity, nor part of Him, nor the body of the Deity.
- The world manifests the wisdom, power, and goodness of God.
- The world which is visible to us was formed gradually, in order, from the lower to the higher and more perfect.
- In the created world "everything was very good"; the world in its entirety is harmonious, excellent, wisely and bountifully ordered.
- Man is an earthly being, made from earth, and appointed to be the crown of earthly creation.
- Man is made after the image and likeness of God, and bears in himself the breath of life from God.

From these truths the logical conclusion follows that man is obliged to strive towards moral purity and excellence, so as not to deface and lose the image of God in himself, that he might be worthy to stand at the head of earthly creation.

Of course, the revelation about the creation of the world supplanted in the minds of the Hebrews all the tales they had heard from the peoples surrounding them. These fables told of imaginary gods and goddesses, who a) are themselves dependent on the existence of the world and are in essence, impotent, b) who are replete with weaknesses, passions and enmity, bringing and spreading evil, and therefore, c) even if they did exist would be incapable of elevating mankind ethically. The history of the creation of the world, which has its own independent value as a divinely revealed truth, deals, as we see, a blow to the pagan, polytheistic, mythological religions.

The Old Testament concept of God is expressed with vivid imagery in the book of the Wisdom of Solomon: *For the whole world before Thee is as a little grain in the balance, yea, as a drop of the morning dew that falleth down upon the earth!* (Wis. 11:23). The book of Genesis confesses pure, unadulterated monotheism. Yet Christianity brings out a higher truth in the Old Testament accounts: the truth of the unity of God in a Trinity of Persons. We read: *Let us make man according to our image*; *Adam is become as one of us*; and later, God appeared to Abraham in the form of three strangers.

Such is the significance of this short account. If the whole book of Genesis consisted only of the first page of the account of the world and mankind, it would still be a great work, a magnificent expression of God's revelation, of the divine illumination of human thought.

The Dawn of Humanity, According to the Bible

The second and third chapters of the book of Genesis unfold a new theme; we can say that they begin a new book: the history of mankind. It is understandable why Moses speaks twice about the creation of man. It was necessary for him to speak of man in the first chapter as the crown of creation, in the general picture of the creation of the world. Now, after concluding the first theme: *And the heavens and the earth were finished, and the whole world of them* — it is natural that he should begin the history of humanity by speaking again of the creation of the first man and of how woman was made for him. These are the contents of the second chapter, which also describes their life in Eden, in paradise. The third chapter tells of their fall into sin and their loss of paradise. In these accounts, together with the literal meaning, there is a symbolic meaning and we are not in a position to indicate where precisely events are related in their natural, literal sense, and where they are expressed figuratively, we are not in a position to separate the symbol from the simple fact. We only know that, in one form or another, we are being told of events of the most profound significance.

A symbol is a relative means of expression, which is convenient in that it is pictorial, and therefore makes an impression on the soul. It does not require great verbal means to express a thought. At the same time, it leaves a strong impression of the given concept. A symbol gives one the possibility of penetrating more deeply into the meaning of the thought. Thus, in quoting the Psalmic text, *Thy hands have made me*, Saint John of Kronstadt accompanies it with the remark: "Thy hands are the Son and the Spirit." The word "hands" in relation to God suggests to him the idea of the Most-holy Trinity (*My Life in Christ*). We read similar words in Saint Irenaeus of Lyons: "The Son and the Holy Spirit are, as it were, the hands of the Father" (*Against Heresies*, Bk. 5, Ch. 6).

It is essential to make a strict distinction between Biblical symbol and imagery, with the special meaning which is hidden within it, and the concept of myth. In the Bible there is no mythology. Mythology belongs to polytheism, which personifies as gods the phenomena of nature and has created fantastic tales on this basis. We are justified in saying that the book of Genesis is a "de-mythologizing" of ancient notions, the unmasking of mythology, that it was directed against myths.

It might be said that one can also see symbolism in mythology. This is true. But the difference here is that the truth — often deeply mysterious — lies behind Moses' figurative expressions; but mythological stories present fiction inspired by the phenomena of nature. These are symbols of the truth; the others are symbols of arbitrary fantasy. For an Orthodox Christian this is similar to the difference between an icon and an idol: the icon is the depiction of a real being, whereas an idol is a depiction of a fictitious creation of the mind.

The symbolic element is felt most strongly where there is the greatest need to reveal an essential point. Such, for example, is the account of the creation of the woman from Adam's rib. Saint John Chrysostom teaches us:

> And He took, it says, one of his ribs. Do not understand these words in a human way, but know that crude expressions are used in adaptation to human infirmity. Indeed, if Scripture did not use these words, then how could we come to know the ineffable mysteries? Let us not, then, dwell only on the words, but let us take everything in an appropriate way, as relating to God. This expression 'took' and all similar expressions are used on account of our infirmity (*loc. cit.*, pp. 120–1).

The moral conclusion of this story is comprehensible to us. Saint Paul points it out: woman is called to be in submission to man. *The head of the woman is the man; the head of every man is Christ…; for the man is not of the woman, but the woman of the man* (I Cor. II:3,8). But why did Moses speak specifically of the manner in which woman was created? He undoubtedly had the intention of protecting the minds of the Hebrews from the fictions of mythology and, in particular, from the mythology of ancient Mesopotamia, the homeland of their ancestors. These sordid and morally corrupting tales tell of how the world of gods, the world of man and the world of animals are in some way merged together: goddesses and gods form unions with men and animals. We find a hint of this in the depictions of lions and bulls with human heads, which are so widespread in Chaldeo-Mesopotamian and Egyptian art.[4] The Biblical account of the creation of woman supports the concept that the human race has its own, absolutely unique, independent origin and keeps its physical nature pure and distinct from the beings of the supernatural world, and from the lower realm of animals. That this is so is evident from the preceding verses of the account: *And the Lord God said, It is not good that the man should be alone; let us make for him a help suitable for him* (Gen. 2:18). And He brought all

---

4) According to the myths of ancient pagan Mesopotamia, the principal goddess Anaph is herself the "Ancestress of men." She turned into a cow and gave birth to a bull, which was sired by Zeus (W.F. Albright, *Archaeology and the Religion of Israel*, Baltimore, 1942, pp. 75, 85).

the wild beasts to Adam, and Adam gave them names, *but for Adam there was not found a helpmate like to himself* (Gen. 2:21). Then it was that God put a trance upon Adam and made him a wife out of one of his ribs.

Thus, after the truth of the unity of God, the truth of the unity, independence, and distinctness of the human race is confirmed. It is with these two basic truths that Saint Paul begins his sermon on the Areopagus in Athens: God is one, *and He hath made of one blood all nations of men for to dwell on all the face of the earth* (Acts 17:26). The account of the creation of man and of the origin of the human race which is given in the book of Genesis deals just such a blow to polytheistic, mythological concepts, as did the story of the creation of the world.

The first people lived in paradise, in Eden, that most beautiful garden. The dawn of humanity is illumined by rays of the Sun of Grace in Moses' account. Now, under the influence of some cave discoveries, early man is usually depicted for us in the gloom of a cave, so as to make a repugnant impression with his animal-like shape, with a protruding lower jaw, with a threatening or frightened expression in his eyes, with a cudgel in his hand, hunting for raw meat. However, the Bible tells us that, although man was in a childlike state in the spiritual sense, he was still a noble creature of God from the beginning of his existence; that from the beginning, his countenance was not dark, not gloomy, but radiant and pure. He was always intellectually superior to other creatures. The gift of speech gave him the opportunity to develop his spiritual nature further. The riches of the vegetable kingdom presented him with an abundance of food. Life in this most beneficent climate did not require much labor. Moral purity gave him inner peace. The process of development could have taken on a higher form, one which is unknown to us.

In the animal world, although it stands lower than man, we observe many noble-featured, harmoniously built species in the kingdoms of four-legged animals and birds which express beauty and grace in their external features. We observe so many gentle animals, prepared to show attachment and trust and, what is more important, to serve in almost a disinterested way. There is also much harmony and beauty before us in the plant world and, one could say, the plants compete to be of service with their fruits. Why then is it necessary to conceive of early man alone as deprived of all the attractive and beautiful features with which the animal and plant kingdoms are endowed?

The Fall into Sin

Man's blessedness and his nearness to God are inseparable, "God is my protection and defense: whom shall I fear?" (cf. Pss. 26:1, 31:7).

God "walked in paradise," so close was He to Adam and Eve. But in order to sense the beatitude of God's nearness and to be aware that one is under God's protection, it is necessary to have a clear conscience. When we lose it, we lose this awareness. The first people sinned and then they straightway hid from God. *Adam, where art thou? — I heard Thy voice, as Thou walkedst in the garden, and I feared, because I am naked, and hid myself.*

The Word of God tells us that God is omnipresent, and He is always near. The awareness of this nearness is dimmed only because of man's corruption. However, it does not become extinguished completely. Throughout all the ages, it has lived and continues to live in holy people. It is said of Moses that God spoke with him face to face, as a man would speak with his friend (cf. Deut. 34:10). *Near art Thou, O Lord*, we read in the psalms (Pss. 118:151; 144:12). "My soul lives in God as a fish lives in water or a bird in the air, immersed in Him on all sides and at all times; living in Him, moving in Him, at rest in Him, finding in Him breathing room," writes Saint John of Kronstadt. In another place he reasons: "What is the meaning of the appearance of the three strangers to Abraham? It means that the Lord, in three Persons, continually, as it were, travels over the earth, and watches over everything that is done on it; and that He Himself comes to those of His servants who are watchful and attentive to themselves and their salvation, and who seek Him, sojourning with them and conversing with them as with His friends (*We will come unto him, and make Our abode with him* — John 14:23); while He sends fire upon the ungodly" (*My Life in Christ*).

This closeness was lost, and so was blessedness. Blessedness was lost and suffering appeared. Moses' account of the fall into sin is essentially the same as the Lord's parable about the Prodigal Son. He left the father, hid himself from him, that he might be satiated with the sweetness of a free life. But instead of pleasure, he was rewarded with husks, which were used to feed animals, and these not to satiety. It was the same with our forefathers; their fall was followed by grief and sufferings. *I will greatly multiply thy pains and thy groanings; in pain thou shalt bring forth children... In pain..., in the sweat of thy face shalt thou eat thy bread, until thou return to the earth, out of which thou wast taken...*

Eating the forbidden fruit, it would seem, was such a minor offense. Could it really have such consequences or bring such a punishment? But everything in life has its beginning; great things arise from insignificant, small ones. An avalanche in the mountains begins from a slight tremor. The Volga originates from a little spring, and the broad Hudson from the "tear clouds" which are lost in the mountains.

Simple observation tells us that there is a connection between vices and suffering, that they lead to suffering and that man thus punishes himself. If death and many of the hardships of life constitute a chastisement from God, still it must be recognized that the majority of man's sufferings are created by humanity itself. This applies to savage wars, accompanied with the terribly inhuman treatment of the vanquished. Wars, in fact, constitute the entire history of humanity. It also applies to those types of suffering inflicted by man on man, which have accompanied the peaceful periods of history: slavery, the yokes of foreign invaders, and the various kinds of violence, which are caused not only by greed and egoism, but also by a kind of demonic passion for cruelty and brutality. In a word, all this is expressed in the old proverb: man's worst enemy is man.

Would man have enjoyed complete blessedness on earth if the fall had not occurred? Would he be free from worries, annoyances, sadness, accidents? Apparently the Bible does not speak of such tranquility in life. Where there is light, there is also shadow; where there is joy, there must also be sorrow. But what sorrows can last long, if the Lord is near?... if He commands His angels to protect His supreme creatures, those who bear His image and likeness in themselves? The Church teaches that man in paradise was created for immortality, not only that of the soul, but also of the body. Yet even if he were not eternal in his earthly body, what woe could there be if he perceived his immortality with all the powers of his soul? If he knew and felt that a transformation into a yet higher form of life awaits him?

The Problem of Evil

Now we have touched upon one of the very broadest questions, that of the general problem of suffering in the world which is so very difficult for religious philosophy to explain. Why is the law of the constant renovation of life, the beneficent law of the life of the world, conjoined with suffering? Is it inevitable that creatures should mutually destroy each other? That some should be eaten by others to support their own life? That the weak should be in fear of the strong, and brute force should triumph in the animal kingdom? Is the struggle of one creature with another an eternal condition of life?

The Bible does not give a direct answer to our questions. However, we do find indirect indications of a solution. Here is what is said about the first law of nourishment which God gave His creatures. God appoints the seeds of plants and the fruit of trees as food for man. Only after the flood does he also make meat lawful for him. For animals, God declares: *And to all the wild beasts of the earth, and to all the fowls of heaven, and to every reptile creeping on the earth, which has in itself the breath of life,* [I have given] *every green plant for food; and it was so* (Gen. 1:30).

But the fall occurred. Before the flood, the human race had become corrupt. This corruption also touched the world of earthly creatures: *And the Lord God saw the earth, and it was corrupted; because all flesh had corrupted His way upon the earth* (Gen. 6:13). The law of concord gave way to the law of struggle. And Saint Paul writes: *For the earnest expectation of creation awaiteth the manifestation of the sons of God. For creation was made subject to vanity, not willingly, but by reason of Him Who hath subjected the same in hope, because creation itself also shall be delivered from the bondage of corruption into the glorious freedom of the children of God. For we know that the whole creation groaneth and travaileth in pain together until now. And not they only, but ourselves also, who have the first fruits of the Spirit, even we ourselves groan within ourselves, waiting for adoption, to wit, the redemption of our body* (Rom. 8:19–23). This means that the groaning of creation is not eternal; obviously then, neither is the law of conflict, the right of the strongest. And is it, indeed, indisputably a law of life? Do we not observe that the ferocious, bloodthirsty, and formidably strong representatives of the animal world disappear more quickly from the face of the earth than the apparently defenseless, gentle creatures, which continue to live and multiply? Is this not an oblique indication to humanity itself not to rely on the principles of force? The holy Prophet Isaiah speaks of the temporary nature of the principle, when he prophesies about the time (of course not in this sinful world) when *the wolf shall dwell with the lamb, and the leopard shall lie down together with the kid* (Is. 11:6).

The account of the origin of evil in the world, of moral evil, and physical and spiritual sufferings, is given in the third chapter of the book of Genesis, and constitutes a new, third blow against pagan mythology. According to the mythological tales, the gods experienced passions and vices and the sufferings which resulted; conflicts, treachery and murders take place among them. Then there are religions which postulate that there is a god of good and a god of evil; but one way or the other, evil is thus primordial. Hence, suffering is a normal condition of life, and there is no path to genuine moral perfection. This is not what the Bible tells us. *God did not create or cause evil.* What was created was "very good" by nature. Sin came into the world through temptation; that is why it is called "sin," i.e., a missing of the mark, losing of the way, a deviation of the will to the wrong side. After sin came suffering.

The author of the Wisdom of Solomon says: *For God made not death: neither hath He pleasure in the destruction of the living. For He created all things that they might have their being; and the generations of the world were healthful, and there is no poison of destruction in them, nor the kingdom of Hades upon the earth... For God created man for incorruption, and made him to be the image of His own eternity. But through the envy of the devil, came death into the world; and they that are of His portion experience it* (Wis. 1:13–14; 2:23–24).

But the moral law is not destroyed by man's fall. It continues to shine, the distinction between good and evil is not lost. Man retains the possibility of returning to his lost riches. The path to it lies through that grief which leads to moral purification and rebirth, through the sorrow of repentance, which is depicted at the end of the third chapter of Genesis, in the account of the expulsion from Paradise. From the last verses of the third chapter of Genesis, we begin to see the radiant horizon of the New Testament far in the distance, the dawn of the salvation of the human race from moral evil and, at the same time, from suffering and death, through the appearance of the Redeemer of the world.

Thus, the story of the fall into sin is of exceptional importance for understanding the entire history of humanity, and is directly connected with the New Testament. A direct parallel arises between the two events: Adam's fall into sin and the coming of the Son of God on earth. This is always present in Christian thought, in general and particular terms. Christ is called the Second Adam; the tree of the Cross is contrasted with the tree of the fall. Christ's very temptations from the devil in the desert recall, to a certain extent, the temptations of the serpent: there it was "taste of the fruit" and "ye shall be as gods"; here, *If thou be the Son of God, command that these stones be made bread.* The Church Fathers prefer a direct, literal understanding of the story of the fall into sin. However, even here the real element, the element of the direct meaning, is so closely intertwined with the hidden, spiritual sense, that there is no possibility of separating them. Such, for example, are the mystical names "tree of life" and "tree of the knowledge of good and evil." The Church, rejoicing in her salvation in Christ, turns her gaze towards the same "Paradise of old," and she sees the Cherubim, who were placed at the gates of Paradise when Adam was expelled, now no longer guarding the tree of life, and the flaming sword no longer hindering our entry into Paradise. After repenting on the cross, the thief hears the words of the Crucified Christ: *Today thou shalt be with Me in Paradise.*

Biblical History and Archaeology

The book of Genesis speaks extremely briefly about the initial period of the life of humanity. After the story of Cain and Abel, the period before the flood is limited almost to a genealogy, to names alone. Calculating the number of years the antediluvian patriarchs lived, we count a span of approximately 1600 years.[5]

Thus, the history of many centuries occupies only a single chapter — the fourth of Genesis. Hence we see how Moses protects his account from arbitrary, popular, or mythological tales. As a source for his genealogies, Moses undoubtedly had very ancient and, of course, very brief lists, whose place of origin was Mesopotamia. From the beginning of its existence, mankind preserved its history as the apple of its eye. Families preserved the memory of their ancestors. But the whole history could express itself only in one thing, in the recording of names and length of life. In contemporary excavations in Mesopotamia, cuneiform fragments are being discovered which go back to the third millennium before Jesus Christ,

---

5) The longevity of the patriarchs causes perplexity in some people. We will not enter into an examination of this question but will permit ourselves to point out a certain analogy. We usually determine the age of trees in tens of years and speak with respect of oaks a hundred years old. However, in western North America, there are whole forests of living trees which are reckoned to be as much as five thousand years old!

which means several hundred years before Abraham. In addition to these records, antiquity tried to preserve from generation to generation the memory of its greatest ancestors, the heads of families, and built tombs and similar monuments in their memory. After a detailed account of the flood, the book of Genesis again returns to its genealogical history, again embracing almost two thousand years, and again it is just as laconic. It just as strictly follows data from sources — unknown to us — in enumerating the heads of generations until Abraham. These records are interrupted by two accounts: that of the flood and Noah and his sons, and that of the building of the tower of Babel and the dispersion of the nations.

If Moses paused to give details of the event of the flood, then obviously he had grounds for it. The principal basis was a direct tradition about the flood among the Hebrew people of that time. They took the account into Egypt and preserved it amongst themselves, while in the monuments of the ancient Egyptians it has not been preserved; evidently they had lost it. Then it comes to light with a mythological coloring in Mesopotamian (Sumerian, not Hebrew) written monuments (from the library of Assurbanipal). This concord about the basic fact clearly demonstrates that the memory of this event was still alive in Mesopotamia. Taking into account the spirit of the language of antiquity, we can assert that Moses uses the expressions in the text of the Bible "all the earth," "all types of animals," in the sense in which they were customarily then understood, at the time when the concept of "the world" was limited to the region in which one lived, when that which was before one's eyes was taken to be everything. We can, therefore, take the words "all," "everyone" in a relative sense. Even in the time of the Roman Empire and early Christianity, the word "universe" referred to that part of the earth's surface which had been explored and was known to the ancients. However, this is only one of many possible explanations regarding the question of the flood.[6]

Moses' account of the flood is subject to three basic tenets, which, in general, are expounded throughout the whole Bible: a) that the world is

---

6) Christian thought again sees here a mystical parallel between the account of the book of Genesis and the Gospel. In the beginning of Genesis, there is depicted the flood which drowned sinful humanity. In the first pages of the Gospel, we have the Lord's Baptism in the Jordan, which drowned man's sin and guilt. We hear concerning this in the services for the Feast of Theophany: "We know that, in the beginning, Thou didst bring upon the world the all-ruining flood, unto the lamentable destruction of all things, O

subject to God's will, b) that national disasters are a chastisement for man's impiety, and c) that one tribe (and subsequently — nation) was chosen to preserve the true faith.

The account of the original unity of language, of the building of the tower of Babel and the dispersal of peoples is another detail amid the short scheme of genealogies. The existence of the tower of Babel is confirmed by contemporary archaeology.[7]

When it reaches the time of Abraham, the book of Genesis begins a continuous historical account. From this point, the history of the Hebrew people begins. It continues to the end of Genesis, then into the other four books of the Pentateuch, and then into the cycle of the historical books of the Old Testament, and in part, into the books of the prophets. It then proceeds without interruption, until, at the end, it draws near New Testament times.

Archaeology provides rich material parallel to the biblical history which begins in Abraham's time. A few decades ago, liberal biblical criticism formulated a theory that the book of Genesis constitutes a collection of pious legends. Now however, archaeological science takes Genesis under serious consideration as one discovery after another confirms the biblical accounts. They prove the great antiquity of names and customs referred to by Moses, like the names of Abraham himself (Abram-ram)

God Who revealest wonders most great and strange. And now, O Christ, Thou hast drowned sin in the waters unto the comfort and salvation of mortal men" (Second Canon, Ode 7). The divinely-inspired writer of the book of Genesis, as it were, foresaw this future parallel, and the importance of the account of the flood because of its significance as a prefiguring.

At first glance, building an ark of such large proportions several decades before the flood, in accordance with God's revelation given to Noah alone, seems to be too unusual and complex a matter for that age. However, we can propose a hypothesis about the conditions which will solve the enigma.

There is no doubt that the technology for such a wooden construction and the essential tools were already available. The topographical conditions were also favorable. The Tigris and Euphrates valleys were subject to periodic floods, like the valley of the lower Nile in Egypt. After the flood, the ground dried out, presenting superb grazing land for animals, and was extremely fertile when cultivated (Herodotus, in the VIIth century B.C., speaks of the amazing fertility of the region). The population engaged in cattle-raising and primitive agriculture in these water meadows (in their depictions, we see ploughs harnessed to small antelopes), had to adapt themselves to local conditions. It is very natural to suppose that, in places like these, they knew how to build their houses not fastened to the ground but on tar-coated floats, like rafts, which could also be used

and Jacob (Iakov-El), which are encountered as personal names in ancient Mesopotamia. There is a connection between the names of Abraham's ancestors and relatives and the names of towns, since towns were named after their founders. These names, in turn, passed from the towns to the people who came from them. Thus, in the names of towns, the following names have been found: Tharrha (Abraham's father), Seruch (Tharrha's uncle), Phaleg (one of their ancestors), Nachor, Arrhan (Abraham's brothers — Charrhan was the region of Mesopotamia from which they came). In observing the morals and customs of that time, the so-called "tables of Nusa," which were found in Mesopotamia, throw some light on such facts as Abraham's intention to adopt his "home-born servant" Eliezer before Isaac was born, Esau's sale of his birthright, the Patriarch's blessings before death, and the story of the Teraphim (the idols which Rachel brought from the house of her father Laban) (Wright, *op. cit.*, p. 41–3). Of course, later periods give more archaeological material. If there are difficulties in making some details agree, this is natural. The title of one book in German on this subject, *In Spite of All, the Bible Is Still True*, expresses our general conclusion, as does the remark of one of the American biblical archaeologists: "There is no doubt now that archaeology confirms the essentially historical nature of the Old Testament tradition" (Albright, p. 176).

---

to store supplies of food for livestock and even for the animals themselves during the floods. We should take into account that, in that region, waterways, rivers and canals were the principal means of transport; in the drawings of this epoch, sea and river animals occupy a principal place (S. P. Handcock, *Mesopotamian Archaeology*, NY, 1912, pp. 4, 11, 14-7, 27, 46 and 53).

We can suppose that these floats served as a prototype for the construction of the ark built by Patriarch Noah and his sons at the Lord's command. Water and the dug-out canoe were, generally speaking, the first means of transport that man had over considerable distances.

Here is an interesting comparison. Who would have thought that a large ship or barge could be preserved in one of the pharaoh's tombs, as was discovered several years ago? This burial practice shows that he was frequently on the royal barge, and this was a favorite place, since the channels of the Nile among the reeds provided excellent conditions for hunting, a special privilege reserved for pharaoh's court. As we have already remarked, Egypt and Mesopotamia are similar in their topological condition (G.E. Wright, *Biblical Archaeology*, Philadelphia, 1957, p. 45).

7) The "ziggurat," the Tower of Babel, was built around the twenty-fourth century B.C. and was destroyed by the Hittites between 1800 and 1600 B.C.

The historical books of the Old Testament, like the Pentateuch of Moses, propound the concept of the causal relationship between the people's piety and the people's prosperity. In other words, they show that national disasters are always brought on by apostasy from the faith and moral decline. Therefore, the sacred history of the Old Testament remains very instructive for everyone, even in the Christian era. In her services, the Church indicates many events from this history as examples for us. In the series of historical books, there are some in which the national Hebraic element places the purely religious element in the background, such as the books of Esther and Judith. The Church does not use these books in the services, although, of course, they still remain edifying for us. Thus, the historical material of the Old Testament is no longer important of itself for us, for *old things are passed away* (II Cor. 5:17), but its importance lies in its edifying content.

In their historical accounts, the prophet Moses and the sacred writers who follow after him speak of many manifestations of God's power, of miraculous phenomena. But rarely do they make use of the term "miracle" or "wonder" (although in the Psalter we encounter it frequently). They instill in us the idea that the whole of history takes place before God's eyes, and that everything consists of events which only seem to be divided into usual and unusual events, into the natural and the miraculous. For the believing soul, openly miraculous events are only an opening in the veil, behind which the interrupted miracle of God's Providence continues and the writ of each man's course is recorded without omission.

Old Testament Wisdom

The didactic books constitute the third group of writings in the Old Testament. They teach man to organize his personal, earthly life in such a way that it will be blessed by God and by men, and may give him prosperity and peace of soul. The wisdom which proceeds from God imparts such a life.

When Solomon, beginning his reign, offered up his prayers and burnt sacrifices, God appeared to him at night and said: "Ask, what am I to give thee" (cf. III Kings 3:5). And Solomon asked God only for wisdom and knowledge, in order that he might rule the people of God. And God said to Solomon, "Because thou hast not asked for riches, property, glory, victories, or long life, but hast asked for wisdom and knowledge, wisdom and knowledge shall be given thee; and I shall also give thee such riches, possessions and glory as former kings have never had, nor will have after thee" (cf. III Kings 3:11–13).

The didactic books are full of practical advice about how to establish one's life and the life of one's family intelligently, wisely, in the fear of God, in righteousness, honesty, labor and abstinence, and how to be a useful participant in society. These precepts are extremely instructive, apt, and true. In their expression there is much imagery, liveliness, and wit; although, of course, one encounters statements which accord with the requirements of distant times, and with customs which are foreign to us. Practical guidance for everyday life constitutes the characteristic feature of the Old Testament teaching on wisdom.

However, it would be a mistake to think that Biblical wisdom is the wisdom of earthly prosperity. The Bible sees true wisdom in humble devotion to God in the most severe sufferings and in recognizing the unfathomable nature of God's ways when suffering innocently. *I myself came forth naked from my mother's womb, naked also shall I depart hence; the Lord hath given, the Lord hath taken away. As it seemed good to the Lord, so hath it come to pass: blessed be the name of the Lord... If we have received good things from the hand of the Lord, shall we not endure evil things?* (Job 1:21; 2:10). This is the wisdom of the righteous Job. But there is no true wisdom in the dialectical logic of his friends, for the very reason that they self-confidently consider that they understand God's thoughts. In their arguments there is what could be called rationalism based on a religious foundation. They are told to ask forgiveness of God through Job.

However attractive prosperity, wealth, success, or glory may be, it is senseless to become attached to anything of this sort; such is the conclusion of Solomon's wisdom. Death awaits everyone, and then it will appear that everything was only an outward show, only vanity, *vanity of vanities, all is vanity!* (Eccles. 1:2).

There is in life something higher, more valuable, more worthy of praise, which comes from wisdom. This is the striving to know the works of God, to study nature, and finally, the striving for pure knowledge: *To know the composition of the world, and the operation of the elements; the beginning, end and midst of the times; the alterations of the turning of the sun, and changes of the seasons; the cycles of the years and the positions of stars; the natures of living creatures, and the tempers of wild beasts; the vio-*

lence of winds and the reasonings of men; the diversities of plants, and the virtues of roots... And should a man desire much experience, she (wisdom) *knoweth things of old, and doth portray what is to come; she knoweth the subtleties of speeches and can expound dark sentences; she foreknoweth signs and wonders, and the issue of seasons and times... And if one love righteousness, her labors are virtues; for she teacheth temperance and prudence, justice and fortitude, which are such things as men can have nothing more profitable in their life* (Wis. 7:17–20; 8:8; 8:7). Here is a recognition of the degrees of knowledge in its many branches.

Possessing such wisdom is not due to personal merit; it is a gift of God. *I prayed,* testifies the author of the Wisdom of Solomon, *and the spirit of wisdom came to me... And all such things as are either secret or manifest, them I know. For wisdom, which is the fashioner of all things, taught me; for she is a noetic spirit, holy, only-begotten, manifold, subtle, agile, clear, undefiled, harmless, loving of the good, penetrating, irresistible, beneficent, kind to man, steadfast, sure, free from care, almighty, overseeing all things, and spreading abroad through all noetic, pure, and most subtle spirits... For she is the effulgence of the everlasting light, the unspotted mirror of the energy of God, and the image of his goodness. And though being but one, she can do all things; and remaining in herself, she maketh all things new; and in every generation, entering into holy souls, she maketh them friends of God, and prophets. For God loveth none save him that dwelleth with wisdom* (Wis. 7:7; 21–23; 26–28).

It is not surprising that such a perfect image of Wisdom, as is given in the didactic books of the Old Testament, demands the attention of the Christian, especially in those passages where she is represented as *sitting beside God Himself. The Lord made me the beginning of His ways for His works,* we read in Proverbs. *He established me before time; in the beginning, before He made the earth, even before He made the depths, before the fountains of the waters came forth, before the mountains were established, and before all hills, He begat me. The Lord made lands and uninhabited tracts and the uttermost inhabited parts under heaven. When He prepared heaven, I was present with Him; and when He prepared His throne upon the winds, and when He made the clouds above mighty, and when He secured the fountains of the earth, and when He strengthened the foundations of the earth, I was by Him, arranging all things; I was that wherein He took delight, and daily I rejoiced in His presence continually. For He rejoiced when He had*

*completed the world, and rejoiced in the children of men… For my outgoings
are the outgoings of life, and in them is prepared favor from the Lord* (Prov.
8:27–31; 35).

Here Wisdom is personified as if it were a divine being; there are other
similar expressions in the passages about Wisdom. Under the influence of
this image, in the Christian religious philosophy of antiquity, the Middle
Ages, and of more recent times, there has arisen an attempt to introduce
into theological thought the idea that Wisdom here refers to a special
divine, personal force, or hypostasis, created, or uncreated, perhaps the
soul of the world, the "Divine Sophia." Within Russian religious thought,
the doctrine of Sophia has been accepted and developed by Vladimir S.
Soloviev, Fr. Paul Florensky, and Archpriest Sergei Bulgakov. It must,
however, be realized that these thinkers develop their thoughts basing
them on their own philosophical presuppositions. Wishing to justify them
[presuppositions] by Scripture, they do not pay sufficient attention to the
fact that personifying abstract concepts was a customary device in Old
Testament writing. The writer of the book of Proverbs warns that, while
reading the book, it will be necessary to *understand a parable, and a dark
speech, the saying of the wise also, and riddles* (Prov. 1:56); i.e., do not take
figurative expressions literally.

In those passages where Wisdom is depicted in an especially vivid way,
as a personal being, as the hypostatic Wisdom, the New Testament accepts
this as a reference to the Son of God, Jesus Christ, *the power of God and the
wisdom of God*, as we read in Saint Paul (I Cor. 1:24). Such an interpretation is given, for example, to the passage from Proverbs which is often
read in church during Vespers, and which begins, *Wisdom has built a
house for herself, and set up seven pillars…* (Prov. 9:1–6). Thus, the sacred
author is transferring our thoughts directly into the New Testament, to
the preaching of the Gospel, to the mystery of the Eucharist and the organization of the Church of Christ; here the Old Testament is already on the
threshold of the New.

Old Testament Prayer and Chant

Among the didactic books, there is one special book, a book of prayer.
What Christian — not only Orthodox, but of any confession or sect —
does not know the Psalter, or at least the penitential Fiftieth Psalm? Here
is a book for all, for prayer in all its forms, for all occasions: in grief, in

times of hopelessness and desperation, when one is afraid, surrounded by enemies, surrounded by unbelief and crime; in personal woes and communal disasters; for tears of repentance after a fall, and in the joy after receiving consolation; when feeling reverent exultation, the need to give thanks, to bear witness to one's faith, to strengthen one's hope and to send up pure praise to God when contemplating the greatness and beauty of His creation. In the Psalter, there are many thoughts addressed to one's own soul, much advice, and many words of consolation. Therefore, the exceptionally extensive use of the Psalter in the Church of Christ is not surprising. Not a single divine service could be conducted without psalms. Some of the psalms are read several times during the course of one day's cycle of divine services. And besides this, the entire Psalter is read through in church in the form of the *kathismata* not less than once a week. Finally, all Orthodox services are also interspersed with individual verses from the psalms, in the form of prokeimena, alleluia verses, verses for "God is the Lord," refrains to stichera, and other short prayers of petition, repentance and praise. Christian prayers recorded in the New Testament very often borrow expressions from the psalms. The Psalter is *Christianized* in the full sense of the word. This means that the Church puts a Christian meaning into all its expressions, and the Old Testament element retreats into the background. The words "rise up" and "arise, O Lord," direct our thoughts to the Resurrection of Christ; words about captivity are understood in the sense of captivity to sin; the naming of peoples hostile to Israel as spiritual enemies; the name of Israel as the people of the Church; the appeal to slaughter our enemies as an appeal to struggle with passions; the salvation from Egypt and Babylon as salvation in Christ from idolatry. In almost every verse of the Psalter the Church finds a reflection of the New Testament, of some event, or thought, feeling, or confession of faith, hope and love. By citing verses from the psalms in their New Testament sense, the Apostles themselves in their writings, have taught us to approach the Psalter in this way.

　　Some psalms contain expressions and even groups of verses which are not clear, not only in the Slavonic text, but even in their ancient languages, in the original Hebrew and in the Greek translation; but next to them are verses which are brilliantly expressive. How many psalms there are which are completely clear and beautifully express our states of soul, and express them in prayer so fully that it is as if the divinely inspired chanter composed them not in some distant age, but in our times and for us!

Finally, there is one book among the didactic which speaks not of wisdom, not of prayer, but of love. This is the "Song of Songs," about the bride and her beloved. At first impression, this book can appear to be just a beautiful, lyric song. Many liberal commentators, who do not subscribe to the voice of the Fathers of the Church, interpret it in just this way. However, if we read the prophets, we see that, in the Old Testament, the image of the bride and her beloved is used in an elevated sense of the covenant between God and the chosen people. If this book entered the canon of the Israelite's sacred books, it did so because Old Testament tradition understood it in a lofty, symbolic sense. In the New Testament, without using the poetic form, Saint Paul employs the same symbol when, speaking of the husband's love for his wife, he compares it with Christ's love for the Church. In church hymns we often hear the same image of the bride and her betrothed, as a symbol of the burning love of a Christian soul for the Saviour: "Thy lamb, O Jesus, crieth out with a loud voice: I long for Thee, O my Bridegroom, and I endure sufferings as I seek for Thee,..." we sing in the dismissal hymn to a woman martyr. A similar expression of the soul's love for Christ is also encountered in the writings of the Christian ascetics.

Heralds of the New Testament

The fall of the kingdoms of Israel and Judah, and especially the destruction of Jerusalem and the Babylonian captivity, were most terrible blows and upheavals on an unprecedented scale for the Hebrew people. This was God's judgment for the betrayal of their covenant with Him and for their profound moral corruption. A night of utter darkness and, it seemed, hopelessness had begun for the people. Then there appeared a whole galaxy of persons to console them in their sufferings. Reproof and consolation; these are the two subjects of their proclamations and of their prophetic books, which comprise the last grouping of the books of the Old Testament.

The prophets' reproofs precede the last blows that sealed the fate of the Hebrew people, when there were still some remnants of prosperity, and the people's conscience was still slumbering. These reproofs are incomparable in their force, in their unsparing veracity.

Woe, O sinful nation, a people full of sins, an evil seed, lawless children... Why should ye be smitten any more, transgressing more and more? The whole head is pained, and the whole heart is sad. From the feet to the head there is no soundness in them; a wound, a bruise, a festering ulcer: they have not been cleansed, nor bandaged, nor mollified with ointment... Though ye bring fine flour, it is vain; incense is an abomination to me; I cannot bear your new moons, and your sabbaths, and the festival assemblies... Wash ye, be clean, remove your iniquities from your souls before mine eyes; cease from your iniquities, learn to do good, diligently seek judgment, deliver him that is suffering wrong, plead for the orphan, and obtain justice for the widow. And come, let us reason together, saith the Lord, and though your sins be as purple, I will make them white as snow; and though they be as scarlet, I will make them white as wool, proclaimed the Prophet Isaiah (Is. 1:4–6; 13; 16–8).

The Prophet Jeremiah castigates, and he laments the people's fall with even stronger words. *Trust not in yourselves, in lying words, for they shall not profit you at all, when ye say, The temple of the Lord, the temple of the Lord... But whereas ye have trusted in lying words, whereby ye shall not be profited; and ye murder, and commit adultery, and steal, and swear falsely, and burn incense to Baal, and are gone after strange gods whom ye know not, so that it is evil with you. Yet have ye come, and stood before Me in the house whereon My name is called, and ye have said, We have refrained from doing all these abominations. Is My house, there whereon My name is called, a den of thieves in your eyes?* (Jer. 7:4; 8–11).

Who will give water to my head, and a fountain of tears to my eyes? then would I weep for this, my people, day and night, even for the wounded of the daughter of my people. Who would give me a most distant lodge in the wilderness, that I might leave my people and depart from them? for they all commit adultery, an assembly of treacherous men... Every one will mock his friend; they will not speak truth; their tongue hath learned to speak falsehoods; they have committed iniquity and they have not ceased, so as to return... Shall I not visit them for these things, saith the Lord?... And I will remove the inhabitants of Jerusalem, and make it a dwelling place of dragons; and I will utterly lay waste the cities of Judah, so that they shall not be inhabited. Who is the wise man, that he may understand this?... Thus saith the Lord, Be ye prudent and call ye the mourning women, and let them come;... and let them take up a lamentation for you, and let your eye pour down tears, and your eyelids drops of water! (Jer. 9:1,2,5,9,11,12,17,18).

And when the disasters befell them and unheard-of woes were heaped upon them, the Babylonian captivity came and there was no longer any consolation and then those same prophets became the people's only support.

Comfort ye, comfort ye, My people, saith God. Speak, ye priests, of the heart of Jerusalem; comfort her, for her humiliation is accomplished, her sin is put away; for she hath received at the Lord's hand double the amount of her sins... O thou that bringest glad tidings to Sion, go up on the high mountains; lift up thy voice with strength, thou that bringest glad tidings to Jerusalem. Lift it up, fear not; say unto the cities of Judah, Behold your God! Behold the Lord. The Lord is coming with strength, and His arm is with power. Behold, His reward is with Him, and the work of each man is before Him. He shall tend His flock as a shepherd, and He shall gather the lambs with His arm and hold them in His bosom, and shall soothe them that are with young (Is. 40: 1–2; 9–11).

Thus the Prophet Isaiah comforts, becoming in those days of lamentation a prophet of God's future deliverance and good will.

One cries to me out of Seir: Guard ye the bulwarks. I watch in the morning and the night. If you wouldst inquire, inquire and dwell by me.

The night will pass, God's anger will pass. *Be glad, thou thirsty desert; let the wilderness exult, and flower as the lily. And the desert places of Jordan shall blossom and rejoice... Be strong ye hands and palsied knees. Comfort one another, ye faint-hearted, be strong and fear not; behold, our God rendereth judgment, and He will render it; He will come and save us. Then shall the eyes of the blind be opened, and the ears of the deaf shall hear. Then shall the lame man leap as a hart, and the tongue of the stammerers shall speak plainly; for water hath burst forth in the desert, and a channel of water in a thirsty land... But the redeemed and gathered on the Lord's behalf shall walk in it, and shall return, and come to Sion with joy, and everlasting joy shall be over their head; for on their head shall be praise and exultation, and joy shall take possession of them; pain and sorrow, and sighing have fled away* (Is. 35:1–6; 10).

What is it that especially inspires the prophets with bright hopes in these distant visions of the future? Is it the political might of their people, her victories and triumphs which they see before them? Or is it a vision of plenty, riches and abundance in the future which is presented to them? No, it is not these objects of material prosperity or national pride that

attract their attention. Could these holy men, who had resigned themselves to a life of suffering, and sometimes even to a martyr's death (the
Prophet Isaiah was sawn in two with a wooden saw), really inspire their
people with these earthly desires alone? They were contemplating another
revelation of God: an unprecedented spiritual rebirth, times of justice and
truth, meekness and peace, when *the whole world is filled with the knowledge of the Lord* (Is. 11:9). They proclaimed the coming of the New Testament.

*But this is the covenant that I shall make with the house of Israel; after
those days, saith the Lord, Giving, I will give My laws into their minds, and
write them on their hearts; and I will be to them a God and they shall be to
Me a people. And they shall teach no more every man his neighbor, and every
man his brother, saying, Know the Lord; for they shall all know Me, from the
least of them unto the greatest of them, for I will be merciful to their iniquities, and I will remember their sins no more* (Jer. 31: 33–34).Thus prophesies Jeremiah.

The same is proclaimed by Ezekiel. *And I will give you a new heart, and
will put a new spirit in you; and I will take away the heart of stone out of your
flesh, and will give you a heart of flesh. And I will put My Spirit in you, and
will cause you to walk in Mine ordinances and to keep My judgments, and do
them* (Ezek. 36:26–7; and 11:19–20).

The prophets speak much about the requital of the other nations, the
enemies of Israel, the pagan peoples, who were only the instruments of
God's anger and His chastisement of Israel. They will receive their cup of
wrath. But the future blessing of Israel will be a light for them also. *And in
that day, there shall be a root of Jesse, and He that shall arise to rule over the
nations; in Him shall the nations hope, and His rest shall be a reward*, pre-
dicts Isaiah (Is. 11:10).

The fulfillment of these hopes is linked with the mystical promise of
granting Israel an eternal king. *My servant David shall be a prince in the
midst of them; for there shall be one shepherd of them all; for they shall walk
in Mine ordinances… And David My servant shall be their prince for ever.
And I will make with them a covenant with them*, we read in Ezekiel (Ezek.
37:24–26).

In consoling their contemporaries, the prophets direct the attention of
all towards their future King. They present His image before them in these
colors: in the light of meekness, gentleness, humility, righteousness. *Jacob*

is My servant, I will help him: Israel is my chosen, My soul hath accepted him;
I have put My Spirit upon him; he shall bring forth judgment to the Gentiles.
He shall not cry, nor lift up his voice, nor shall his voice be heard without. A
bruised reed shall he not break, and smoking flax shall he not quench; but he
shall bring forth judgment to truth (Is. 42:1–3).

In such and similar words, the prophets depict the coming of the Saviour of the world. Before us, scattered throughout various passages of the prophets' writings, but abundant when taken all together, is a depiction of the future events of the Gospel and its portrayal of the Lord Jesus Christ Himself.

Here, in Isaiah, is a reference to Galilee, the place where the Saviour first dwelt on earth and appeared to people: *Do this first, do it quickly, O land of Zabulon, land of Naphtali, and the rest inhabiting the seacoast, and the land beyond Jordan, Galilee of the nations. O people walking in darkness, behold a great light: ye that dwell in the land of the shadow of death, a light will shine upon you… For unto us a Child is born, and unto us a Son is given, Whose government is upon His shoulder. And His name is called the angel of great Counsel, Wonderful, Counsellor, the Mighty One, the Potentate, the Prince of Peace, the Father of the age to come* (Is. 9:1–2, 6).

Here is a reference to the Lord's glorification of Jerusalem: *Shine, shine, O Jerusalem, for thy light is come, and the glory of the Lord is risen upon thee. Behold, darkness shall cover the earth, and there shall be thick darkness upon the nations; but the Lord shall appear unto thee, and His glory shall be seen upon thee. And kings shall walk in thy light, and nations in the brightness* (Is. 60:1–3).

Here is the prophecy about Christ by this same prophet, which Christ Himself used in the synagogue of Nazareth to begin His earthly preaching: *The Spirit of the Lord is upon Me, because He hath anointed Me; He hath sent Me to preach good tidings to the poor, to heal the broken-hearted, to proclaim deliverance to the captives, and recovery of sight to the blind, to declare the acceptable year of the Lord* (Is. 61:1–2).

Does the prophet foresee that the Saviour will not be recognized or accepted by the leaders of the Jewish people, or by those people that follow them? Yes, he makes an oblique reference to this in the great depiction of Christ's sufferings which he gives in Chapter 53 of his book, which is one of the greatest prophecies, if not the greatest of them all:

O Lord, who hath believed our report? and to whom hath the arm of the Lord been revealed? We brought a report of a Child before him; He is as a root in a thirsty land; He hath no form nor comeliness; and we saw Him, but He had no form nor beauty. But His form was ignoble, and forsaken by all men; He was a man of suffering, and acquainted with the bearing of sickness, for His face is turned away from us; He was dishonored and not esteemed. He beareth our sins and is pained for us: yet we accounted Him to be in trouble, and in suffering, and in affliction. But He was wounded on account of our sins, and was bruised because of our iniquities; the chastisement of our peace was upon Him; and by His bruises we were healed. All we as sheep have gone astray; every one hath gone astray in his way; and the Lord gave Him up for our sins. And He, because of His affliction openeth not His mouth. He was led as a sheep to the slaughter, and as a lamb before the shearer is dumb, so He openeth not His mouth. In His humiliation, His judgment was taken away; who shall declare His generation? for His life is taken away from the earth, because of the iniquities of My people He was led to death. And I will give the wicked for His burial, and the rich for His death; for He did no iniquity, neither is there guile in His mouth (Is. 53:1–9).

The Gospel narrative testifies that the Jewish people did not recognize the time of its visitation. However, we cannot say that the prophecies of consolation were not fulfilled. For no one can take away from the Jewish people the boast that from their race came the Most-holy Virgin Mary, that Jesus Christ was of the seed of David, that Christ's Apostles were of the same people, and that Jerusalem has become for all time the place of the glory of the Risen Christ. From Jerusalem, the preaching of the Gospel went forth into the whole world, and of her the Church sings: "Rejoice, holy Sion, thou mother of the churches, and dwelling place of God: for thou wast first to receive remission of sins through the Resurrection" (Octoechos, Tone 8, Sun. Sticheron on "Lord, I have cried").

A full explanation of the fact that it was principally people from the pagan nations who entered the Church of Christ, and that the majority of the Jews remained in unbelief, is given to us in the New Testament by the Apostle Paul. In his writings, we find an exhaustive interpretation of the Old Testament prophecies concerning this. The Apostle writes:

What if God, willing to show His wrath and to make His power known, endureth with much long suffering the vessels of wrath fitted to destruction, and that He might make known the riches of His glory on the vessels of mercy, which He had afore prepared unto glory, even us, whom He hath called, not of the Jews only, but also of the nations? As He saith also in Hosea, I will call them My people, which were not My people; and her beloved, which was not beloved. And it shall come to pass, that in the place where it was said unto them, ye are not My people, there shall they be called the people of the living God. Isaiah also crieth concerning Israel: Though the number of the children of Israel be as the sand of the sea, a remnant shall be saved... What shall we say then? That the nations which have followed not after righteousness, have attained to righteousness, even the righteousness which is of faith. But Israel, which followed after the law of righteousness, hath not attained to the law of righteousness. Wherefore? Because they sought it not by faith, but as it were by the works of the law. For they stumbled at that stumbling stone; as it is written, Behold, I lay in Sion a stumblingstone and rock of offense, and whosoever believeth in Him shall not be ashamed... But I say, continues the Apostle in the next chapter, *did not Israel know: First Moses saith, I will provoke you to jealousy by them that are no people, and by a foolish nation will anger you. But Isaiah is very bold, and saith: I was found by them that sought Me not; I was made manifest unto them that asked after Me. But to Israel He saith: All day long I have stretched forth My hands to a disobedient and gainsaying people* (Rom. 11:22–27; 30–33; 10:18–21).

This would seem to be too harsh a fate and too strict a sentence for the chosen people of old. But the Apostle Paul himself becomes a comforter of his people, saying, *For I wish not, brethren, that ye be ignorant of this mystery, lest ye be wise in your own conceits; that hardness in part is happened to Israel, until the fullness of the nations be come in. And so all Israel shall be saved; as it is written: There shall come out of Sion the Deliverer, and He shall turn away ungodliness from Jacob... For God hath enclosed them all in disobedience, that He might have mercy upon all. O the depths of the riches, both of the wisdom and knowledge of God! How unsearchable are His judgments, and His ways past finding out!* (Rom. 11:25–26; 32–33).

An Inseparable Part of the Church's Heritage

"The shadow of the law hath passed, and Grace hath come" (Octoechos, Dogmatic Theotokion of the 2nd Tone). The prefiguring paled before the Truth; the shadows that come just before dawn were dispersed when the Sun shone forth. There are no more Old Testament sacrifices; not only in the sense that they have lost their significance, but they no longer exist even physically. There is no tabernacle; there is no Old Testament temple in Jerusalem; the Jews have no high priest or priesthood according to the Law.

The Kingdom of Christ has come. And the very core of the Old Testament law — God's Ten commandments, which were given on Mount Sinai — yield their place to the commandments which were proclaimed on another mountain, the Beatitudes of the Sermon on the Mount.

Two ancient commandments remain unshaken: that concerning loving God with all one's heart, all one's soul, and all one's mind, and the second concerning loving one's neighbor as oneself. They constitute the ideological essence of the Old Testament: the Saviour said that all the Law and the Prophets were based in them. But concerning love for one's neighbor, the Lord gave us a new, more exalted commandment, during His parting discourse with His disciples: *A new commandment I give unto you, that ye love one another, as I have loved you. Greater love hath no man than this, that a man lay down his life for his friends.* Here the previous commandment is not abolished, but is exalted by the concept of love to the level of self-denial, of love which is greater than the love one has for oneself.

At the Mystical Supper, the Lord revealed the mystical truth of the establishment of the New Testament: *This cup is the New Testament in My blood.* This truth became the subject of the Apostles' preaching.

Nevertheless, the Old Testament remains the foundation on which the Church of Christ stands and rises up to the heavens. The cornerstones of this foundation are the books of the Old Testament Bible: the nomothetic[8], historical, didactic and prophetic books. They contain great prophecies about Christ and an almost unlimited number of foreshadowings and reflections of the coming New Testament. In them, we hear early calls to repentance, meekness, and mercy, which were later proclaimed in all their force and depth in the preaching of the Gospel. In them, we find numerous examples of piety and an abundance of moral edification. Eternal truths about God, the world, man, sin, about the necessity of redemption and about the coming awaited Redeemer are here revealed to mankind.

Illuminated by the light of the Gospel, and with its full meaning revealed by the New Testament Church, the Old Testament Bible remains an inseparable part of the heritage of Christianity.

---

8) The five books of law, the Pentateuch.

The Church of Christ and the Contemporary Movement for Unification in Christianity

Address to the XVth Diocesan Assembly
of the Russian Orthodox Church Outside of Russia, 1962.

We should not be astonished at the search for ways to unite un-united Christianity in our times. In communist nations a direct campaign against Christianity is being waged before our very eyes; but, in a form more externally moderate, the campaign against Christianity also has spread to the nations of the so-called free world. A struggle is imminent, and it will demand a unification of those people who are true to Christ and a firm stand in the truth. The enemies today are prepared to bury Christianity. In vain! The words of the Lord are given: *Take heart! for I have overcome the world.* They should be engraved within our hearts in fiery letters. But the imminent struggle will be lengthy and fierce. Who among the faithful does not regret that in these grave historical hours such masses of Christians remain outside the walls of the Church created by the Lord? Who among the faithful would not take joy in the unification of all Christianity, un-united and scattered about, into the one, holy, catholic and apostolic Orthodox Church?

But frightful temptations lie ahead if the noisy, externally strong unification process proceeds along a deceitful way and, in particular, if in proceeding along its false way it should even partly touch our Holy Orthodoxy.

Protestantism has declared itself the initiator of the unification movement in our days. What has inspired the movement there? The motives were not exclusively of one sort, they were varied in different individuals.

It is natural to think that one of the reasons, benign and justified by life itself, is the one already indicated, namely, the demand of the times to prepare for Christianity's self-defense. It is possible to see yet another inspiration. In the depths of the strivings of many Protestants there are searchings for the one, apostolic, Christian Church of long ago. After four hundred years of divisions, Protestantism has arrived at a dead end. In America alone there are more than 250 sects; the time for the opposite movement has arrived, not towards any center, but towards the organic center.

There is also another reason, however, not directly expressed, but nonetheless allowing itself to be felt: an extreme weakening of faith in contemporary Protestantism. While in the lower echelons of Protestantism there are those that to an extent still live by simple faith, the theological faculties have become the vehicles of positivism in biblical and church-historical science, a method which considers even miracles and the element of the supernatural in history to be foreign. They have made religion a support for "objective science." The leaders and instructors of Protestantism, the pupils of these faculties, vacillate between faith and faithlessness in the basic truths of the Gospel, concerning which they sometimes openly declare: beliefs in the truths of the divinity of the Lord Jesus Christ, His resurrection, in the immortality of the soul is vanishing. The interest in questions concerning eternal life is vanishing in Protestantism. So among the motives for unification, there is the subconscious searching for a healing source of renewed faith, similar to a renewal of powers in physical organisms that takes place through a transfusion of blood. However, if one observes this from the sidelines, one cannot but already see in these searchings a host of false harbingers.

One of these delusions is the idea in the contemporary world that there is no true repository of the unsullied Christian Truth; that all subdivisions of Christianity are defective. In this error is to be found the main delusion of the strivings for unification in Protestantism. This false principle in particular has been accepted as the basis of the ecumenical movement, concerning which a discussion is to follow.

Another false supposition, clearly a paradox, is that if one combines all the defective parts into one complete whole, a fullness of the truth will be attained.

A third similar mistake: if one combines the various Christian confessions which are weak in faith, weak in spirit, and weak in their influence on social life, then, in our age of religious skepticism, a power will be created, a power which would be able to oppose the anti-Christian powers of the world.

The Idea of the Establishment
of a Kingdom of God on Earth. Ecumenism.

In one way or another, the striving for unification in Protestantism has been aroused. But how is it to be realized? Through what means is one to arouse the will of people to activity? By what means is one to replace the moving force of faith when faith itself ceases to move the heart? A new idea that would enliven the mind and heart was needed. It was discovered and proclaimed as the ecumenical movement, and Christianity is summoned to make it a reality. This is in fact an old idea revitalized, which the Roman Catholics tried to realize in a monarchistic manner through the papacy, and now Protestantism is trying to bring it into movement in a democratic manner through ecumenism. This idea is "the establishment of the Kingdom of God on earth."

In terms of ecumenism, what does "the establishment of the Kingdom of God on earth" mean? It means the social erection of the future world on earth. The new world must replace the former, old, decrepit, and supposedly destined-for-wreckage, social structure on earth. Now all attention, all strivings of Christianity, must be directed towards the idea, not of the personal salvation of each person, not concerning one's soul, not about the future eternal life, but of building a society on new foundations. From this it is determined that the church of our time is the "serving church," *dienende Kirche*, i.e., is to serve social aims.

Even before the formation of ecumenical organizations these ideas were born in the minds of those active in Protestantism. In order to understand the origin of the ecumenical movement, let us present the ideas of two important figures in Protestantism, ideologists of the Kingdom of God on earth: a) the German pastor, called among Protestants "the great prophet of our times," Christoph Blumhardt, who called for unification on this basis, although he did not live to see it realized, and b) the present leader of ecumenical movement, the general secretary of the Council of the Ecumenical Movement, W. A. Vissar d'Hooft. We shall present a brief excerpt from an address given before representatives of the press at Bad Boll, Germany in 1946 in the Evangelical academy.

Christoph Blumhardt died in 1919, before the formation of the ecumenical movement, but in his appeals the ideas now being carried through in ecumenism are very clearly expressed, Vissar d'Hooft cited Blumhardt repeatedly in his address at Bad Boll.

"We have no need to tremble in fear that the old is coming to an end," Blumhardt announced during the First World War. "Yes, it is dying! All that is dear, all that is beautiful, to what we were tied, which we loved, is past! For all time, for all eternity, it is past! The old world caved in and a new one is arising on its ruins. Christianity must take a most active part in its construction" (Easter sermon of 1915). Blumhardt posed three problems before Christianity: the realization of a better social structure; secondly, the overcoming of confessional contradictions and, finally, collaboration in the formation of a completely peaceful co-existence between peoples, with the complete eradication of wars between nations. The realization of the first issue, a just social structure, he imagined in the form of socialism realized peaceably, with the help of Christianity.

With regard to the second issue, the eradication of confessional barriers, Blumhardt wrote in 1895: "We must finally divorce ourselves from the idea that the Lord Jesus Christ would have allowed Himself to be cloistered up in some one of many churches or sects which have arisen, and would want to bring happiness to the world only through this one... For the omnipotent God, through Jesus, we are obliged to clear out much more space than any one of the churches could offer... Christ does not meddle in the quarrels of churches. His Kingdom is much higher... Now, in our century the question of creeds and churches should not be posed: the time for that is past, it had meaning forty years ago. All this is far from me, this is already ruins!" Blumhardt ecstatically exclaimed.

The third problem: the creation of a peaceful state of co-existence between all nations. According to Blumhardt, the first step towards this should be in the mutual repentance of peoples before each other, and in the unification of churches, i.e., the repentance of churches. Away with anti-Christian fatalism, which has the view that wars are unavoidable and that humanity's history consists of such wars. For this peoples and nations must be prepared to sacrifice their nationhood as Abraham was ready to give up his son Isaac, and offer him in sacrifice. As it is said of the apos-

tles: *they forsook all and followed Him.* Of course do not expect the fulfillment of this hope in our time, — we are only at the threshold. Says
Blumhardt: "We must receive a new Spirit, enter upon a new era. There is
no other help but help from God, Who directs the world, and His victory
will come in Jesus Christ." [1]

The present general secretary of the Council of the Ecumenical Movement, Vissar d'Hooft, confirms the ideological tie of the ecumenical
movement with the mood expressed by this evangelical pastor.

In an address given in 1946 in Bad Boll, the homeland of Blumhardt,
d'Hooft formulated the task of ecumenism in those very same three
points, although in more reticent words, since the results of the Second
World War were too far removed from the previous optimistic expectations. He calls the "church," firstly to social service in the world. He sets
forth the task of the "serving church," i.e., the church which has entered
into the service of social aims. "The world says to the church: your concern is private life; religion is something to do with the beyond and, specifically speaking, there is nothing for it to seek on this earth. No, the church
has to be the soul of humanity, her task is service in the decisive affairs of
the world." Vissar d'Hooft brings to mind Blumhardt's call to Christianity, that it should enter the world as the creative source for the erection of
the Kingdom of God on earth. However, for this, he says, the church itself
has to become renewed: it must pass through repentance. And this repentance has to have practical consequences. Renewed, it has the possibility,
for example, of preparing a path to socialism. Unfortunately, churches
after the war again manifested weariness, a spirit of restoration, social and
political reactions, adjustment to the post-war situation; in many countries the churches became overly bourgeois. This is why a *metanoia* is
needed (*metanoia*: a change in thought process, repentance). He points to
Holland, where during the war a friendship arose between the 'people of

---

1) Blumhardt saw the godlessness of the proletariat, but felt that often under the visible
surface of the godlessness a subconscious yearning for God and His kingdom is concealed. With this disposition, toward the end of his life he entered the ranks of the German Social-Democratic party, which was too bold a move for that time and it caused
him to lose his title as pastor of the evangelical church. The thought occurs that might
not this life journey of Blumhardt, starting enthusiastically on a religious foundation
and ending with submission to a socialist-political party, be symbolic of the ecumenical
movement, for its beginning and for its end? (Dr. Alo Münch. *Die Aufgaben unserer
Zeit im Licht der Botschaft von Christoph Blumhardt.* 1946. P. 1–16)

the church' and the socialistic parties. The serving church should preach that Jesus Christ is the Lord not only of the church but also of the world. The Bible must become a cosmic book, i.e., to serve all of humanity. That form of piety where all accent is placed upon the salvation of separate souls and of the internal world of the human represents a lack of understanding of the breadth of the Bible. Christ must penetrate into the life of all people; we are in need of Christian physicians, artists, journalists... Thus, according to Blumhardt, serving social problems is the first task of the church.

Secondly, he says that the serving church must overcome confessionalism and become one church. Service to one's neighbor is something to be shared by all. The ecumenical assembly is a society of churches which in many aspects are different from one another, but in the ultimate sense are unified by the Lord Himself.

Thirdly, he says that the serving church is a church which, calling things by their proper names, declares: we have chosen false paths, we have gone in directions that gave us no promise, no future, for the very reason that we have chosen such paths; and now nothing else remains but to make a complete turn, a 180 degree turn. Repentance is required in order to change the thought process, to come to our senses. Is it possible that only now we have come to learn that we are on a false path? The church must make deductions from the experience of past centuries and say: turn about, for the Kingdom of God is near! What does this mean? That the Kingdom of God desires to enter this world and that Jesus Christ even waits to be our king (W. A. Vissar d'Hooft: *Der Dienst der Kirche in der grossen Entscheidungen der Welt* — in *Zeitwende*, März 1947, München). In these rather unclear, enigmatic words is seen the idea of the establishment of a single world government as the Kingdom of God on earth

We could regard these plans, expressed by two outstanding representatives of Protestantism, simply as fantasy, as a utopia, not the first in the history of social thought. But such people as the present leader of the ecumenical assembly can hardly be called dreamers: they, apparently, are headed towards realistic goals. There can be no doubt but that the ecumenical movement is being joined and supported by, if not directed by, secret and overt world organizations who are alien to religious tasks, and perhaps even inimical to them. Finally, while there is expressed a hope that ecumenism may help to oppose the advance of godlessness and anti-Christian forces in the world struggle, the USSR sends its own people to the ecumenical council and the World Council of Churches, as if in the name of the Soviet Church. A permanent representative from this church has been dispatched to Geneva as a member of the secretariat of the World Council of Churches (Archpriest Borovoy). In such a manner the Soviets will control all the activities of the World Council of Churches. It is evident that participation of representatives from the Soviet Church was expressed at the ecumenical assemblage at New Delhi, and likewise at the Orthodox gathering on the island of Rhodes, in that no one had the right to raise a voice concerning a struggle with atheism. Red Moscow, according to the directives of Lenin, utilizes such doubtful coalitions until it sees benefit for itself, in the conviction that such a doubtful ally can easily be discredited, discarded, and destroyed at the opportune time.

So at first, separate Orthodox individuals entered into the world organization of the ecumenical assembly, as if merely representatives of Orthodox theological science, and then later clergymen and hierarchs, as representatives of a series of local Orthodox churches, and these churches themselves are included in the World Council of Churches and the ecumenism connected with it.

Of course, in ecumenism the Orthodox Church is regarded as its most conservative member. However, its entry into the organization was very much stressed and even boisterously acclaimed. Why? On the one hand, because it has apostolic succession, and by this it brings into the world organization — into this conglomerate of Protestant sects — an element lacking: apostolic succession. According to the ecumenical view, defectiveness of some parts of a given whole is covered over or filled by the appearance of that element which is lacking in the membership of the organization, in the given case by the entry of the Orthodox Church. On the other hand, the entry of the Orthodox Church annuls its possible opposition to ecumenism. For the local Orthodox churches, their entry into the given supraconfessional organization, claiming itself to be the Church of Christ, has no justification.

This step is not justified from the point of view of practicality: not by sermons on Orthodoxy, since in the given conditions it would be an absolute fantasy to hope to convert these Protestants to the Orthodox Faith, to draw them nearer to the authentic Orthodox Church. Ecumenism has a ready-made, already worked-out creed, and the Orthodox representatives are aligned into a ready-made frame within which they are allowed to function. But more importantly, the recognition of all the Christian confessions and sects as being part of a single church, and of equal status, means a distortion of the dogma of the Church. In such a case neither dogmas, nor the canons of councils are obligatory, nor succession from apostles. Such an attitude is equal to self-destruction for the Church.

Now we have the result before our eyes: we do not see Orthodoxy witnessing to itself in ecumenism; on the contrary, and unheard of in Orthodoxy, the new, ecumenical, teaching about the Church has already infilltrated into us and is energetically being spread among us by Orthodox ecumenists.

Is it possible to accept the idea of the establishment of a kingdom of God on earth?

Is the teaching of a Kingdom of Christ on earth acceptable to Orthodoxy? What does the Gospel say about the Kingdom of God?

Everywhere in the Gospel of St. Matthew, the Kingdom of God is directly called the "Kingdom of Heaven." Throughout the course of the whole Gospel according to the evangelist John the Theologian it is called "eternal life."

In the evangelists Mark and Luke it is called the Kingdom of God, but with that very same meaning: *And seek not ye what ye shall eat, or what ye shall drink..., for all these things do the nations of the world seek after;... prepare for yourselves... incorrupted treasure in heaven; Let the dead bury their dead* (Luke 12:29–30, 33; 21:34; 9:60). *They did eat, they drank, they married wives, they were given in marriage, until the day that Noe entered into the ark, and the flood came, and destroyed them all. Likewise also as it was in the days of Lot; they did eat, they drank, they bought, they sold, they planted, they builded;... it rained fire and brimstone from heaven, and destroyed them all. Even thus shall it be in the day when the Son of man is revealed* (Luke 17:27–29). These are the words of the Saviour.

At the tribunal of Pontius Pilate *Jesus answered, My kingdom is not of this world: if My kingdom were of this world, then would My servants fight, that I should be delivered...* (John 18:36). Here is my answer to the question concerning the building of earthly well-being: Although the blessedness of the life in Christ, not only the personal life of each separate Chris-

tian, but also the life of Christian communities, a life thoroughly influenced by the Church, already begins here, on earth, the Kingdom of Christ
is not of this world. This has been tried and tested through innumerable
examples of holy people. Father John of Kronstadt many times speaks of
himself concerning his feeling during the Church services: "Where am I? I
am in heaven." This is the feeling of many pure souls. Here heaven is
brought down upon the earth; but for this one has to raise oneself to heav-
en, and not turn away from it towards earthly interests, earthly plans. The
Gospel calls us to build our life in such a manner that earth becomes part
of heaven in a moral sense, as the Earth is a particle of the heavens in a
physical sense. Tikhon of Zadonsk, makes a general summation of Orthodox Christian thought of all ages concerning the Kingdom of God when
he writes:

"Our life is in heaven, and it is from heaven that we are awaiting our
Saviour, the Lord Jesus Christ. The life of Christians in this world is nothing but a wandering and continual moving and hurrying towards one's
homeland, as the Apostle says: *For here we have no continuing city, but we
seek one to come.* This is why we are wanderers and strangers, and are so
called in this world, as it is written of Abraham, Isaac and Jacob: *They were
strangers and pilgrims on the earth...* The Christian homeland is heaven,
where the glory of the Heavenly Father is to Whom we pray *Our Father
Who art in the Heavens,* where His most glorious abode is, in which *there
are many mansions,* where is *the great holy city of Jerusalem, possessing the
glory of God...;* with the eye we view *and sigh, desiring to assume our heavenly dwelling.*"

What a difference in interpretation of the Kingdom of God in the
above understanding, and there in modern Christianity!

Well, well! — they interrupt us — to hand over the earth to blind and
evil forces, and think only for the salvation of one's own soul! This is what
you continue to call for... — No, we answer. We continue merely by indicating the words of Christ: *Seek ye first of all the Kingdom of God and His
righteousness and all these things will be added to you,* seek the heavenly and
the earthly will be added. For Christians the heavenly kingdom begins
already here, bright and blessed, a pledge of the future eternal life. It blesses earthly life, not only individual life, but also the life of Christian communities. It orders it, lightens it, makes it blessed. It introduces brotherly
relations into society and transforms the most difficult experiences in life

into light ones, as it already has been tested through numerous examples in the history of Christianity. This earthly reflection of heaven may indeed take on broader dimensions, spreading to the life of the society and the state. But for this there must be faith and prayer in the first place. Nothing of this sort will be attained if we turn our gaze away from heaven and towards the earth. Without faith and prayer, let life even be happy and without sorrow, yet it will not be the Kingdom of God.

Why does ecumenism, for the sake of the idea of building the Kingdom of God on earth, abandon Christian teaching concerning the salvation of the soul? For the reason that faith in external life has completely weakened it, if not caused it to be lost altogether, because their total view of reality is limited to earthly life. But is not the Orthodox Christian teaching concerning the salvation of the soul connected with the idea of humanity as a whole? The teaching on the soul is a teaching of the moral perfection of humanity, of the good of all humanity attained by each separate individual through the path of working on oneself. This perfection aims not only at eternity: it is necessary also for the improvement of relations in the human society of this world. How is it possible to build the Kingdom of God under conditions of contemporary depraved morality, in an atmosphere of faithless, materialistic, immoral license? Is it really possible to seriously assert that if people will begin to think less of heaven they will become better Christians? Unfortunately, in the theological editorials of Orthodox ecumenists the idea is resolutely being preached that it is time to renounce the teaching of "the salvation of the soul beyond the grave" and turn to the concern of building a Kingdom of Christ on earth.

The Orthodox dogma of the Church.

The most dangerous element, however, connected with the entry of the Orthodox churches into the ecumenical movement is the acceptance of the Protestant-ecumenistic conception of the Church. Indeed, such a conception is repeated in spoken addresses and in the printed matter of Orthodox ecumenists. Along with the destruction of the authentic Orthodox understanding of the Church the significance of the seven Ecumenical Councils is undermined, and this means that the firmness of Christian dogmas established by them is undermined, and in such a manner Orthodoxy is undermined and destroyed at its foundations.

With cautious circumspection the apostles erected the structure of the Church of Christ on earth. They clearly determined who belongs to it and who does not belong. They likened the Church to an ordinary building: *We are the laborers...ye are God's building*, the Apostle instructs us. The basis of the structure is Christ. *Now if any man build upon this foundation gold, silver, precious stones, wood, hay, stubble; Every man's work shall be made manifest* (I Cor. 3:9–13). Apparently there may be more than one structure, but the true Church is one. There will come the time of the last day, and the truthfulness of this Church *the day shall declare,* as the apostle teaches *because it shall be revealed by fire; and fire shall try every man's work of what sort it is,* whether it will stand or will be consumed! (I Cor. 3:13–14). For this reason we must firmly believe in the single apostolic building, in the one apostolic Church.

A believing person enters the Church through Baptism with water. However, it is necessary for the Baptism to be recognized and affirmed. For it may happen that he who performs the Baptism is a heretic or schismatic, himself not in the Church. So it was also at the time of the apostles. When the Apostle Paul first came to Ephesus there were about twelve people who regarded themselves as disciples of the Christian faith and as having been baptized. But with questioning it turned out that they were baptized only with the Baptism of John. The Apostle Paul explained to them the insufficiency of their Baptism. He himself baptized them and then placed his hands on them in order to bring down upon them the Holy Spirit (Acts 19:1–7). The laying on of hands for this bringing down of the Holy Spirit, being a Mystery [sacrament], was at the same time a confirmation of a correctly performed Baptism and a uniting to the Church; being a Mystery, it also had the formal significance of the stamp of acceptance into the Church. So it was called by the ancient Church: a "seal" or "impress". The Mystery of the laying on of hands, soon taking on the form of anointment, was always carried out by the apostles themselves: in imparting the gift of the Holy Spirit, the apostles simultaneously confirmed the acceptance of the given individual into the Church. In the book of the Acts it is related how the Apostles Peter and John had to undertake a journey from Jerusalem to Samaria in order to personally carry out the Mystery of the laying on of hands upon people there who had already received Baptism.

Through understanding the significance of this Mystery as a seal, it is evidently explained why in the post-apostolic age the right to carry out this Mystery passed on to the bishops, as the superiors and administrators of the Church. When it became evident that it was impossible to bring each baptized person to the apostles and their successors, the bishops, this Mystery, as the sign of a blessing from the bishop, took the form of granting the presbyters Chrism which had been blessed by the bishops themselves — perhaps even the apostles themselves — for the anointment of those baptized. In the Apostolic Canons, one of the earliest manuscripts of the ancient Church, we read: "water is the symbol of death; anointment, the seal of the covenant" *sigillum pactonis* (*Constitutionis Apostilicae*, [book] 7, 22:2). This shows how the ancient Church expressively and clearly determined the composition and limits of the Church and how the membership of separate individuals was indicated. *And of the rest, durst no man join himself to them*, the book of Acts emphasizes (Acts 5:13).

Furthermore, unanimity in faith and a singleness of thought concerning teachings was demanded of the Christians who entered the Church. The apostles exhort *to labor for the faith once delivered to the saints, to stand in faith*, not to accept any innovations of that which was declared by the apostles, even though the initiator of the innovation be an angel from heaven. Of course, individuals who separated themselves from the unity of the faith did appear in the Church. They introduced dissension and made it necessary for the apostles to excommunicate them from church gatherings or to completely exclude them from the Church. And such individuals who were alien to the general spirit of the Church had to remove themselves from association with the Church. *They went out from us, but they were not of us; for if they had been of us, they would no doubt have continued with us: but they went out, that they might be made manifest that they were not all of us* (I John 2:19). This spiritual unity, this concordance in all, and especially unity in faith, the apostle again compares with the strictness in adherence to a plan in building a structure, rejoicing spiritually at the proportions of the erected spiritual temple: *all the building fitly framed together groweth into a holy temple in the Lord*, we read in the epistle to the Ephesians.

And thus this understanding of the Church as a spiritual orderly building forever remains in the consciousness of the Orthodox Church. The manuscript of the second century, *The Shepherd of Hermas*, gives the following descriptive image of the building of the Church. On the waters, i.e., through Baptism, a great fortress is being erected: the Church. It is being built out of stones. Some stones are smooth, cut, all alike, and are used in the construction. Others, which are uneven, are worked over or laid aside. The square and white stones represent the apostles, teachers, bishops, deacons, who walk undefiled in the holy teaching of God. Those laid aside are those who have sinned but desire to repent. This is how Christian antiquity understood the unity of the Church: not a unity of dissent, but a strict concordance, similar to the pattern of bricks of one and the same form during construction.

The durability and correctness of what followed after the apostles, the erection of the Church, is based upon hierarchal succession. Apostolic succession of hierarchy is the primary sign of the Church. It creates the organic identity of the Church of all ages; it shows, we may say, in the sense of transference, "the inheritance of blood," the inheritance of nature, similar to that which goes from ancestors to descendants. Further, it supports the unity of tradition in the teaching within Church customs, in canons, and in the order of the Church service. But what is most important is that in this way the succession of the Grace of the Holy Spirit is preserved, as received by the apostles on Pentecost. *Neglect not the gift that is in thee, which was given thee by prophecy, with the laying on of the hands of the presbytery; Wherefore I put thee in remembrance, that thou stir up the gift of God, which is in thee by the putting on of my hands,* the Apostle Paul instructs Timothy. The Grace of God remains, lives, and is given in the apostolic Church of Christ. The Grace of God, however, is in no way obliged to impart salvation where the teaching and life of the Apostolic Church is violated. Although "physically" succession is preserved, apostolic succession is not an automat or calling card. Here, in this temporal, universal, externally and internally unified temple, *According as His divine power hath given unto us all things that pertain unto life and godliness* (II Peter 1:3), and from us who are led into the constructed building of the Church, we are obligated to *preserve the Grace* in us given by the Church *whereby we may serve God acceptably with reverence and godly fear* (Hebrews 12:28).

It is likewise extremely important to remember that the foremost element, hierarchic succession, by way of successive laying on of hands of the apostles, has not left the Church. The apostles, having entered the heavenly Church, do not cease simultaneously to participate in the Church on earth. Between the Church on earth and the heavenly Church there is a close, constant, and living tie. *But ye are come into mount Sion, and unto the city of the living God, the heavenly Jerusalem, and to an innumerable company of angels, To the general assembly and church of the firstborn, which are written in heaven* (Hebrews 12:22–23). For the Orthodox Church these are not dead words but real life, a life in unity with the heavenly Church. Apostles, saintly hierarchs, martyrs, and the righteous, having departed into eternal life do not cease being participators in the Church on earth. "The glorious firmament of the Church you do now radiate as most great stars and always illumine the faithful, O divine martyrs, warriors of Christ." In the Orthodox divine service (troparia, stichera, canons, kontakia) the Apostles are glorified as the foundations of the Church, forever; saintly hierarchs are called pillars of the Church, i.e., ramparts, strengthening its walls; martyrs are stars, shining in the dome of the Church firmament, of the Church arch extending into heaven; and the righteous, spiritual ascetics, and saints are lamps within the Church. For this reason when the Church is called Apostolic, then it is so not only in the sense that the apostles laid its foundation or were its first builders, not only because they left in it evangelic teaching, gave it order, or even (what is more important for organization) transferred to it an uninterrupted succession of hierarchy, but, we repeat, also because they themselves continue to remain in her, although having entered the heavenly dwelling of Christ. The same applies to all the saints. When we stand before the Icon of the Mother of God, is it only Her Icon with us here on earth and not She Herself in the Church on earth? When we sing "Now the heavenly hosts serve with us invisibly," are these only words? Does not a guardian angel accompany us in our earthly life?

All these qualities of the Church: its oneness, the unity of its teaching, its succession from the apostles, the recognition of the Holy Spirit's Grace remaining in the Church, living in her, and the tie with the heavenly Church — how far removed all this is from the Protestant concept of the Church! How is it possible to neglect such glaring discontinuity for the sake of planning spiritual unity? And furthermore, how is it possible to neglect these qualities of the Church for the sake of ecumenical unity?

It is also remarkable that Protestantism, having broken ties with the Church of apostolic succession, does not even have pretensions of belonging to the hereditary organism of the apostolic Church, in the direct sense of the word. In this respect it is honest with itself. Protestantism — at least in the new sects such as the Adventists, the Baptists — does not pretend to have the Grace of Baptism: there Baptism is only "a promise of good conscience to God," and the submersion into water a simple symbol. Anointment, that seal of unification with the Church, and the granting of the divine gift of the Holy Spirit that resides in the Church, is regarded as being unnecessary. This is logical since there is no union with that Church which maintains the order of apostolic succession. In the most recent large sects, the Eucharist is, according to their personal understanding, a simple remembrance of the events of the Last Supper. They understand it as a simple eating of bread and wine: such a remembrance can be outside the Church. Protestantism contents itself with the ministry of lay preachers for the reason that it has no successive laying on of hands, as a Grace-filled Mystery remaining within the Church. In them there is no association with the heavenly Church. Further yet, they refuse to honor the Most Holy Mother of God and consciously demean Her, even to the extent of falsifying the Holy Scriptures (thus, in the German Protestant translation of the Gospel, the words of the Lord: *Woman, what have I to do with thee? Mine hour is not yet come* received the following sense "What is there in common between you and me?"). The concept of spiritual struggle associated with carrying one's cross according to the Lord's commandment is also absent. The idea of attaining holiness as the aim of the earthly life of a Christian (according to the Apostle Paul: *Holiness, without which nobody will see the Lord*) is absent. The Church, as a guide and repository of the Grace of God, becomes unnecessary. If there is a dreamy faith in a revelation to one or another individual or some illumination by the Holy Spirit, then it is an individual contact with heaven independent of the Church. Christianity becomes primarily something outside of the Church itself, and the name "church" turns out to be a plain symbol and, finally, only an empty sound. If you want to be a Christian in the Protestant sense, simply call yourself such and own a Gospel. You are a Christian, you already are in the invisible spiritual Church. If you receive Baptism, then you do so only in order that others recognize you as a Christian. From here arises the facility of the Protestant missionary task in heathen nations, the ease of transition from one sect to another. But it does not lead to union with the

Church of Christ. Ecumenism as a progeny of Protestantism bears all its features to the fullest extent.

The Church of Christ is *the foundation of God — [it] standeth sure, having this seal, The Lord knoweth them that are His* (II Timothy 2:19). The Church is the fortress of Christianity in the world. It is a citadel around which free settlements of Christian and non-Christian trends have spread. It is a bastion which is predestined for the task of enduring all the onslaughts of hell, as the Saviour foretold concerning it and as it is depicted in the Apocalypse of St. John the Theologian — hell in the form of a dragon, effluxing a river out of its jaws in order to captivate and drown the Woman-Church (Rev 12:15). The angel preserved the Church, and the earth swallowed up the river.

Personal salvation is within the Church. And the salvation of the world is through the Church. This first truth must be brought into agreement with a second truth: the apostolic consolation to the people outside the Church, that *God, Who is the Saviour of all men, specially of those that believe;* that He shed His blood for the sins of the whole world; that *in every nation he that feareth Him, and worketh righteousness, is accepted with Him,* is accepted with God. At the same time, we must understand as well that *many are called, but few are chosen* and that *sons of the Kingdom* may be cast into outer darkness.

What should be our relation to the movement for unification in Christianity?

We Orthodox, I repeat once more, must not flatter ourselves with the thought that we are capable of directing the movement for unification in ecumenism into a course towards Orthodoxy. Rather, it is easier to think that when the ecumenical movement is exhausted, then the more sincere groups in Protestantism will be drawn towards those sources from which Protestantism originated, to which it is more related in spirit, from whence it carried forth the idea of building the Kingdom of God on earth, i. e., towards Latinism.

However, if we are approached it is our obligation to "give an answer concerning [the content] of our hope." Protestantism still continues to be prejudiced against the Orthodox Church and does not understand its essence: but it is as if ready to learn about Orthodoxy. Appearing as an open forum, the Orthodox Church must be completely free of the paths, boundaries, and regulations into which ecumenism places its own members, allowing them to function only in an already designated direction. The Church must act independently, standing outside of ecumenism, perhaps associated with it as with a member of mutual discussion, but not subject to it.

The late and most Blessed Metropolitan Anthony Khrapovitsky, when he was invited to London on the occasion of the 1600th Anniversary celebration of the first Ecumenical Council, and an opportunity was offered to him to express himself concerning the question of "unification of Christianity," formulated his opinion: "To carry out such a request is incomparably easier than if you had offered to me to speak of the unification of churches... We from childhood have become accustomed to believe in the one, holy, catholic, and apostolic Church... It is another matter if we speak of the unification of Christianity. Such a unification, first of all, must be expressed in the freedom of our souls not only from every shade of inimical feeling towards those who might think differently, but also from the dominant striving in our minds to refute them." Having in view the Anglican church, Metropolitan Anthony advised to make attempts towards clarifying all that which we have in common (*Life of the Blessed Metropolitan Anthony*, Vol. VII, page 85 [in Russian]).

If, indeed, separated Christianity was amiably inclined to meet our Church [halfway], then what else could our relationship be to it except to aid it in uniting to the one, holy, catholic, and apostolic Orthodox Church? This means: to unify un-united Christianity not to "us," not to Russians, Greeks, Syrians or Serbians, but to help them become unified with the Orthodox Church of all times, with the Church in which such hieromartyrs as Ignatius the God-bearer, hierarchs such as Sts. Athanasius the Great, Basil the Great, Gregory the Theologian, John Chrysostom served, where there were hosts of martyrs, where there were great ascetics: Anthony, Euthymius, Macarius, John of the Ladder, and others. In short, to help them enter into the kingdom of holiness, the kingdom of Grace, the kingdom of prayer, the kingdom of asceticism, into the Church which in its holiness is the *pillar and ground of truth*.

Our intense attempts would consist of 1) indicating to un-united Christianity, that without union with the Heavenly Church there can not be completeness in the body of Christ, and that there cannot be true catholicity without this union that without it there is not a true Church;

2) the calling of Orthodox churches to help grant apostolic Church succession and, in such a manner, 3) to help begin a Grace-filled life, united with a 4) confession of the fullness of Church teaching. Thus it should be.

How do those Orthodox proceed, who from the beginning have declared themselves to be friends of the ecumenical movement, and likewise those who have already entered this movement, as if in the name of the Orthodox Church? These individuals, have been carried away by the idea of ecumenism, have adjusted to the situation, desiring to please a fashionable movement, and have quickly changed the teaching of the Church, all for the sake of the dreamy aim of unifying Christianity. They not only falsely inform the non-Orthodox, but strive to convince us, the Orthodox, to accept a disfigured teaching of the Church — to introduce, as if a new revelation form the Holy Spirit, as a moving wind of a new Pentecost, the new ecumenical view of the essence of the Church and its structure. This would replace the truth about the unity of the body of the Church with the conception of some kind of a spiritual Church, embracing all dissension, conflicting teachings, and all divisions in contemporary and historical Christianity. Individuals of a modernistic frame of mind or individuals who have passed through Protestant theological schools and have assimilated their spirit make appearances at gatherings in the name of the Orthodox Church and have been accepted as Her representatives.

Between the First and Second World Wars a book appeared, published by the YMCA, under the heading, *Christian Unification: the Ecumenical Problem in Orthodox Consciousness*. In it we find a series of editorials in Russian by Orthodox authors of different nationalities. The most liberal point of view is advanced by Russian theologians. Archpriest Sergey Bulgakov argues for an ecumenical conception of the Church. "Thus," he expresses himself, "we speak of churches quite often in the sense of different Christian denominations" ("we" — evidently, he himself and those in agreement with him). He concludes: "the evidence of the genius of a language cannot be reduced to simple politeness or hypocrisy for the sake of courtesy and amiability before the non-Orthodox." This argument is weak; a reference to the spirit of modernized languages.

Professor Kartashev offers historical information in his article to the effect, that supposedly "all the reunions of the Church, after mutual anathematizations and excommunications, were accomplished on the level of equality, without any hint of being joined to something, without

an 'unia,' without recalling excommunications, and without lifting anathemas, which shows that anathemas have a conditional character." However erudite the late Parisian Professor Kartashev may be in Church history,
this assertion is not true. Of course, if in some local church a heretical or
schismatic bishop was replaced by an Orthodox bishop, then this church
became Orthodox: why then should the anathema be lifted from the
Church? For, in general, it is heretics and heresies that were anathematized
and not churches. But there was no way for a heretical bishop to be reunited to the Church except he reject the heresy or schism. In the decisions of
the Ecumenical Councils we constantly read of reunifications, for example, in the following form: I, so and so, having repented, enter the holy,
catholic, and apostolic Church of God" or: "We reunited to the holy,
catholic, and apostolic Church" (see the Acts of the 3rd Ecumenical Council). And thus it is proper to apply the words of the Rev. Bulgakov to Kartashev — i.e. in the author's [Kartashev's] extremely exaggerated historical premise one feels either affection or hypocrisy in reaction to the ecumenists. Professor Kartashev kindly affirms that membership in the
Church is preserved "even with defects and mutilations in the dogmatic
teaching both in canonical and ritual practice... Even Protestant communities," Kartashev continues, "mercilessly breaking contact with apostolic
hierarchic succession and the living sacred tradition of the Church, but
having preserved the Sacrament of Baptism in the name of the Holy Trinity, continue through this mystagogical door to introduce their members
into the bosom of the one invisible Church of Christ, and to commune to
them that very same Grace of the Holy Spirit. All this gives ground for
posing the question of a unification of churches on the basis of their equal
rights in their mystic realism, and not on the basis of "uniatism," i.e.
reuniting heretics to Orthodoxy. The reunification of churches should be
a manifestation and a concrete incarnation in visible reality of an already
invisibly existing unity of the Church." When one reads these deliberations by Professor Kartashev one involuntarily would like to inquire: if,
then, all of Protestantism is already a part of the Church, if there already
is a unity, then why the need for reunifications? Why is there need for
decades of stubborn exertion for reunification? Kartashev here goes further than the expectations of the Protestants, and his assertions annul all
Orthodox Christian dogmas. The very same trend of thought, though not
as clear, is followed by the Bulgarian Protopresbyter Stephan Tsankov.

The point of view of the teaching of the spiritual church is supported by Archpriest V. Zenkovsky. He writes: "In its entire historical content the visible historical Church naturally leans towards divisions into various 'confessions'…: this dismemberment does not affect the unity of the heavenly Church, but, " he adds, "dismemberment also is not healed through uniting."

In his dialogues "At the Feast of the Gods" of 1921, the Rev. Bulgakov says: "It is with a kind of freshness and captivation that the old problem of unification of churches arises before us, towards which the terrible historical hour that has arrived for all of Christianity is calling and coercing us… Having as an analogy the epoch of the persecutions and the catacomb period of the Church." Is not Fr. Bulgakov calling forth before this terrible hour for the destruction of the fortress and rock of Christianity, the apostolic Church, for the breaking down of its walls, for its abolishment?

At the first sessions of the ecumenical gatherings its Orthodox members seemingly tried to stand in defense of the view that for them the Orthodox Church is *Una Sancta*; but then gave in to the general trend. In Edinburgh, during 1950 at the ecumenical assembly, the Orthodox delegates gave "a clear answer," as is described in the report of the convocation of the World Council of Churches in Toronto in that very same year: "Notwithstanding all our differences, we have a common Teacher and Lord, Jesus Christ, Who will lead us towards increasingly more intimate common work in the building up of the body of Christ." With regard to this "clear" answer there remains to be said that unfortunately the ecumenical conception of the body of Christ is too different from the conception of the Orthodox Church.

In that very same ecumenical direction and on those very same principles various separate high representatives of the Greek church are advocating the idea of the reunification of churches, at least as far as one is capable of judging according to the reports of the press. Thus, Archbishop Iakovos (USA) now sees the Church in the divided multiplicity of churches as one organism, one body of Christ. He sees nothing but human pride as the cause of divisions. He sees a way out in living together and praying together, not raising any walls of division determined by racial and religious prejudices. The Orthodox Church, according to his words, must cease making known its "universal teaching" (*Church Life*, May–July, 1961).

In such a manner there is taking place an obvious disfiguration of the dogmas of the Church and a simultaneous attraction of local Orthodox churches into a completely alien channel, subjecting them to Protestantism, and, in addition, towards a movement directed not only by the mere idea of reunification, but also by different social ideas and plans completely alien to us.

At this time the Moscow Patriarcte is preparing to announce itself as the sole protector of the immutability of the dogmas of Christianity, and she will be listened to with interest, having been accepted as the voice of the historical Russian Church.

At this grave historical moment much courage, firmness, conscientiousness, and readiness for sacrifice are demanded from those who are faithfully preserving themselves in Orthodoxy, and a strong faith in the words of the Saviour concerning the unshakeableness of the Church. There is no doubt that in the depth of each local Orthodox church there is a true understanding of Orthodoxy and a readiness to stand up in defense of it. These voices will be raised and will be heard. One should not become discouraged by the apparent weakness and meagerness of these voices.

In his time St. Gregory the Theologian characterized the state of Orthodoxy in the Church of Constantinople thus: "This field once was small and poor...it was not at all a field. It was worth, perhaps, neither a granary, neither a thrashing floor, nor a sickle, but instead only small unripened sheaves..."

Such it was at the time when St. Gregory began to preach in Constantinople in the house church of St. Anastasius; yet this period ended during his lifetime with the triumph of Orthodoxy in all of Constantinople (see his farewell address).

At another time the same hierarch asks: "Where are those who reproach us for our poverty and boast of their wealth? They accept great numbers as sign of the Church, and scorn a small flock. They measure divinity (concerning the Arians, who say that the Son is less than the Father) and weigh people. They highly value grains of sand and degrade the star; they collect into the treasure chest simple stones and ignore the gems." (Chapter 33, Against the Arians). Thus, also as our support we do not have Protestantizing theologians, but the stars of both the Universal and Russian Church, Her holy pastors and teachers.

If it will not be fated for us to attract the non-Orthodox confessions into the one, apostolic and Orthodox Church of Christ, then in any case we must preserve ourselves and guard our brothers in Christ who belong to the same Church from false ways, from being captivated by over extended goals, from being bought out at the expense of betrayal to the teaching of the Church. With sorrow one is forced to admit that there is no possibility of a sufficient exchange of ideas with the non-Russian Orthodox world yet free from the communist yoke, because of difference of language and for other reasons. In part, there is not a sufficient exchange of ideas with the Greek Orthodox world. We are forced to silently observe with bitterness how easily forces unfavorable for Orthodoxy are at work in its midst.

We believe, however, that at the meeting of true ideas with false ideas, both there and also in our midst, living forces will be aroused and will repulse temptations; and faith itself, tested in temptation, will become a firm rock. For many, and many in our own Orthodox milieu, perhaps now yet cool in heart and almost indifferent towards questions of the Church and its dogmas, this faith, made firm through temptation, will become, as the first apostle expresses himself, *more precious than gold that perisheth, though it be tried with fire...* (I Peter 1:7), i.e., more dear than material earthly wealth.

Our War is not Against Flesh and Blood

On the Question of the "Toll-Houses"

We are fools for Christ's sake,
but ye are wise in Christ.
— ICor. 4:10

Our life among a population which, although it is nominally Christian, in many respects has different conceptions and views than ours in the realm of faith. Sometimes this inspires us to respond to questions of our Faith when they are raised and discussed from a non-Orthodox point of view by persons of other confessions, and sometimes by Orthodox Christians who no longer have a firm Orthodox foundation under their feet.

In the limited conditions of our life we unfortunately are unable fully to react to statements or to reply to the questions that arise. However, we sometimes feel such a need. In particular, we now have occasion to define the Orthodox view of the "toll-houses," which is one of the topics of a book which has appeared in English under the title, *Christian Mythology* by Canon George Every. The "toll-houses" are the experience of the Christian soul immediately after death, as these experiences are described by the Fathers of the Church and Christian ascetics. In recent years a critical approach to a whole series of our Church beliefs has been observed; these beliefs are viewed as being "primitive," the result of a "naive" world view of piety, and they are characterized by such words as "myths," "magic," and the like. It is our duty to respond.

The subject of the toll-houses is not specifically a topic of Orthodox Christian theology: it is not a dogma of the Church in the precise sense, but comprises material of a moral and edifying character, one might say pedagogical. To approach it correctly, it is essential to understand the *foundations* and the spirit of the Orthodox world-view. *For what man knoweth the things of a man, save the spirit of man which is in him? Even so, the things of God knoweth no man, but the Spirit of God* (I Cor. 2:11–12). We must ourselves come closer to the Church, *that we might know the things that are freely given to us of God* (I Cor. 2:12).

In the present question the *foundation* is: We believe in the Church. The Church is the heavenly and earthly Body of Christ, pre-designated for the moral perfection of the members of its earthly part and for the blessed, joyful, but always active life of its ranks in its heavenly realm. The Church on earth glorifies God, unites believers, and educates them morally so that by this means it might ennoble and exalt earthly life itself — both the personal life of its own children, and the life of mankind. Its chief aim is to help them in the attainment of eternal life in God, the attainment of sanctity, without which *no man shall see the Lord* (Heb. 12:14).

Thus, it is essential that there be constant communion between those in the Church on earth and the heavenly Church. In the Body of Christ all its members are interactive. In the Lord, the Shepherd of the Church, there are, as it were, two flocks: the heavenly and the earthly (Epistle of the Eastern Patriarchs, 17th century). *Whether one member suffer, all the members suffer with it; or one member be honored, all the members rejoice with it* (I Cor. 12:26). The heavenly Church rejoices, but at the same time it sympathizes with its fellow members on earth. St. Gregory the Theologian gave to the earthly Church of his time the name of "suffering Orthodoxy"; and thus it has remained until now. This interaction is valuable and indispensible for the common aim that we *may grow up into Him in all things...from Whom the whole body fitly joined together and compacted by that which every joint supplieth, according to the effectual working in the measure of every part, maketh increase of the body unto the building of itself in love* (Eph. 4:15–16).

The end of all this is deification in the Lord, that *God may be all in all* (I Cor. 15:28). The earthly life of the Christian should be a place of spiritual growth, progress, the ascent of the soul towards heaven. We deeply grieve that, with the exception of a few of us, although we know our path, stray far away from it because of our attachment to what is exclusively earthly. And, although we are ready to offer repentance, still we continue to live carelessly. However, there is not in our souls that so-called "peace of soul" which is present in Western Christian psychology, which is based upon some kind of "moral minimum" i.e., having fulfilled my obligation that provides a convenient disposition of soul for occupying oneself with worldly interests.

However, it is precisely there, where "peace of soul" ends, that there is opened the field of perfection for the inward work of the Christians. *If we sin wilfully after that we have received the knowledge of the truth, there remaineth no more sacrifice for sins, but only a certain fearful expectation of judgement and fiery indignation, which shall devour the adversaries... It is a fearful thing to fall into the hands of the living God* (Heb. 10:26–27, 31). Passivity and carelessness are unnatural to the soul; by being passive and careless we demean ourselves. However, to rise up requires constant vigilance of the soul and, more than this, warfare.

With whom is this warfare? With oneself only? *We wrestle not against flesh and blood, but against principalities, against powers, against the rulers of the darkness of this world, against the spirits of wickedness under the heaven* (Eph. 6:12).

Here we approach the subject of the toll-houses.

It is not by chance, that the Lord's Prayer ends with the words: *Lead us not into temptation, but deliver us from the Evil One.* Concerning this Evil One, in another of His discourses the Lord said to His disciples: *I beheld Satan as lightning fall from heaven* (Luke 10:18). Cast down from heaven, he became thus a resident of the lower sphere, *the prince of the power of the air,* the prince of the *legion* of unclean spirits. *When the unclean spirit is gone out of a man* but does not find rest for himself, he returns to the home from which he departed and, finding it unoccupied, cleaned and put in order, *he goeth and taketh with himself seven other spirits more wicked than himself, and they enter in and dwell there; and the last state of that man is worse that the first. Even so shall it be also unto this wicked generation* (Matt. 12:43, 45).

Was it only a generation? Concerning the bent-over woman who was healed on the Sabbath day, did not the Lord reply: *Ought not this woman, being a daughter whom Satan hath bound, lo, these eighteen years, be loosed from this bond on the Sabbath day?* (Luke 13:16).

The Apostles in their instructions do not forget about our spiritual enemies. St. Paul writes to the Ephesians: *In past times ye walked according to the course of this world, according to the prince of the power of the air, the spirit that now worketh in the children of disobedience* (Eph. 2:2). Therefore, now *put on the whole armor of God, that ye may be able to stand against the wiles of the devil* (Eph. 6:11), *for the devil, as a roaring lion, seeketh whom he may devour* (I Peter 5:8). Being Christians, shall we call these quotations from the Scripture "mythology"?

Those warnings to previous generations found in the written word of God also relate to us. Therefore the hindrances to salvation are the same. Some of them are due to our own carelessness, our own self-confidence, our lack of concern, our egoism, to the passions of the body; others are in the temptations and the tempters who surround us: in people, and in the invisible dark powers which surround us. This is why, in our daily personal prayers , we beg God not to allow any "success of the evil one" (from the Morning Prayers), that is, that we be not allowed any success in our deeds that might occur with the help of dark powers. In general, in our private prayers and also in public Divine Worship, we never lose sight of the idea of being translated into a different life after death.

In the times of the Apostles and the first Christians, when Christians were more inspired, when the difference between the pagan world and the world of Christians was much more distinct, when the suffering of the martyrs was the light of Christianity, there was less concern to support the spirit of Christians by preaching alone. But the Gospel is all encompassing! The demands of the Sermon on the Mount were meant not only for the Apostles! And therefore, in the writings of the Apostles we already read not simple instructions, but also warnings about the future, when we shall have to give an account.

Put on the whole armour of God, that ye may be able to stand against the wiles of the devil...that ye may be able to withstand in the evil day, and having done all, to stand (Eph. 6: 11, 13). *For if we sin wilfully after that we have received the knowledge of the truth, there remaineth no more sacrifice for sins, but a certain fearful looking for of judgment and fiery indignation, which shall devour the adversaries.. It is a fearful thing to fall into the hands of the living God* (Heb. 10:26–27, 31). *On some have compassion, and others save with fear, pulling them out of the fire, hating even the garment spotted by the flesh* (Jude, the brother of James, 22–23). *It is impossible for those who were once enlightened, and have tasted of the heavenly gift, and were made partakers of the Holy Sprit, and have tasted the good word of God, and the powers of the world to come, if they shall fall away, to renew them again unto repentance, seeing they crucify to themselves the Son of God afresh, and put Him to an open shame* (Heb. 6:4–6).

Thus it was in the Apostolic age. But when the Church, having received freedom, began to be filled with masses of people, when the general inspiration of faith began to weaken, there was a more critical need for powerful words, for denunciations, for calls to spiritual vigilance, to fear of God and fear for one's own fate. In the collection of pastoral instructions of the most zealous archpastors we read stern homilies giving pictures of the future judgement which awaits us after death. These homilies were intended to bring sinners to their senses, and evidently they were given during periods of general Christian repentance before Great Lent. In them was the truth of God's righteousness, the truth that nothing unclean would enter into the kingdom of sanctity; this truth was clothed in vivid, partly figurative, close to earthly images which were known to everyone in daily life. The hierarchs of this period themselves called these images of the judgement which follows immediately after death the "toll-houses." The tables of the publicans, the collectors of taxes and duties, were evidently points for letting one go on the road further into the central part of the city. Of course, the word "toll-house" in itself does not indicate to us any particular religious significance. In patristic language it signifies that short period after death when the Christian soul must account for its moral state.

St. Basil writes, "Let no one deceive himself with empty words, for *sudden destruction cometh upon them* (I Thess. 5:3) and causes an overturning like a storm. A strict angel will come, he will forcibly lead out your soul, bound by sins. Occupy yourself therefore with reflection on the last day... Imagine to yourself the confusion, the shortness of breath, and the hour of death, the sentence of God drawing near, the angels hastening towards you, the dreadful confusion of the soul tormented by its conscience, with its pitiful gaze upon what is happening, and finally, the unavoidable translation into a distant place" (St. Basil the Great, quoted in "Essay in an Historical Exposition of Orthodox Theology," by Bishop Sylvester, Vol. 5, p.89).

St. Gregory the Theologian, who guided a large flock only for short periods, limits himself to general words, saying that "each one is a sincere judge of himself, because of the judgement-seat awaiting him."

There is a more striking picture found in St. John Chrysostom: "If, in setting out for any foreign country or city we are in need of guides, then how much shall we need helpers and guides in order to pass unhindered past the elders, the powers, the governors of the air, the persecutors, the chief collectors! For this reason, the soul, flying away from the body, often ascends and descends, fears and trembles. The awareness of sins always torments us, all the more at that hour when we shall have to be conducted to those trials and that frightful judgement place." Continuing, Chrysostom gives moral instructions for a Christian way of life. As for children who have died, he places in their mouths the following words: "The holy angels peacefully separated us from our bodies, and having good guides, we went without harm past the powers of the air. The evil spirits did not find in us what they were seeking; they did not notice what they wished to put to shame; seeing an immaculate soul, they were ashamed; seeing an undefiled tongue, they were silent. We passed by and put them to shame. The net was rent, and we were delivered. Blessed is God Who did not give us as a prey to them" (St. John Chrysostom, Homily 2, "On Remembering the Dead").

The Orthodox Church depicts the Christian martyrs, male and female, as attaining the heavenly bridal chamber just as freely as children and without harm. In the fifth century the depiction of the immediate judgement upon the soul after its departure from the body, called the Particular Judgement, was even more closely joined to the depiction of the toll-houses, as we see in St. Cyril of Alexandria's "Homily on the Departure of the Soul," which sums up the images of this kind in the Fathers of the Church which preceded him.

It is perfectly clear to anyone that purely earthly images are applied to a spiritual subject so that the image, being impressed in the memory, might awaken a man's soul. "Behold the Bridegroom cometh at midnight, and blessed is the servant whom He shall find watching." At the same time, in these pictures the sinfulness that is present in fallen man is revealed in its various types and forms, and this inspires man to analyze his own state of soul. In the instructions of Orthodox ascetics the types and forms of sinfulness have a special stamp of their own;[1] in the Lives of Saints there is also a characteristic stamp.

---

1) In ascetic literature sometimes the passions and evil demons are almost identified: the spirits who settle in the bodies of living men are the arousers of the passions; while the passions become infirmities not only of the body, but also of the soul, and therefore they remain in the soul as enticers of earthly passions even after death. Therefore one may also depict the toll-houses as an inward personal battle in the soul which has been separated from the body.

Due to the availability of the Lives of Saints, the account of the toll-houses by the righteous Theodora, depicted by her in detail by Saint Basil the New in his dream, has become especially well known. Dreams in general express the state of soul of a given man, and in special cases are also authentic visions of the souls of the departed in their earthly form. The account of Theodora has characteristics both of one and the other. The idea that good spirits, our guardian angels, as well as the spirits of evil under heaven participate in the fate of man (after death) finds confirmation in the parable of the rich man and Lazarus. Lazarus immediately after death was brought by angels to the bosom of Abraham. In another parable the unrighteous man heard these words: *Thou fool, this night thy soul shall be required of thee* (Luke 12:20); evidently, the ones who "require" are none else than the same "spirits of wickedness under the heavens."

In accordance with simple logic and as also confirmed by the Word of God the soul immediately after its separation from the body enters into a sphere where its further fate is defined. *It is appointed unto men once to die, but after this the judgment,* we read in the Apostle Paul (Heb. 9:27). This is the Particular Judgement, which is independent of the universal Last Judgement.

The teaching concerning the Particular Judgement of God enters into the sphere of Orthodox dogmatic theology. As for the toll-houses, Russian writers of general systems of theology limit themselves to a rather stereotyped note: "Concerning all the sensual, earthly images by which the Particular Judgement is presented in the form of the toll-houses, although in their fundamental idea they are completely true, still they should be accepted in the way that the angel instructed Saint Macarius of Alexandria, being only the weakest means of depicting heavenly things." (See Macarius, Metropolitan of Moscow, *Orthodox Dogmatic Theology*, Saint Petersburg, 1883, vol. 11, p.538; also the book of Bishop Sylvester, Rector of the Kiev Theological Academy. Archbishop Philaret of Chernigov, in his two volume work on dogmatic theology, does not comment on this subject.) [2]

2) However, Metropolitan Macarius does speak quite in detail on the subject of the toll-houses, devoting ten pages of his second volume to it (pp.528–538), and giving extensive quotes from Saints Cyril of Alexandria, Ephraim the Syrian, Athanasius the Great, Macarius the Great, John Chrysostom, Maximus the Confessor, and a number of other sources, including many texts from the Divine service books, and concluding that "such

If one is to complain of the frightening character of the pictures of the toll-houses — are there not many such pictures in the New Testament scriptures and in the words of the Lord Himself? Are we not frightened by the very simplest question: *How camest thou in hither not having a wedding garment?* (Mat. 22:12).

We respond to the discussion on the toll-houses, a topic which is secondary in the realm of our Orthodox thought, because it gives an occasion to illuminate the essence of our Church life. Our Christian Church life of prayer is uninterrupted mutual communion with the heavenly world. It is not simply an "invocation of the saints," as it is often called; it is an interaction in love. Through it the whole body of the Church, being united and strengthened in its members and bonds, *increaseth with the increase of God* (Col. 2:19). Through the Church we *are come unto the Heavenly Jerusalem, and to an innumerable company of angels, to the solemn assembly and the church of the first-born, which are written in heaven, and the God the Judge of all, and to the spirits of just men made perfect* (Heb, 12:22–23). Our prayerful interaction extends in all directions. It has been commanded us: *Pray for one another.* We live according to the principle of Faith: *Whether we live or die, we are the Lord's* (Rom. 14:8). *Love never faileth* (I Cor. 13:8). *Love shall cover a multitude of sins* (I Peter 4:8).

For the soul there is no death. Life in Christ is a world of prayer. It penetrates the whole body of the Church, unites every member of the Church with the Heavenly Father, the members of the earthly Church with themselves, and the members of the earthly Church with the Heavenly Church. Prayers are the threads of the living fabric of the Church body, for *the prayer of the righteous man availeth much* (James 5:16). The twenty-four elders in heaven at the throne of God fell down before the Lamb, each having harps and vials filled with incense, *which are the prayers of saints* (Apoc. 5:8); that is, they offered up prayer on earth to the heavenly throne.

Threats are necessary; they can and should warn us, restrain us from evil actions. The same Church instills in us that the Lord is compassionate and merciful, long-suffering and plenteous in mercy, and is grieved over

an uninterrupted, constant, and universal usage in the Church on the teaching of the toll-houses, especially among the teachers of the fourth century, indisputably testifies that it was handed down to them from the teachers of the preceding centuries and is founded on apostolic tradition" (p.535). (Translator's note)

the evil doings of men, taking upon Himself our infirmities. In the Heavenly Church are also our intercessors, our helpers, those who pray for us. The Most Pure Mother of God is our protection. Our very prayers are the prayers of saints, written down by them, which came from their contrite hearts during the days of their earthly life. Those who pray can feel this, and thus the saints themselves become closer to us. Such are our daily prayers; such also is the whole cycle of the Church's Divine services of every day, of every week, and of the Feasts.

All this liturgical literature was not conceived as an academic exercise. The enemies of the air are powerless against such help. But we must have faith, and our prayers must be fervent and sincere. There is more joy in heaven over one who repents, than over others who need no repentance. How insistently the Church teaches us (in its litanies) to spend "the rest of our life in peace and repentance," and to die thus! It teaches us to call to remembrance our Most Holy, Most Pure, Most Blessed Lady Theotokos and all the saints, and then to commit ourselves and one another unto Christ our God.

At the same time, with all this cloud of heavenly protectors, we are made glad by the special closeness to us of our Guardian Angels. They are meek, they rejoice over us, and they also grieve over our falls. We are filled with hope in them, in the state we will be in when our soul is separated from the body, when we must enter into a new life: will it be light or in darkness, in joy or in sorrow? Therefore, every day we pray to our angels for the present day: "Deliver us from every cunning of the opposing enemy." In special canons of repentance we entreat them not to depart from us now nor after our death: "I see thee with my spiritual gaze, thou who remainest with me, my fellow converser, Holy Angel, watching over, accompanying and remaining with me and ever offering to me what is for salvation." "When my humble soul shall be loosed from my body, may thou cover it, O my instructor, with thy bright and most sacred wings." "When the frightful sound of the trumpet will resurrect me unto judgement, stand near to me then, quiet and joyful, and with the hope of salvation take away my fear." "For thou art beauteous in virtue, and sweet and joyous, a mind bright as the sun; brightly intercede for me with joyful countenance and radiant gaze when I am to be taken from the earth." "May I then behold thee standing at the right hand of my wretched soul, bright and quiet, thou who intercedest and prayest for me, when my spirit shall be taken by force; may I behold thee banishing those who seek me, my bitter enemies." (From the Canon to the Guardian Angel of John the Monk, in the Prayer Book for Priests)

Thus, the Holy Church through the ranks of its builders: the Apostles, the great hierarchs, the holy ascetics, having as its Chief Shepherd our Saviour and Lord, Jesus Christ, has created and gives us all means for our spiritual perfection and the attainment of the eternal blessed life in God, overcoming our carelessness and light-mindedness by fear and by stern warnings, at the same time instilling in us a spirit of vigilance and bright hope, surrounding us with holy, heavenly guides and helpers. In the Typicon of the Church's Divine service, we are given a direct path to the attainment of the Kingdom of Glory.

Among the images of the Gospel the Church very often reminds us of the parable of the Prodigal Son, and one week in the yearly cycle of Church services is entirely devoted to this remembrance, so that we might know the limitless love of God and the fact that the sincere, contrite, tearful repentance of a believing man overcomes all the obstacles and all the toll-houses on the path to the Heavenly Father.